D0903115

Visual Basic
Professional 3.0
Programming

Visual Basic Professional 3.0 Programming

Thomas W. Torgerson

A Wiley–QED Publication

John Wiley & Sons, Inc.

New York • Chichester • Brisbane • Toronto • Singapore

ISBN 0 471-60693-6

Printed in the United States of America

10 9 8 7 6 5 4 3 2 1

I would like to thank the QED group and Microsoft for their assistance. I dedicate this book to my wife Christine and our two wonderful children, Carissa and Kendra Torgerson, who, when they grow up, I have no doubt will make my contribution to the world pale in comparison to their contributions. They will help make the world a better place. God bless them!

Contents

PREFACE . . . . **xxiii**

CHAPTER 1. INTRODUCTION 1

1.1   Welcome to Visual Basic 1
1.2.   Who Will Benefit from This Book 2
1.3.   Structure and Style of the Book 2
1.4.   The Two Versions of Visual Basic 3
    1.4.1.   Standard Version 3
    1.4.2.   Professional Version 3
1.5.   Background of Visual Basic 4
    1.5.1.   Version 1.00 4
    1.5.2.   Version 2.00 5
    1.5.3.   Version 3.00 5
1.6.   Multiple Developer Support 6
1.7.   Support from Third Parties 6
1.8.   Two Preview Applications 7
1.9.   Online Documentation 8
    1.9.1.   Context-Sensitive Help 10

CHAPTER 2. GETTING STARTED 11

2.1.   Overview 11
2.2.   Introduction to a Project 11

2.3.   Running Visual Basic 12
2.4.   The Programming Environment 13
    2.4.1.   Menu Bar 14
    2.4.2.   Toolbar 14
    2.4.3.   Form 14
    2.4.4.   Toolbox 17
    2.4.5.   Properties Window......................... 20
    2.4.6.   Project Window 20
2.5.   Your First Application and Project 21
    2.5.1.   Function of the Application 22
    2.5.2.   Create the Interface....................... 22
        2.5.2.1.   *Changing the Size of Controls* 25
        2.5.2.2.   *Moving Controls* 25
    2.5.3.   Set Properties............................. 25
        2.5.3.1.   *Set Control Properties* 27
    2.5.4.   Write Needed Code 28
        2.5.4.1.   *More on the Code Window* 30
    2.5.5.   Running and Saving the Application Project 32

CHAPTER 3.   CONTROLS **33**

3.1.   Controls and Their Use.............................. 33
3.2.   Custom Controls 33
    3.2.1.   Loading a Custom Control................... 34
    3.2.2.   CDK (Control Development Kit) 34
3.3.   A Look at Each Control.............................. 35
    3.3.1.   Other Controls 35
3.4.   Object Naming Formats 39
    3.4.1.   Format Rules 40
    3.4.2.   Professional Edition—*About* Property 40
        3.4.2.1.   *Object Types* 40
3.5.   Buttons and Actions 40
    3.5.1.   Using Command Button Controls.............. 41
    3.5.2.   Image Control Action....................... 42
    3.5.3.   Choosing Command Buttons at Runtime 43
3.6.   Showing Text Information 44
    3.6.1.   Labels 44
3.7.   Text Boxes 46
    3.7.1.   Multiple Line Displays with Text Boxes 46
3.8.   When to Use What Controls.......................... 47
3.9.   Individual Options with Check Boxes 48
3.10.   Grouping Option Buttons 50
    3.10.1.   How to Group Controls in Frames 51
    3.10.2.   Selecting Option Buttons.................... 51

3.11. Combo Boxes and List Boxes 53
    3.11.1. Combo Box Styles. 53
        3.11.1.1. Drop-down Combo Box (Style 0) 53
        3.11.1.2. Simple Combo Box (Style 1) 54
        3.11.1.3. Drop-down List Box (Style 2) 54
    3.11.2. Putting Items in a List 54
    3.11.3. Adding and Removing Items 56
    3.11.4. Getting a List Value with the *Text* Property 57
    3.11.5. Getting a List Value with the *List* Property. 57
    3.11.6. Total Number of Items 58
    3.11.7. Multiple-column List Boxes. 58
3.12. Scroll Bars as an Input Source 61
3.13. Setting Focus and Tab Order 62
    3.13.1. Focus 63
    3.13.2. Tab Order 63
3.14. Control State 64
3.15. Control Arrays. 64
    3.15.1. Making a Control Array at Design Time 65
        3.15.1.1. Set Index *Property*. 65
        3.15.1.2. Assign Same Name 66
        3.15.1.3. Copying an Existing Control 67
    3.15.2. Expanding a Control Array at Runtime 67

CHAPTER 4.   MENU AND DIALOG BOX USAGE **69**
4.1. Introduction to Menus 69
    4.1.1. What Menus Do 70
4.2. The Menu Design Window 71
    4.2.1. Menu Control Properties 72
    4.2.2. Menu Control List Box 72
    4.2.3. Menu Control List Box Positions 74
4.3. Creating a Menu for an Application 74
    4.3.1. Menus and Control Arrays 77
        4.3.1.1. Index Values 77
    4.3.2. Creating a Menu Control Array 77
        4.3.2.1. Example Control Array. 78
4.4. Code Requirements for Menu Controls 78
4.5. Submenus 79
    4.5.1. Creating a Submenu 79
        4.5.1.1. Creating Menu Separators 80
4.6. Access and Shortcut Keys. 80
    4.6.1. Access Keys 80
    4.6.2. Shortcut Keys. 81
4.7. Runtime Control of Menus 81

4.7.1.   Enabling and Disabling Items and Making
Items Invisible 81
4.8.   Dialog Boxes 82
4.8.1.   Predefined Dialog Boxes 82
4.8.1.1.   *MsgBox* 83
The MsgBox Statement 83
The MsgBox Function 84
4.8.1.2.   *InputBox* 85
4.8.2.   Custom Dialog Boxes 85
4.8.2.1.   *Custom Dialog Command Buttons* 87
4.8.2.2.   *Default and Cancel Properties* 87
4.8.2.3.   *Disabling Controls* 88
4.8.2.4.   *Displaying a Custom Dialog Box* 89
4.8.2.5.   *Display Options* 91

**CHAPTER 5.   MANAGING PROJECTS AND CREATING
EXECUTABLES** **93**
5.1.   Introduction to Projects and Executables 93
5.2.   Project Components 93
5.2.1.   What a Project Can Include 94
5.2.2.   The Project Window 94
5.2.3.   The Project File 94
5.3.   New Forms and Code Modules 96
5.4.   Create, Open, and Save a Project 97
5.5.   Actions to Perform with Files 97
5.6.   Text and Binary Forms and Modules 98
5.6.1.   How to Create a Text File 98
5.6.1.1.   *Saving a Form or Module as a Text
File* 98
5.6.1.2.   *Saving Code as a Text File* 99
5.6.1.3.   *Add a Text File as a Form or Module* 99
5.6.1.4.   *Load a Text File as Code* 99
5.7.   Making an Executable File 99
5.7.1.   Making an Executable from Visual Basic 101
5.7.2.   Making an Executable from MS-DOS 101
5.7.3.   Custom Controls, Runtime File,
and Executables 102
5.8.   Environment Settings 102
5.9.   Project Options 102
5.10.   Autoload.mak File 104
5.11.   SetupWizard 104
5.11.1.   Running SetupWizard 104

CHAPTER 6.   VISUAL BASIC PROGRAMMING
BASIC **107**

6.1.   Introduction to Language Fundamentals 107
    6.1.1.   Language Overview 107
6.2.   Introduction to Event-Driven Programming 108
    6.2.1.   Event-Driven Programming in Visual Basic 108
        6.2.1.1.   Normal Event-Driven Scenario *109*
    6.2.2.   Application Startup Code Options 110
    6.2.3.   Quitting Your Application Safely 111
6.3.   Types and Use of Modules 111
    6.3.1.   Event Procedures 112
    6.3.2.   General Procedures 112
    6.3.3.   Managing Procedures 112
6.4.   Types of Procedures 113
    6.4.1.   Sub Procedures 113
    6.4.2.   Function Procedures 115
    6.4.3.   Public vs. Private Procedures 116
6.5.   Code Statements in Procedures 116
    6.5.1.   Comments, Numbers, and Code Statements 116
    6.5.2.   Naming Rules 117
    6.5.3.   Assignment and Retrieval Properties 118
        6.5.3.1.   Controls and Properties on Other
                Forms *119*
    6.5.4.   Value of a Control 119
6.6.   Overview of Variables 120
    6.6.1.   Data Types 120
    6.6.2.   Declaring Variables 120
        6.6.2.1.   Introduction to Variable Lifetimes *121*
6.7.   Control Structures 121
    6.7.1.   Decision Structures 122
        6.7.1.1.   If / Then *122*
        6.7.1.2.   If / Then / Else *122*
        6.7.1.3.   Select Case *123*
    6.7.2.   Loop Structures 124
        6.7.2.1.   Do / Loop *124*
        6.7.2.2.   For / Next *126*
    6.7.3.   Nesting Control Structures 127
    6.7.4.   Exiting Control Structures and Procedures 128
        6.7.4.1.   Exit Control Structures *128*
        6.7.4.2.   Exit Sub and Exit Function
                Procedures *128*

CHAPTER 7.   VARIABLES AND DATA TYPES **131**

7.1.   Introduction to Variables and Data Types 131
7.2.   Declaration of Variables 132
    7.2.1.   Implicit Declaration 132
    7.2.2.   Explicit Declaration 132
7.3.   Scope and Lifetimes of Variables 133
    7.3.1.   Scope of Variables 134
        7.3.1.1.   *Local Variables* *134*
        7.3.1.2.   *Module Level Variables* *134*
        7.3.1.3.   *Global Variables* *134*
    7.3.2.   Lifetime and Static Variables 135
7.4.   Fundamental Data Types 135
    7.4.1.   Variant Type 135
        7.4.1.1.   *VarType* *136*
        7.4.1.2.   *IsNumeric and Other Functions* *136*
        7.4.1.3.   *Concatenation and Addition* *137*
        7.4.1.4.   *Date / Time Variant Example* *138*
        7.4.1.5.   *Empty Value* *139*
        7.4.1.6.   *Null Value* *139*
    7.4.2.   Other Data Types 140
        7.4.2.1.   *Type Declaration Character* *141*
        7.4.2.2.   *Numeric Variables* *141*
        7.4.2.3.   *Strings* *142*
    7.4.3.   Argument Types 143
    7.4.4.   Argument By Value 143
    7.4.5.   Function Data Types 144
7.5.   Arrays 144
    7.5.1.   Multidimensional Arrays 145
    7.5.2.   Dynamic Arrays 146
    7.5.3.   Huge Arrays 147
7.6.   User-Defined Data Types 148
7.7.   Constants 150

CHAPTER 8.   FILES, DATABASES, AND REPORTS **151**

8.1.   Introduction 151
8.2.   Types of Files 151
    8.2.1.   Random Access Files 151
    8.2.2.   Sequential Files 153
    8.2.3.   Binary Files 153
8.3.   Using Random Access Files 154
    8.3.1.   Functions and Statements 155

8.3.2. Defining the Data Type 155
8.3.3. Variables for Random Access 156
8.3.4. Opening Random Access Files 156
8.3.5. Editing Random Access Files 157
    8.3.5.1. Get Statement 157
    8.3.5.2. Editing Data 157
8.3.6. Writing Random Access Files 157
    8.3.6.1. Replacing Records 158
    8.3.6.2. Adding Records 158
    8.3.6.3. Deleting Records 158
8.4. Using Sequential Access Files 159
8.4.1. Functions and Statements 159
8.4.2. Opening Sequential Access Files 159
8.4.3. Editing and Reading Files 160
8.4.4. Text Boxes and Files 161
8.4.5. Placing Strings into Files 162
8.5. Using Binary Access Files 162
8.5.1. Functions and Statements 163
8.5.2. Opening a Binary Access File 163
8.5.3. Records and Fields in Binary Access Files 163
8.5.4. File Output 164
8.5.5. File Input 166
8.5.6. Input$ Statement 167
8.6. Tracking Record Locations 168
8.7. Microsoft Access 1.1 Engine Introduction 170
8.7.1. True Transaction Processing 170
8.7.2. SQL 171
8.7.3. Multiuser 171
8.7.4. Security 171
8.7.5. Programmatic Objects 171
    8.7.5.1. Database Objects 172
    8.7.5.2. Table Object 172
    8.7.5.3. TableDef Object 172
    8.7.5.4. Dynaset Object 172
    8.7.5.5. Snapshot Object 172
    8.7.5.6. QueryDef Object 173
    8.7.5.7. Field Object 173
    8.7.5.8. Index Object 173
8.7.6. Data Control Use 173
8.7.7. Data-aware Controls—Visual Layer 173
8.8. A Data Control Sample Application 174
8.8.1. Placing a Data Control 174

	8.8.2.	Data Control Properties	175
	8.8.3.	Data Control Query	177
	8.8.4.	Placement of Data-aware Controls	177
	8.8.5.	DataField and DataSource	178
		8.8.5.1. *Set DataSource Property*	*178*
		8.8.5.2. *Set DataField Property*	*179*
	8.8.6.	Execute Application	179
	8.8.7.	Validation	180
8.9.		Crystal Reports	182
	8.9.1.	Report Writer Design Environment	183
	8.9.2.	Report Writer Custom Control	183
	8.9.3.	Quick Start	183

**CHAPTER 9.   DEBUGGING AND ERROR
HANDLING** **187**

9.1.		Introduction	187
9.2.		Types of Debugging Errors	188
	9.2.1.	Compile Errors	188
	9.2.2.	Runtime Errors	189
	9.2.3.	Logic Errors	189
9.3.		Toolbar Debugging Tools	189
9.4.		Design, Run, and Break Time Modes	189
	9.4.1.	Changing Modes by the Toolbar	190
9.5.		Break Mode Use	191
	9.5.1.	Breaking on Code Statements	191
		9.5.1.1. *Break Automatically*	*191*
		9.5.1.2. *Break Manually*	*191*
	9.5.2.	Break Variables	191
	9.5.3.	Runtime Errors and Debugging	192
	9.5.4.	Breaking at a Specific Point	193
	9.5.5.	Examination at Breakpoint	193
	9.5.6.	Stop Statement	194
9.6.		Executing Only Selected Code Areas	194
	9.6.1.	Single Stepping	194
	9.6.2.	Procedure Stepping	195
	9.6.3.	Set Next Line to Execute	195
9.7.		Debug Window	196
9.8.		Watch Expressions	197
	9.8.1.	Adding a Watch	197
	9.8.2.	Editing or Deleting a Watch	197
	9.8.3.	Instant Watch	198
9.9.		Immediate Pane Testing	198

9.9.1. Immediate Pane Printing Methods 199

9.9.2. Print Statements in the Immediate Pane 199

9.9.3. Assignments 200

9.9.4. Tips on Using the Immediate Pane 200

9.10. Tips on Avoiding Bugs and Debugging 201

9.11. Reasons for Using Error Handling 202

9.12. Steps in Error Handling 202

9.13. Error Handling Example 203

9.14. Ways to Exit Error-Handling Code 205

**CHAPTER 10. BASICS OF COMMUNICATING WITH
OTHER APPLICATIONS** **207**

10.1. Introduction 207

10.2. DDE 207

10.2.1. Source and Destination 208

10.2.2. Application, Topic, and Item 209

10.2.2.1. Application *211*

10.2.2.2. Topic *211*

10.2.2.3. Item *212*

10.2.3. Links 212

10.2.4. Design Time and Links 212

10.2.4.1. Retrieving Data by Links *213*

10.2.4.2. Sending Data by Links *213*

10.2.5. methods and DDE Operation 214

10.2.5.1. Starting Applications *214*

10.2.5.2. Poking Data *215*

10.2.5.3. Sending Commands *215*

10.2.5.4. Error Handling *217*

DDE and System Sharing *217*

10.2.6. Sending Keystrokes to Applications 218

10.2.7. Activating Applications 219

10.3. DLL 219

10.3.1. Overview of Using DLLs 220

10.3.2. Declaring 221

10.3.3. Calling 221

10.3.4. Declaring Considerations 222

10.3.4.1. Library Specifications *222*

10.3.5. Passing Arguments 222

10.3.6. Flexible Types 223

10.3.6.1. Alias *223*

10.3.7. String Data Types 224

10.3.8. Arrays 224

10.3.9.   User-defined Types 225

10.3.10.   Null Pointers 225

10.3.11.   Handles. 226

10.3.12.   Properties and Objects. 226

10.3.13.   Converting Declarations 226

10.4.   OLE 227

10.4.1.   Using the OLE Control's Pop-up Menus 228

10.4.2.   OLE Automation 228

10.4.3.   Class 228

10.4.4.   Container Application 229

10.4.5.   Linked and Embedded Objects 229

10.4.6.   Objects and OLE 230

10.4.7.   OLE Automation by a Control 231

10.4.8.   OLE Automation by Object Functions 231

10.4.9.   OLE Objects As Controls. 232

10.4.10.   CreateObject Function. 232

10.4.11.   GetObject Function 233

10.4.12.   Files 235

          10.4.12.1. Save *235*

          10.4.12.2. Read. *235*

CHAPTER 11.   ODBC **237**

11.1.   Introducing ODBC 237

11.2.   Components of ODBC 238

11.3.   Applications. 238

11.4.   Driver Manager. 238

11.4.1.   Drivers 239

11.5.   Data Source 239

11.6.   Driver Configurations. 239

11.7.   Reference Overview 239

11.8.   Database Structure. 241

11.9.   Objects 241

11.10. Collections 241

11.10.1.   Create or Delete ODBC Objects 242

11.11. Dynasets 243

11.12. Introduction to Data Manipulation 244

11.12.1.   Opening and Closing a Database 244

11.13. Information about a Database 245

11.13.1.   TableDefs Collection 245

11.13.2.   Information about a Field 246

11.13.3.   Information about Indexes 246

11.14. Changing the Database Structure 247

11.14.1. Adding a Field 248
11.14.2. Adding an Index 249
11.14.3. Deleting a Table or Index 249
11.15. Dynaset Objects 249
11.16. Getting Around in a Dynaset 250
11.16.1. Go to First Record 250
11.16.2. Go to Next Record 250
11.16.3. Go to Desired Record 251
11.16.4. Closing a Dynaset 252
11.17. Manipulating Records 252
11.17.1. Add a Record 252
11.17.2. Edit Current Record 253
11.17.3. Delete a Record 253
11.17.4. Transaction States 253
11.17.5. Data Locking 254
11.17.6. SQL Commands 254
11.18. Large Data Fields 254
11.19. Transactions 255
11.19.1. BeginTrans 255
11.19.2. CommitTrans 255
11.19.3. Rollback 255
11.20. Connect Failure Areas 256
11.20.1. INI Settings 256
11.20.2. ODBC and Driver DLLs 258
11.20.3. Server Information Needed 259
11.20.4. Microsoft and Sybase SQL Servers 259

**CHAPTER 12. LIMITATIONS IN VISUAL BASIC
SYSTEMS** **261**

12.1. Application Limitations 261
12.1.1. Objects 261
12.1.2. Forms 261
12.1.3. Procedures 262
12.2. Form Limitations 262
12.2.1. Control Numbers 262
12.2.2. Open Forms 262
12.2.3. Properties 262
12.3. Control Limitations 262
12.3.1. List 263
12.3.2. Text 263
12.3.3. Caption 263
12.3.4. Tag 263

12.4. Code Limitations 263
12.5. Symbol Tables 264
    12.5.1.   Module 264
    12.5.2.   Global 264
12.6. Data Limitations 264
    12.6.1.   Global 264
    12.6.2.   Form and Code 264
    12.6.3.   Size of Variables 264
12.7. String Data 265
12.8. Arrays 266
12.9. User-Defined Types 266
12.10. Stack Space 266
12.11. Windows Limitations 266
    12.11.1. Resources 266
    12.11.2. Run and Shell Settings 267
    12.11.3. MDI Applications 267

CHAPTER 13.   ADVANCED AREA INTRODUCTIONS **269**

13.1. Graphics 269
    13.1.1.   Fundamentals 269
          13.1.1.1. Twips 269
          13.1.1.2. Coordinate System 270
          13.1.1.3. Color 270
               RGB 271
               QBColor 271
    13.1.2.   Graphical Controls 271
          13.1.2.1. Advantages 271
          13.1.2.2. Limitations 272
          13.1.2.3. Image Control 272
          13.1.2.4. Line Control 272
          13.1.2.5. Shape Control 272
          13.1.2.6. Placing Pictures in Forms 272
          13.1.2.7. Animation 272
    13.1.3.   Graphical Methods 273
          13.1.3.1. Advantages 273
          13.1.3.2. Limitations 273
13.2. MDI 273
    13.2.1.   MDI in Visual Basic 275
    13.2.2.   Creating MDI Forms 275
    13.2.3.   Design-Time Child Forms 275
    13.2.4.   Runtime Child Forms 275
    13.2.5.   Windows Compatibility 275
    13.2.6.   Document-Centered Applications 276

13.3. Objects 276
    13.3.1. Introduction to Objects 276
    13.3.2. Declaring an Object 277
    13.3.3. Object Types 279
    13.3.4. Arrays 279
    13.3.5. Using Objects 279
    13.3.6. System Objects 280
13.4. Printing and Displaying 280
    13.4.1. Fonts 280
        13.4.1.1. Printer and Screen Fonts *280*
        13.4.1.2. Font Characteristics *281*
        13.4.1.3. Setting Fonts *282*
    13.4.2. Print Method 282
    13.4.3. Tabs 282
    13.4.4. Format Number, Time, Date 283
    13.4.5. Introduction to Printing 283
        13.4.5.1. Printer Object *283*
        13.4.5.2. PrintForm *284*
        13.4.5.3. Printing a Printer Object *284*
        13.4.5.4. Multipage Documents *284*
        13.4.5.5. PrintForm Method *284*
13.5. Help Compiler 285
    13.5.1. Features 286
    13.5.2. Tools 286
    13.5.3. Creating the Help System 287
    13.5.4. Topics 287
    13.5.5. Planning the Help System 288
    13.5.6. Creating Topic Files 288
    13.5.7. Hypergraphics 288
    13.5.8. WinHelp Macros 289
13.6. Grid 289
    13.6.1. Grid Control 289
    13.6.2. Sizing 289
    13.6.3. Changing the Grid Size 290
    13.6.4. Text in Grid Cells 291
    13.6.5. Alignment 291
    13.6.6. Adding Graphics 291
    13.6.7. Adding and Removing Rows 291
13.7. Control Development Kit 292
    13.7.1. Custom Control Defined 292
    13.7.2. Needed Software Background 292
    13.7.3. Software System Requirements 292
    13.7.4. Installing CDK 293

13.7.5. Fundamentals 293

13.7.6. Control Class 293

13.8. Data Manager 293

13.8.1. Creating a Database 294

13.8.2. Opening a Database.......................... 295

13.8.3. Modifying Table Data 296

13.8.3.1. *Opening a Table* 296

13.8.3.2. *Adding a Record to a Table* 296

13.8.3.3. *Deleting a Record from a Table* 296

13.8.3.4. *Modifying the Data in a Record* 297

13.8.3.5. *Viewing the Current Records*
         in the Table 297

APPENDIX A. **299**

A.1. Installing Visual Basic 299

A.1.1. Backup Disks and Miscellaneous Issues 299

A.1.2. Running Setup 300

A.1.3. Other Text Files 300

A.1.4. Checking Setup 301

INDEX **303**

'Hello from Visual Basic 3.0 Professional'

Preface

The BASIC (Beginners' All-purpose Symbolic Instruction Code) language first developed between 1963 and 1964, immediately gained worldwide acceptance, and soon thousands of programmers and nonprogrammers were using it. BASIC has continually been updated, and new and improved versions such as BASICA have appeared over the ensuing years. Now with Windows gaining such attention due to its GUI (Graphical User Interface), BASIC has again evolved to run under Windows. Microsoft's Visual Basic takes the older BASIC programmer to a higher and improved level of program writing for the Windows GUI platform.

A slightly different mindset must be used when writing in Visual Basic versus the older BASIC versions. However, many familiar BASIC commands and code still exist for the newcomer to Visual Basic to relate to. This book will explain the similarities and differences and show you how to get up and productive using Visual Basic Professional 3.0 to program in the shortest possible amount of time.

Nonprogrammers will find this book invaluable for learning the essentials of programming and constructing Windows applications. Students and schools of computer science will also find this book a perfect primer for teaching programming basics and terminology for the Windows world. Since Version 3.0 has features that even support Windows NT, this book should be a welcome reference for some time to come.

Introduction

1.1. WELCOME TO VISUAL BASIC

Welcome to the world of BASIC in the form of Visual Basic Professional 3.0 by Microsoft Corporation, which allows you to write professional applications for the world of Windows in a reliable, fast, and efficient way. Version 3.0 offers features that make your Windows programming platform even more powerful without making the previous versions of the language obsolete. Visual Basic Professional 3.0's capabilities may convince MIS departments, database, network, and system managers, and others who use higher-level languages such as COBOL to use the features that this language now provides.

According to Microsoft, Visual Basic is the cornerstone of its applications programming strategy. Many of Microsoft's applications may eventually contain a derivative of Visual Basic as a common macro language that will be able to control the application and other applications through the OLE (Object Linking and Embedding) 2.0 Automation interface included in Visual Basic. Since OLE 2.0 supports Windows NT, Visual Basic can only grow in the number of installed sites.

1.2. WHO WILL BENEFIT FROM THIS BOOK

This book is for those programmers and nonprogrammers who use, or have used, some form of Basic and want to write Windows programs while retaining a link to the BASIC language. The format of this book is such that even those not familiar with BASIC will find it the fast track to learning how to write Windows programs.

All readers, familiar or not with BASIC, should have an end-user's working knowledge of the essentials of Windows 3.x or Windows 4.x. Though you need not have a detailed background in Windows, you should at least have used a Windows-based product long enough to know that when the word "icon" is used it refers to a representative graphic symbol for some process that will take place if you choose it, usually by left-clicking your mouse button.

1.3. STRUCTURE AND STYLE OF THE BOOK

What makes this book different is that it wastes no time telling you how to start writing your own Visual Basic programs. After the usual, general introductory and background material, the minimum details about the language that you need to write and run your first Windows program will be given. You need not know and remember every icon and its meaning to write your first application.

Next, the finer points of Visual Basic will be explained. By this I mean that the areas most programmers use in every program—not every area available in the package—will be dealt with in depth. Only rarely, if ever, are all areas and options of a language used in a single program. Thus my first purpose is to show you the most commonly used features of Visual Basic to get you up and productive *fast*! I have chosen to cover the Professional version here since it has many features that experienced programmers will want to include in their applications but that the Standard version does not offer.

Those features of Visual Basic not used as often during programming will be covered, but only in general terms. Thus you will know all of the features available in the Visual Basic Professional 3.0 language and will learn how to use the majority of them.

1.4. THE TWO VERSIONS OF VISUAL BASIC

Even though this book covers the Professional version of Visual Basic, a look at both available versions is in order here so that you will have sufficient information regarding the features each contains to choose which version best suits your present and future needs.

1.4.1. Standard Version

The Standard version is designed to meet the needs of those who must occasionally write programs but are not programmers by trade or title. These people, on average, spend fewer than fifteen hours per week programming and are not familiar with a large number of programming tools and utilities. Examples of this part-time group include engineers, professionals in the financial industry, and academics involved in instruction or research. The primary need of this group is to get code working fast with as little training and instruction in programming as possible. For example, a stockbroker may need to develop quickly an application that automatically updates spreadsheets for daily inspection from a remote database. Here is a situation where Visual Basic's design tools and OLE 2.0 (Object Linking and Embedding) client controls save time in building a user interface as the user wants to see and use it.

1.4.2. Professional Version

The Professional version contains the same performance features, debugging tools, capacity, and design environment as the Standard edition. However, it also includes a number of tools and development support features that broaden the range of applications you may produce. Thus the Professional version is ideal for consultants, corporate developers, and software vendors who need a comprehensive set of programming tools that quickly enable them to generate and ship a wide variety of Windows applications. Advanced developers must address a more demanding range of user requirements and needs. Additional controls in the Professional edition allow these users to build sophisticated graphical user interfaces and address special needs such as Multimedia or Pen issues. Creating e-mail and work group applications through MAPI (Messaging Application Programming Interface) may be of great interest to some. Others will be attracted by the object-oriented database access that the Professional version provides through its language-based data access object using OLE 2.0 and the ODBC (Open Data Base Connectivity) standard developed by Microsoft and the SQL Access Groups. Also included is the complete set of support and publishing tools required for distributing programs that include the Windows Help Compiler, Setup Wizard, and Setup Toolkit.

1.5.   BACKGROUND OF VISUAL BASIC

Almost from its first release date, Visual Basic has had a large impact on users and programmers alike. The second and third releases merely made a good platform better.

1.5.1.   Version 1.00

When Microsoft Corporation introduced version 1.00 of Visual Basic in May of 1991, it was designed to be a visual programming environment integrating an editor, compiler, and debugger using an event-driven programming model. The goal was to enable programmers trained in traditional languages to create quality Windows applications quickly with little additional training. Combining graphic design tools, event-driven programming, and an open system, Visual Basic offered programmers what is now termed *visual programming*.

A customer survey made one year after Visual Basic 1.00 was released showed that more than 100,000 new Windows applications written in Visual Basic were in use. Each of these applications was used, on average, by 44 people. As for Visual Basic's learning curve, programmers used to third- or fourth-generation languages generally became proficient in Visual Basic in 2–3 weeks. Gauged in terms of production quality applications shipped, Visual Basic quickly emerged as one of the highest productivity development tools available.

1.5.2. Version 2.00

Visual Basic 2.00 expanded the toolset with the additional capabilities necessary for serious part-time and professional programmers, providing significantly increased speed gains and program capacity to meet the requirements of highly reliable business applications. Many power enhancements were added along with a full-featured debugging system. The inclusion of such enhancements as e-mail-based work flow and ODBC (Open Database Connectivity) database features in the Professional version opened up new application areas for custom software developers in nearly any industry.

1.5.3. Version 3.0

Version 3.0 builds upon the foundation of the two previous versions. It is downward compatible, making the conversion of Versions 1.0 and 2.0 applications to Version 3.0 nearly transparent. Version 3.0 also meets the demands of custom solution developers with better ability to access data and to use applications as components with OLE 2.0 Automation. Among the important new features in version 3.0 are:

- The Microsoft Access 1.1 Engine. This feature permits you to access many database and other formats. It supports ODBC, multiple users, SQL, true transaction processing, servers, and more.
- A two-way data access methodology: the programmatic layer and the visual layer. The *programmatic layer* uses code statements to control data access, while the *visual layer* uses toolbox controls.
- Data-aware controls. Using the visual layer, these controls provide ways to create the data access section of custom solutions without writing any code.
- Crystal Reports Version 2.0. This report writer, included in the

Professional edition, allows you to embed reports into your application.

- OLE 2.0 Automation. This feature gives you the ability to send messages, execute methods, and set properties on an OLE 2.0 defined object. Put another way, it is a communication protocol that enables users to create documents using more than one application. OLE 2.0 Automation can be used instead of DDE. Using OLE is faster and constitutes an easier way of exercising interapplication communication and control.

1.6. MULTIPLE DEVELOPER SUPPORT

The following items have been added to Visual Basic to make it more usable by larger development teams.

- ASCII representation of code modules and forms. This feature is particularly important to corporate developers. Since ASCII can be read by nearly any tool, from word processors to databases, it enables you to use source library managers and CASE tools, thereby allowing multiple teams to work on projects with third-party code management tools.
- ASCII make files allowing textual representation of project (.MAK) files. This feature provides programmers better documentation of their applications, allows CASE tools to generate applications created in Visual Basic, and permits Visual Basic for MS-DOS projects to be loaded into Visual Basic for Windows and vice versa.
- The /MAKE$ option. This feature allows code generators to create .EXEs without programmer assistance, thus permitting developers to start large compile jobs automatically.

1.7. SUPPORT FROM THIRD PARTIES

Included in each Visual Basic package you will find a Products and Services Directory, a comprehensive listing of the numerous third-party custom controls and DLLs (Dynamic Link Library), libraries and programming utilities, publications, and services available to Visual Basic users.

1.8. TWO PREVIEW APPLICATIONS

Before you start learning how to use Visual Basic, you may want to see what it can do. Two examples will show you just a few of the features that can be incorporated into your applications. In Figure 1.1 you will see an application to calculate a "Goal." In this case the name of the goal is SPORTS CAR X. The program gives the results "Save Yearly" and "Monthly" by doing calculations based on "Years to goal," "Price of goal," "Annual rate of return," and "Amount already saved." Clicking on the "Calc Results" button after you have entered the requested information will give you the results shown. Two other buttons offer you the options of seeing the results in a grid or in graph format for a more detailed examination of the variables.

Figure 1.2 is an example of a simple database application concerning employees. It allows adding and deleting records and shows information about a person's salary, last review date, and any comments from past reviews.

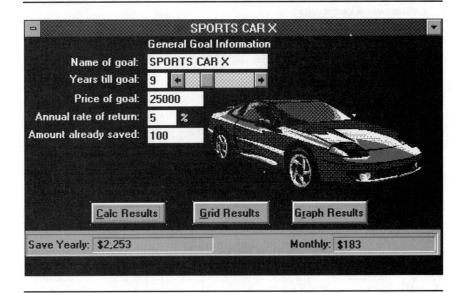

Figure 1.1. Calculations for SPORTS CAR X.

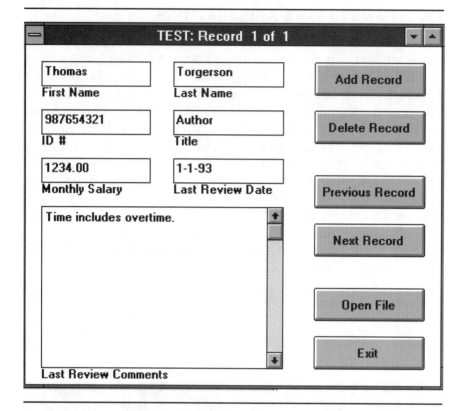

Figure 1.2.   Test: Employee database.

These applications show only a fraction of the Visual Basic features you can use to create applications to fit your particular needs. Visual Basic has been used in such varied areas as corporate information systems, purchasing management, accounting, travel agent support, personal finance, communications, and inventory management.

1.9.   ONLINE DOCUMENTATION

Along with the written documentation manuals that accompany the Standard and Professional versions, Visual Basic also affords access to online documentation of nearly all features during pro-

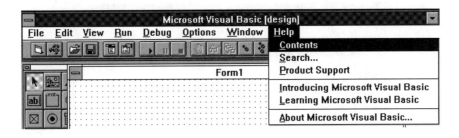

Figure 1.3.   Help menu.

gram development. Many of the Help topics contain code examples that you can copy directly into your application using the clipboard.

Figure 1.3. shows all of the options available under the Help menu. Choosing Product Support advises you how to seek help if you cannot solve a problem yourself. About Microsoft Visual Basic . . . provides interesting facts about the product. However, it is the other options that you will find most useful and informative while developing applications.

Selecting Help+Contents brings up Figure 1.4. This submenu gives you four subject areas from which to choose: Visual Basic Help options, How to Use Visual Basic, Building a Visual Basic Application, and Reference options. The Contents screen is used to jump to topics that tell you how to use Visual Basic, or to access key reference topics quickly. Click on any icon or underlined area for more help concerning the topic on which you want information. For instance, if you are starting to make a user input screen and have a question about your screen interface, you may wish to click (with your left mouse button) on the underlined topic Creating the Interface under the heading Building a Visual Basic Application.

Referring back to Figure 1.3, you may wish to use the Search . . . option, available from any Help topic window, to go directly to a topic. To do so, select the Search button, type the appropriate word in the dialog box (or select a word by scrolling down the topic list under the dialog box), and press ENTER to view the chosen topic.

The two remaining Help menu options, Introducing Microsoft

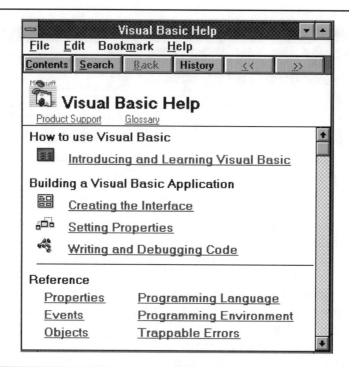

Figure 1.4.   Help contents screen.

Visual Basic and Learning Microsoft Visual Basic, are essentially online tutorials on the fundamentals of Visual Basic and how to use it to produce an application. Both are highly informative and recommended reading for any new Visual Basic owner.

1.9.1.   Context-Sensitive Help

One of the most invaluable aids offered by Visual Basic is the context-sensitive Help option. While you are developing program code, being able to highlight a keyword or command and then press F1 for immediate help on that topic is a tremendous advantage. Context-sensitive areas include every window, all items in the toolbar, the toolbox controls, the objects on a form, properties, event procedures, reserved words, and error messages.

Getting Started

2.1.   OVERVIEW

This chapter covers the fundamental theory underlying Visual Basic Professional 3.0 and other essential information you need to know before building your first Windows application.

2.2.   INTRODUCTION TO A PROJECT

Before you go further, a brief explanation of what a project is and does is in order. A *project* is the collection of files that your application comprises. The different types of files an application may use are distinguished by their file name extensions. A file with the extension .BAS is a code module; a .VBX indicates a custom control file (for instance, a "do an action" routine represented by an icon, a group option box, or even an OLE); the .FRM extension designates forms; and the .MAK extension marks the project file, which keeps track of all the files and provides information on the environment options used. Another extension you may see, .FRX, is for binary data files.

Visual Basic Professional 3.0 also gives you the ability to generate Help files related to your applications. The extensions for such files are .RTF, .HPJ, .BMP, . WMF, .SHG, and .MRK.

With this information, you now have an idea of how the file names relate to each other in the overall scheme of Visual Basic and of what a file with a specific extension is likely to contain. This important information will help you interpret how all the many different file extensions contained in the example projects in your manuals and sample files fit together without digging through pages and pages of manuals to find a file extension's meaning and its relationship to others in an application.

Details on the different file types, by extension use, will be given as needed and in context throughout this book. Remember, though, that the main function of this book is to get you up and programming usefully in the minimum amount of time. You need not know all the details of all the file types to program productively in Visual Basic Professional.

2.3.   RUNNING VISUAL BASIC

Double-clicking on the icon labelled 'Microsoft Visual Basic' brings you into the programming and development area that is the subject of this book. Visual Basic can also be started from the command line, if desired, by using the following syntax:

```
VB [[/R[UN] filename] [/C[MD] commandline]]|[/M[AKE]
projname[.mak [exename]]
```

Option Meaning

/RUN Run the application specified by the *filename*

/CMD Allows an input command-line argument that you can use with the COMMAND function.

/MAK Loads the project named, in *projname* and executes the MAKE .EXE command from the File menu to create an executable file named *exename*.

The *filename* specified with the /RUN option must have a .MAK extension if it is to be seen as a project file. Any other file with a different extension will be loaded as either a Form or Module into a new project.

2.4.   THE PROGRAMMING ENVIRONMENT

When Visual Basic Professional starts, you will see your programming environment with its screens and windows in the basic form shown in Figure 2.1.

There are six main areas in the environment.

1. Menu Bar: Shows and displays the specific commands you use to build an application.
2. Toolbar: An area providing quick access to commands found in the Menu Bar.

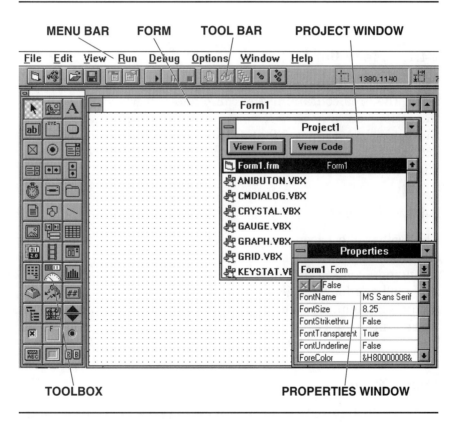

Figure 2.1.   The Visual Basic Professional programming environment.

3. Forms: The window or windows that you customize to produce the user interface to your application.

4. Toolbox: The set of tools used at design or programming time to place controls on your forms such as Text or Combo boxes.

5. Properties Window: Lists the property settings for a particular control or form. A property is some value of an object such as its color or size.

6. Project Window: Lists the control files, basic code modules, forms, and other files that make up the entire application. Recall that a 'project' is the set of files that together make up an application or complete program.

The remainder of this section explains each of these six areas in more detail.

2.4.1.   Menu Bar

The menu bar format should be familiar to any Windows user. To select the area containing the command you wish to execute or the action you want to perform, click on the appropriate word in the menu bar. Figure 2.2 shows the list of subcommands and actions that appears when you select the File menu bar option as an example.

2.4.2.   Toolbar

The toolbar offers icon representations of some of the commands found in the menu bar as shown in Figure 2.3. To execute these commands, click on the particular icon for the command you need. The toolbar's fourteen icons, their actions, and their equivalent menu bar commands are summarized in Table 2.1. Note that it is much quicker to click on the toolbar icon than to use the menu bar.

2.4.3.   Form

You may customize the Form window to serve as the user interface. This window will contain the controls, pictures, graphics, and other elements users will see and with which they will inter-

Figure 2.2.   Options available under File on the menu bar.

The Visual Basic toolbar provides shortcuts for many common design and debugging commands.

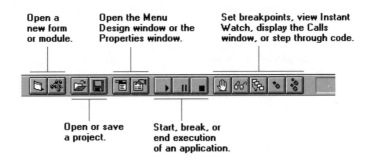

Figure 2.3.   Visual Basic Toolbar

Table 2.1. Toolbar icons and actions and their menu bar equivalents.

Icon	Action performed	Menu Equivalent
	Creates a new form	New Form option under File on the menu bar
	Creates a new module	New Module option under File on the menu bar
	Opens an existing module	Open Project option under File on the menu bar
	Saves the current project	Save Project option under File on the menu bar
	Displays the 'Menu Design' window	Menu Design option under Window on the menu bar
	Displays the 'Properties' window	Properties option under Window on the menu bar
	Starts an application in design mode	Start option under Run on the menu bar
	Stops execution of a program while running	Break option under Run on the menu bar
	Stops an application and returns to design mode	End option under Run on the menu bar
	Toggles breakpoint on the current line	Toggle Breakpoint option under Debug on the menu bar
	Shows value of the current selection in a code line	Instant Watch option under Debug on the menu bar
	Displays the structure of active cells	Calls command under Debug on the menu bar
	Executes code one line at a time	Single Step option under Debug on the menu bar
	Executes code one procedure or statement at a time	Procedure Step option under Debug on the menu bar

You can use forms in many different ways:

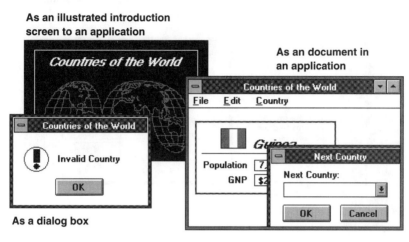

As an illustrated introduction screen to an application

As an document in an application

As a dialog box

Figure 2.4. Example forms.

act. Figure 2.4 shows how forms may be used in different ways, and that there can be multiple forms in an application.

2.4.4. Toolbox

Figure 2.5 shows all Toolbox controls contained in the Standard version of Visual Basic. Note that there are fewer controls than in the Professional version. Your first application will use only a few controls, all of which we will now consider.

Figure 2.6. is the Label control, used for making headings for your application. The command button control in Figure 2.7 is used frequently. Examples are the OK and CANCEL buttons. You may also devise command buttons for your applications that allow the user to choose among optional actions. The Text Box control, shown in Figure 2.8, is also used frequently to allow the user to enter text information such as a name or address. This tool is also used for outputting text messages, instructions, and so forth.

Controls are tools such as boxes, buttons, and labels you draw on a form to get input or to display output. They also add visual appeal to your forms.

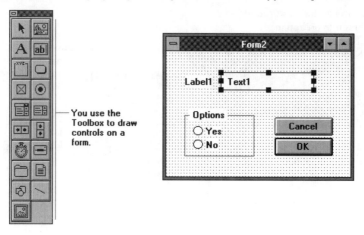

You use the Toolbox to draw controls on a form.

Figure 2.5. Toolbox example controls.

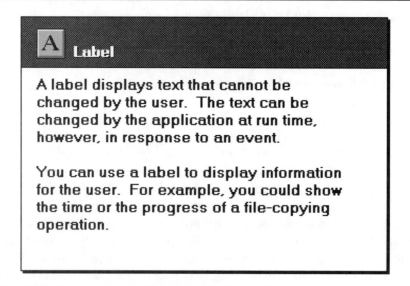

Label

A label displays text that cannot be changed by the user. The text can be changed by the application at run time, however, in response to an event.

You can use a label to display information for the user. For example, you could show the time or the progress of a file-copying operation.

Figure 2.6. Label from the Toolbox.

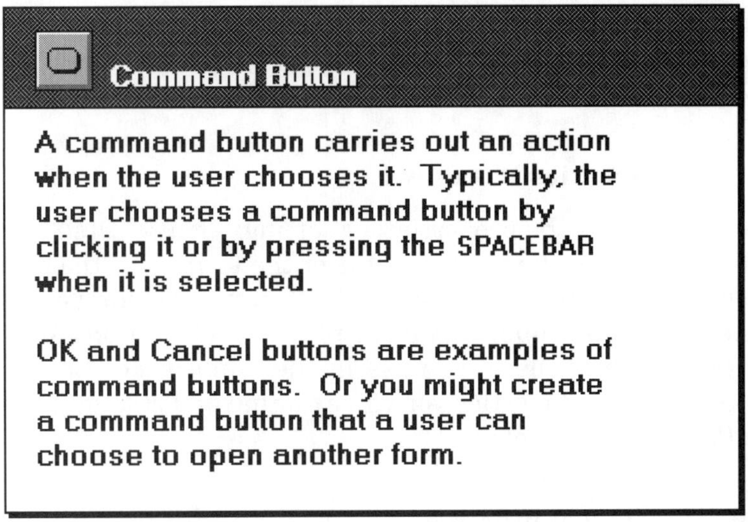

Command Button

A command button carries out an action
when the user chooses it. Typically, the
user chooses a command button by
clicking it or by pressing the SPACEBAR
when it is selected.

OK and Cancel buttons are examples of
command buttons. Or you might create
a command button that a user can
choose to open another form.

Figure 2.7.   Command button from the Toolbox.

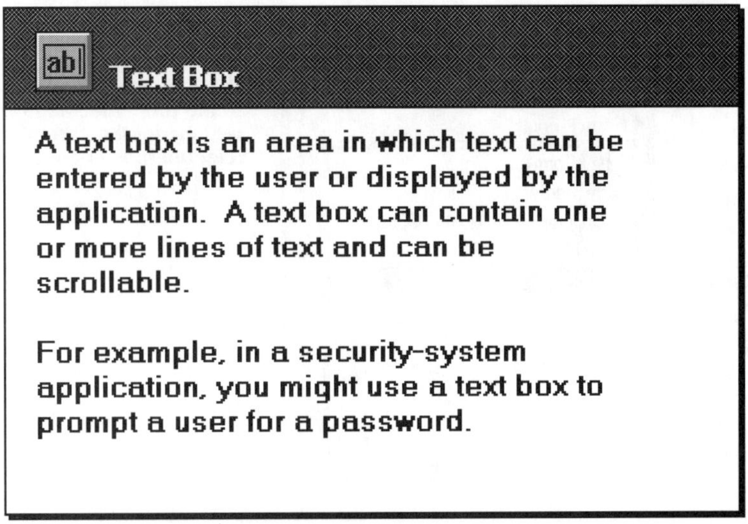

Text Box

A text box is an area in which text can be
entered by the user or displayed by the
application. A text box can contain one
or more lines of text and can be
scrollable.

For example, in a security-system
application, you might use a text box to
prompt a user for a password.

Figure 2.8.   Text Box from the Toolbox.

Most of the remaining Toolbox controls will be shown and discussed later, as you progress in learning Visual Basic. For now, however, it is best to master using these basics first, before moving on to use more advanced features!

2.4.5.   Properties Window

Figure 2.9 shows the properties, or settings, of a selected form or control. You may change the name of the form with the caption setting, highlighted in the figure. You may, for example, decide to change the caption from Form1 to FormCalculations for more clarity regarding the form's use in the application. Each form and control has properties you can examine and change by using this Properties window.

2.4.6.   Project Window

The Project window serves two purposes. One is to give you an overall list of the files involved in a project or application. The second purpose is to allow you either to look at the Visual Basic

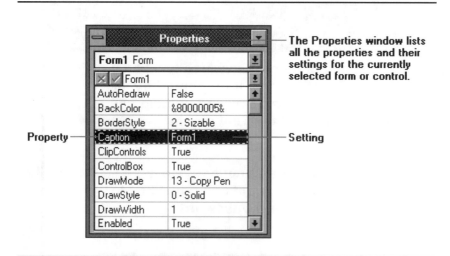

Figure 2.9.   Properties window.

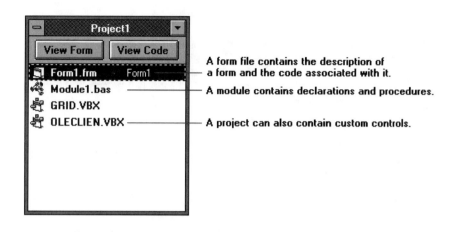

Figure 2.10. Project window files.

code for a given module or to examine a chosen form from the user's perspective instead and make any needed changes on the form.

Figure 2.10. shows a sample project and gives you some information regarding its files. Note that this is a hypothetical project created only for purposes of illustration. Your files will differ in number and name. Figure 2.11 illustrates where to click either to view a form or to view actual Visual Basic code for the project called Project1.

2.5.   YOUR FIRST APPLICATION AND PROJECT

In this section you will use what has been shown and explained thus far to build your first Windows application in Visual Basic Professional. You will do all of the three processes that must be done for every new application: create the interface, set properties, and write the code. You will then save the application as a project so that you may load and run the application program at any later date. Remember, a project is nothing more than the total collection of different files needed to run, use, or change an application.

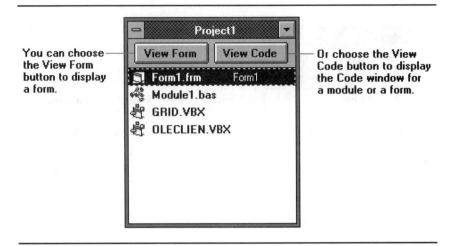

You can choose the View Form button to display a form.

Or choose the View Code button to display the Code window for a module or a form.

Figure 2.11. Project window viewing options.

2.5.1. Function of the Application

The function of this program is the usual 'Hello World . . .' type of routine. When a user clicks on a certain button, the text "Hello World" will appear in what used to be a blank text area. A heading will also be visible at all times near the top of the form window.

To make sure that no other old files will be included in your new application, click on New Project under File on the menu bar. After successfully running the application, you will use the Save Project As . . . option under File on the menu bar. Name the project *Prog1.prj* or another name of your choice. Name the form, when asked, with the same prefix as your project prefix name to avoid confusion, for example: *Prog1.frm*.

2.5.2. Create the Interface

An interface must first be constructed on a form, or user window, before anything else can be done. By using the Toolbox controls (see Table 2.1) you pick which control(s) you want on a form. In this instance there is only one form with three controls, but most applications have multiple forms with which the user interacts.

Tip: An easy way to add a control is to double-click the icon for that control in the Toolbox. This will create a default-sized control located in the center of the form.

Click on the Label control icon from the Toolbox. Move the pointer onto the form where you want the upper left corner to be and click. The pointer will become a cross-hair. Drag the cross-hair down and to the right until the control is where you want it (see Figure 2.12), and release the mouse button. Note that small rectangular boxes appear at the corners of the control. These are called *sizing handles*.

Click on the Text box control icon from the Toolbox. Follow the same steps as previously to position the control where you want it on the form (see Figure 2.13).

Finally, click on the Command button control icon from the Toolbox and repeat these steps to obtain the result shown in Figure 2.14.

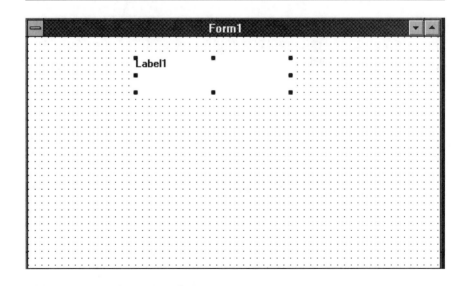

Figure 2.12. Label control.

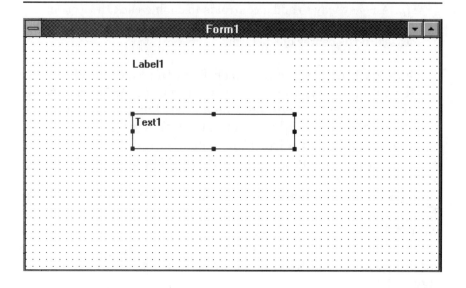

Figure 2.13. Text box control.

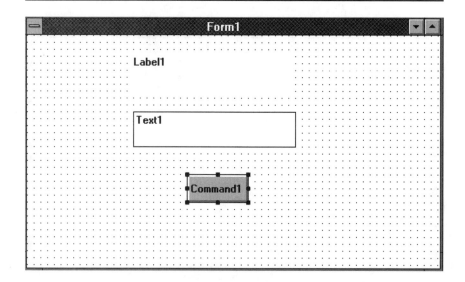

Figure 2.14. Command button control.

2.5.2.1. Changing the size of controls. If you find that a control is too large or small on the form you can resize it. To do so, click the control you want changed on the form to display the sizing handles. Now place the mouse pointer on one of these handles, click, and drag until the control is the size you want it to be. Release the mouse button when the control size has changed sufficiently. Experiment with the different handles, paying attention to where they are on the control and what each does to the control's shape and size.

2.5.2.2. Moving controls. Sometimes the size of a control is exactly as you want it, but you wish to move the entire control to a different position on the form. To do this, place your mouse pointer on any point *other than* a sizing handle on the control you want to move, and drag the whole control to its new position. Release the mouse button when the control is at the desired location.

2.5.3.   Set Properties

Your application now has four objects: a form, a label area, a text box, and a command button. Each of these has a unique set of associated properties. *Properties* include captions, color, and font type, to name but a few. All objects have default values that can be changed. To make your application more understandable to a user, you will only need to change captions and a text value for the objects. To do this you first need to pick an object, then pick the property you wish to change from the property list in the Properties window.

For this lesson, first click on any blank area in the form. This makes the object *form* the active object. Next, open the Properties window, either by choosing the Properties command from the Windows menu, or clicking on the Properties icon from the Toolbar (see Table 2.1), or right-click on the object. The aim at this point is to rename the form caption, Form1, to HELLO. Right click anywhere in the form's object to bring up the property inspector, which contains all properties belonging to that particular object. You will work with three areas in the Properties window. The first, the *Object box* (see Figure 2.15), contains the line "Form1 Form." In this line, Form1 is the name of the object

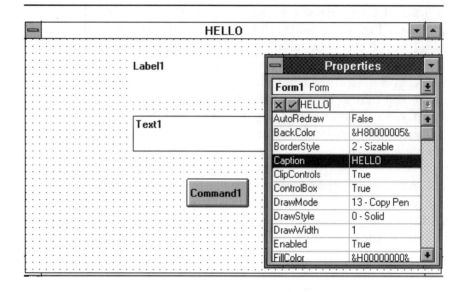

Figure 2.15. Changed Form caption property.

whose properties you can set and Form is the type of object with which you are working. So, here you are working with the form object called Form1. If you click on the down arrow on the right side of this top line, you will see all the objects you can choose to modify for the active form. This is a shortcut way to move to the next property control you wish to change when you are done with the current object's properties. Second is the Settings box where you type in new values or text properties. You can also edit the content of this box by clicking on its down arrow, again on the right. If there are multiple choices, you can click on the one you wish to select. Third is the Properties list, where you click on the desired property to change it or simply to check its current value.

Your goal here is to change the caption of this object to HELLO. Left, then right click in any area of the form that has no object. As shown in Figure 2.15, the way to accomplish this is first to click on the property Caption, then click on the Settings box and type in HELLO, replacing the caption Form1. Note that as you type in the new caption, the form's caption changes immediately, letter by letter, so you see exactly what the new caption looks like instantly, not sometime later. Seeing your changes take effect as soon as you make them is invaluable. Now that you have completed your first change, leave the Properties window active and proceed to the next steps.

2.5.3.1. Set Control Properties. Now that the form object has been changed to what you wish, the three control captions and text will be changed to reflect your particular application.

The command button caption is the next to be changed. Click on the command button to give it the focus, then right click on the command button. Click on the right down arrow on the object box and find and click on the command button line (see Figure 2.16.). Click on Caption from the Property list and enter "OK" in the Settings box. This will signify to the user that clicking on OK will start the application.

Next, click on the down arrow in the object box and find and click on the Text box line. Since this is the area where "Hello

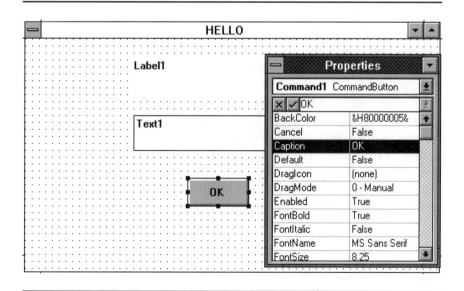

Figure 2.16.   Changed command button caption.

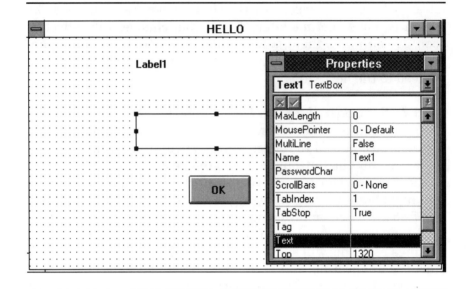

Figure 2.17. Changed Text box caption.

World" will appear when OK is clicked, no caption or information should appear in this box when the program is started, so you must blank it out. In the Settings box, where you normally backspace and then enter new text, this time just backspace all the way to the left. This leaves a blank area, as shown in Figure 2.17.

Finally, click on the down arrow in the object box and find and click on the Label line. The label acts basically as a heading and cannot be changed by the user. Click on the Text property, and go to the Settings box text line. Backspace all old information and then type in "When you click on OK a Hello message should be seen . . ." Note that, depending on the length of your label, at the end of each line, automatic wordwrapping occurs (see Figure 2.18).

2.5.4. Write Needed Code

The final thing you must do is to write the code to execute language statements. Without the appropriate code, the program so far is nothing more than a shell of a GUI (graphical user inter-

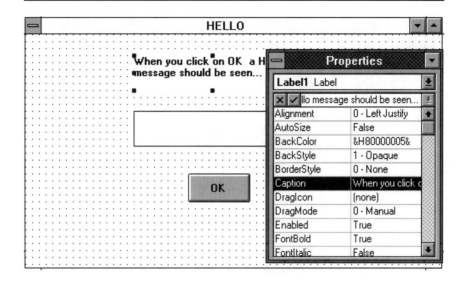

Figure 2.18.   Changed Label caption.

face). Our goal is to put a message on the screen when the user clicks on the OK button. This means we need only write code that belongs to the OK button.

Code in a Visual Basic program is divided into small blocks called *procedures*. An *event procedure*, the category to which the OK button belongs, contains code that is executed when an event such as clicking on the OK button occurs. To create an event procedure, you first pick an object in the Object box by clicking on its down arrow, and then pick a procedure from the Procedure list box (see Figure 2.19). A template will appear into which you must insert your own code. A template usually consists of just the first and last lines of a procedure, but it saves you time since you need only fill in the action code that will be executed between the first and last lines of any procedure.

In general, to open the Code window, double-click the form or control for which you wish to write code, or open it from the Project window by selecting the form's name and picking the View code button. Figure 2.19 shows the Code window after

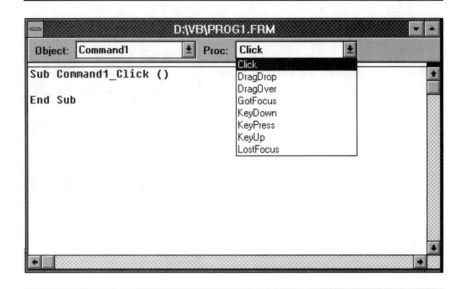

Figure 2.19. Code window events drop-down options.

double clicking on the control with its caption, OK. The drop-down list contains the events available for Command1 object. In this case the default, Click, is what you want, since when you click on this object you want the upcoming code to be executed.

2.5.4.1. *More on the code window.* The Code window has two main areas, the Object box and the Procedure list box. The Object box displays the name of the selected object. Clicking on this box's down arrow shows all objects contained in the active form. The Procedure list displays the selected procedure or event, and clicking on its down arrow shows all the procedures for the object.

You need to insert the line

```
Text1.Text = "Hello World."
```

between the two template lines as shown in Figure 2.20. Be sure to enclose in quotes the text that you wish to appear in the text box when your application executes.

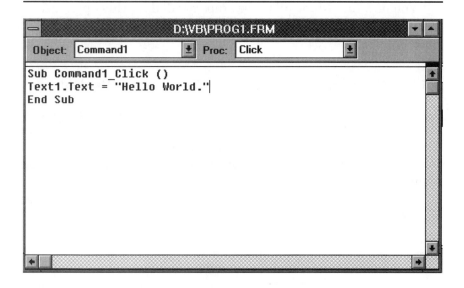

Figure 2.20.   Completed routine.

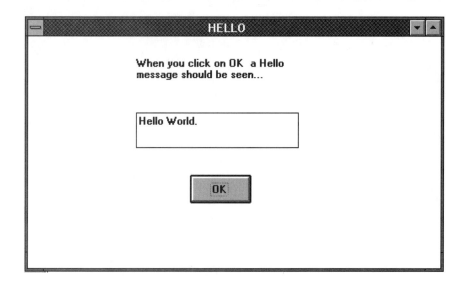

Figure 2.21.   Result of running the application.

You now have done all three steps needed for this application: created the interface, set properties, and written the required code.

2.5.5.   Running and Saving the Application Project

You can start an application in any of the following three ways: (1) pick Start from the Run menu; (2) click the start icon (see Table 2.1); or (3) press the F5 function key. If all steps described in the preceding section were done correctly, the result will be as shown in Figure 2.21.

Congratulations! You have just completed your first application in Visual Basic Professional 3.0!

3

Controls

3.1. CONTROLS AND THEIR USE

Controls are used to receive input and display output. You used controls in the last chapter to build your user interface. Command buttons, labels, and text boxes were used to communicate to the user and output results. This chapter takes a further look at the controls available in Visual Basic Professional. Many of the example applications shown in this chapter can be found in the Visual Basic subdirectory Samples. If possible, load and examine these programs as they are discussed here. Doing so will give you a well-rounded understanding of the topics and reduce your learning curve.

As mentioned before, the first step in building an application is to create the interface. The interface of forms, controls, and other objects the user will see and interact with, must be done first.

3.2. CUSTOM CONTROLS

A *custom control* is an extension to the toolbox. Custom controls are used just as any other built-in controls found in the Standard version of Visual Basic. In the Visual Basic Professional edition, you have access to controls not found in the Standard version. Gauges, graphs, and create MAPI (Messaging Application Program Interface) are but a few of the controls found in the Professional version of Visual Basic that are not included in the Standard version.

3.2.1. Loading a Custom Control

A custom control file is a DLL (Dynamic Link Library) containing all the information needed to provide one or more new types of controls. To load a custom control file, first choose Add File from the File menu. The Add File dialog box displays three file extension options: *.FRM, *.BAS, and *.VBX. Custom control files use the *.VBX extension. Now select or type the name of the custom control file you want to open. In the Professional version, custom control files should be located in the \Windows\System directory.

As the file is loaded, note that the control file appears in the Project window, and all the new controls are added to your Toolbox in the form of icons.

At this point you can now use these new controls just as you used the standard controls that you first saw upon running Visual Basic after the install process.

> *Tip:* Running the demonstration programs under the Help menu option will add most custom controls to your system, so you will not have to load them manually as described above.

3.2.2. CDK (Control Development Kit)

The CDK, available only in the Professional edition, lets you write your own custom control files. Custom controls you write extend the application development tools provided by Visual Basic by defining new controls with new properties, events, and functionality. These become part of the tools provided in the Toolbox, so that your new functions are only a key click away.

The CDK also allows you to create a *bound custom control*. A bound control gives you the ability to create a link between a property in the custom control and a data value in a database.

Custom controls can also be created from an existing DLL. This feature allows you to use custom controls in both the Visual Basic and the Visual C++ languages.

To write your own controls and use CDK, you must have and know how to use the Microsoft SDK (Software Development Kit)™ Version 3.0 or later, and a programming language such as C or C++ that can create Windows DLLs.

The CDK consists mainly of examples, documentation, header files, and a library file. Since this book is a primer and not all readers will know the C or C++ language, the details of CDK are not discussed here. If you wish to use this feature, the CDK is described in detail in the documentation accompanying the Professional edition of Visual Basic.

3.3.   A LOOK AT EACH CONTROL

The Toolbox (see Figure 3.1) contains the tools used to draw controls on your forms. Each of the thirty-nine tools shown represents a control. Table 3.1 lists the Standard version's controls and most of the Professional version's controls by icon, control name, and function.

3.3.1.   Other Controls

One control not in the Toolbox is the Menu control, used to create menus for your applications. You can access this control either by selecting the Menu Design option under Window on the Menu bar, or by clicking on the Menu Design icon from the Toolbar (see Table 2.1).

You may see other controls in the Toolbox depending on what sample programs you have run and what external hardware accessories you have. Controls not shown here include Pen applications, MAPI (messaging interface), and Multimedia applications. Only the Professional version offers these controls, and depending on your system, some or all may appear as icons in the Toolbox when you use your copy of Visual Basic.

Figure 3.1. Toolbox.

Table 3.1. Partial listing of the Visual Basic Professional Toolbox controls.

Icon	Control Name	Function
	Pointer	This is not a control, but gives a way to move and resize forms and controls.
	Picture Box	Provides an area to display text and picture forms; can also act as a visual container of other controls.
	Label	Displays text that a user cannot modify.
	Text box	Provides an area to display or input text.
	Frame	Is a visual and functional container for controls.
	Command button	When a user chooses this, it carries out a command.
	Check box	Displays a yes/no or true/false option to the user.
	Option button	Used with option groups to allow user to pick one option from the group.
	Combo box	Allows user to type in a selection or pick an item from a drop-down list.
	List box	Displays a list of items from which the user can pick.
	Horizontal scroll bar	Allows a user to pick a value from a range of horizontally arrayed values. (*Not* the same as controls with built-in scroll bars.)
	Vertical scroll bar	Allows a user to pick a value from a range of vertically arrayed values. (Similar to the horizontal scroll bar.)
	Timer	Executes events at specified time intervals.
	Drive list box	Allows a user to pick the desired disk drive.
	Directory list box	Allows a user to pick the desired disk directory.

Table 3.1. *Continued*

Icon	Control Name	Function
	File list box	Allows a user to pick the desired file.
	Shape	Adds a rectangle, ellipse, square, or circle to a form.
	Line	Adds a straight line to a form.
	Image	Acts as a command button to show icons, bitmaps, or Windows metafiles.
	Data control	Provides access to databases through bound controls on your form.
	Grid	Shows a series of columns and rows so user can manipulate a cell's contents.
	OLE 2.0	Puts an OLE 2.0 object in an application.
	Animated button	Displays multiple bitmaps to create the illusion of animation.
	Common dialog	Displays one of the standard Windows dialog boxes.
	Crystal report	Calls Crystal Reports to make a custom report.
	Gauge	Creates a user-defined indicator in needle or linear style.
	Graph	Displays many types of graphs.
	Key status	Displays or modifies the status of the CAPS LOCK, NUM LOCK, and SCROLL LOCK keys.
	Communications	Allows transmission and reception of data through the serial port.
	Masked edit	Allows editing or restricting data input and auto formatting of output data.
	Outline	Displays items in a hierarchical list.
	Picture clip	Displays a portion of a source bitmap in a picture box or form.

Table 3.1. *Continued*

Icon	Control Name	Function
	Spin button	Increases or decreases numbers.
	3D check box	Similar to a standard check box; allows use of 3D text.
	3D frame	Simulates the standard frame control, and displays 3D text. The frame can be displayed as raised or inset.
	3D option button	Simulates the standard option button; also allows use of 3D text that can be aligned to the left or right of the control.
	3D command button	Simulates the standard command button; also allows display of a 3D caption, an icon or a bitmap.
	3D panel	Displays a 3D text on a 3D background.
	3D group push button	Simulates functionality of the Ribbon in Excel™ or toolbar in MS Word™ for Windows.

3.4.   OBJECT NAMING FORMATS

All created objects, forms, and controls have a default value for their Name property. For example, in the application presented in Chapter 2, the OK command button object was named Command1. If you had made two other command buttons, they would have been named Command2 and Command3, respectively. Visual Basic keeps track of the number of buttons and automatically adds 1 to the name of each command button you create. In the program in Chapter 2 we did not need to change the object's name from Command1, since there was only one command and you knew what and where it was. However, in a complex application with multiple forms and many command button objects, it would be hard to keep track of what did what and in which form. In such a case, descriptive names other than Command*N* are essential.

3.4.1.   Format Rules

The format to be used for naming objects consists of a prefix describing the object type followed by a descriptive name for the control. This convention makes code more self-documenting and easier to follow.

The object names must conform to these rules:

- All names must start with a letter.
- No name may be longer than 40 characters.
- A name may contain only letters, underscores, and numbers; no spaces or punctuation marks are permitted.

Table 3.2 summarizes the standard naming formats that will be followed in the remainder of this book and gives examples of their use.

3.4.2.   Professional Edition—*About* Property

Many third-party software vendors provide add-on kits for Visual Basic, and some of the controls in the Professional edition are made by these companies. Every custom control in the Professional edition has an *About* property box that you can read for information about a particular control and its maker. To see an example of this, select the *About* property in the Properties list box, then click on the ellipsis to open a dialog box showing the abovementioned information.

3.4.2.1. Object Types.   Each control's object type must be used with the TypeOf keyword in If...Then...Else code statements. The TypeOf keyword is used in situations where it is necessary to determine the type of a given control, as when a control is passed as an argument. For example, consider the source argument of a DragDrop event—*What* is being dragged? Table 3.3 lists each control in the Professional edition and its object type.

3.5.   BUTTONS AND ACTIONS

The most common way a user communicates with a form is to click a button. Such was the case in the application in Chapter 2 where clicking on the OK button caused a message to appear.

Table 3.2.   Object Naming Formats.

Object	Prefix	Example
Check box	chk	chkWriteOnly
Combo box	cbo	cboLanguage
Command button	cmd	cmdOK
Directory list box	dir	dirTarget
Drive list box	drv	drvSource
File list box	fil	filPick
form	frm	frmStart
Frame	fra	fraPrinters
Grid	grd	grdQuantities
Horizontal scroll bar	hsb	hsbHueColor
Image	img	imgBitMap
Label	lbl	lblHelpUser
Line	lin	linHighLightText
List box	lst	lstColorCodes
Menu	mnu	mnuFileSave
Option button	opt	optSpanish
Picture box	pic	picMemoryLeft
Shape (squares, circle, oval, rectangles)	shp	shpOval
Text box	txt	txtInputText
Timer	tmr	tmrStartAlarmCount
Vertical scroll bar	vsb	vsbRatios

There are two ways to use buttons to cause this action. The most common way is to use the command button control as described in Chapter 2. The second way is to create your own button using an image control containing a graphic, usually an icon.

3.5.1.   Using Command Button Controls

In the application presented in Chapter 2, clicking the OK button called the Click event procedure, which told the application to

Table 3.3. Professional controls and object types.

Control	Object type
3D check box	SSCheck
3D command button	SSCommand
3D frame	SSFrame
3D group push button	SSRibbon
3D option button	SSOption
3D panel	SSPanel
Animated button	AniPushButton
Communications	MSComm
Gauge	Gauge
Graph	Graph
Key status	MhState
MAPI	MapiSession, MapiMessages
Masked edlt	MaskEdBox
Multimedia MCI	MMControl
Outline	Outline
Pen edit	VBedit, VHedit
Pen ink on bitmap	InkOnBitmap
Pen onscreen keyboard	SKBButton
Picture clip	PictureClip
Spin button	SpinButton

display a message. In Figure 3.2, the caption property of one of the command buttons has been changed from *Command1* to *Change Signal*. Each time the user clicks on this button, the code in the command button Click event procedure is executed, causing each of the three colored icons in the signal light to change in turn, thus simulating a real traffic light.

3.5.2. Image Control Action

An *image control* also recognizes the Click event. Image controls enable you to trigger the same actions that a command button per-

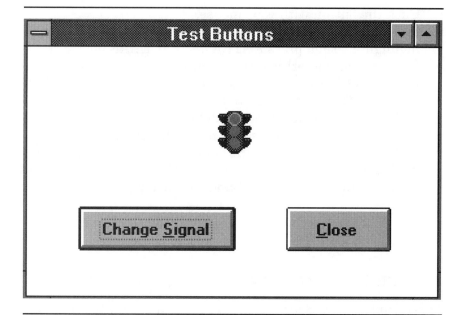

Figure 3.2. Change signal colors using command button control.

forms by clicking on an image. In the traffic light program, clicking on any of the three colored icons in the picture of the traffic light will accomplish the same thing as clicking on the Change Signal button.

Grouping several such image controls horizontally at the top of your form allows you, in effect, to make a toolbar specifically for any of your applications. Each image in the toolbar will have its own function and purpose. Because the procedure for building toolbars is beyond the scope of this book, I refer readers interested in this notion to the Visual Basic *Systems Manuals*, where it is explained in detail. I mention image controls here only to give you an idea of how versatile Visual Basic can be, and an overview of how images may be used as more than just pictures on the screen.

3.5.3. Choosing Command Buttons at Runtime

The various ways to choose a command button are:

- Click the button with your mouse.
- Press the TAB button until the desired command button is highlighted, then press ENTER or SPACEBAR.
- If there is an underlined character in the caption of the button, press ALT+the underlined character.
- Set the button's Value property to TRUE.
- If the command button is the default button, press ENTER even if the command button is not highlighted.
- If the command button is the default CANCEL button, press ESC to choose the button. You specify the default Cancel button by setting the button's Cancel property to TRUE.

Any of these alternatives will invoke the Click event procedure.

3.6.   SHOWING TEXT INFORMATION

Labels and *text boxes* are used to display and input text for your forms. In general, use text boxes for text that may be edited by the enduser, and labels for text intended only to be read.

3.6.1.   Labels

A label control displays text that the user cannot change at runtime. Labels can also be used to identify controls such as scroll bars and text boxes that do not have their own caption property.

Labels have two properties, AutoSize and WordWrap, that help size captions of variable lengths. Figure 3.3 shows the start of a program to demonstrate these two properties. Though single-line captions may be designated as such with the Properties Window during design time, this approach can cause problems. If you need a caption that is longer or may change at runtime, it is better to use AutoSize or WordWrap.

If a label's AutoSize property is set to TRUE, the label will grow horizontally as needed to fit its content, as shown in Figure 3.4. Conversely, the WordWrap property makes the label grow vertically, retaining the original width of the label established during program startup. Both check boxes must be checked to use the WordWrap property, as shown in Figure 3.5. The reason

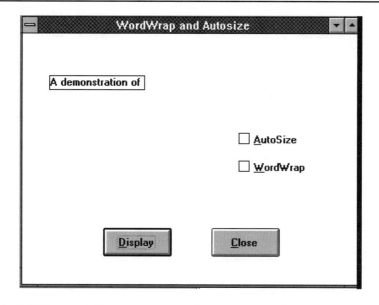

Figure 3.3.   Start of the AutoSize and WordWrap example.

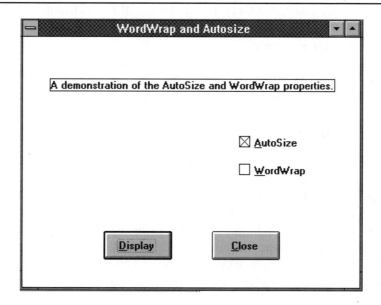

Figure 3.4.   AutoSize example.

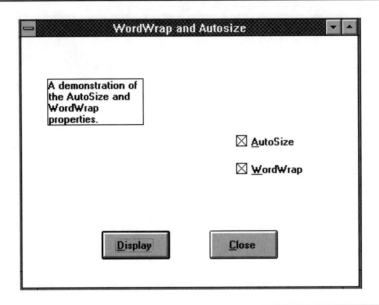

Figure 3.5. WordWrap example.

for this is that the width of the label increases only if the width of a single word exceeds the current width of the control.

3.7. TEXT BOXES

Text boxes are extremely useful controls because they can both display text data and receive user input.

3.7.1. Multiple Line Displays with Text Boxes

MultiLine and *ScrollBars* are two important properties in determining how a text box looks and operates. Note that the text box property ScrollBars is not the same as the scroll bar controls. These are two different entities.

When MultiLine is set to TRUE, the text box can accept the input of user data or display multiple lines of text if need be. When there is no horizontal scroll bar in the text box, MultiLine will also automatically handle word wrap for you. Normally, there won't be any horizontal scroll bar since the ScrollBars property is set to 0 (none) by default. The automatic wordwrap feature of MultiLine means that the user need not insert line breaks at the end of lines—MultiLine autowraps automatically to the next line. When displaying text from within your program, MultiLine will also autowrap, so you need not explicitly code in the line breaks.

Because you cannot enter linebreaks in the Properties window at design time, you must program in a newline character, that is, a carriage return (ANSI 13) and a linefeed (ANSI 10). The following code displays two lines of text in the multiline text box Text9 when this form is called and loaded.

```
Sub Form1_Load()
    NL = Chr(13) + Chr(10)   'Now NL means a NewLine.
    Text9.Text = "First Line" & NL & "Second Line"
End Sub
```

3.8.   WHEN TO USE WHAT CONTROLS

The following set of conditions will help you pick the right control for a specific need. All of the controls suggested for use here are explained in the remaining sections of this chapter. Also, refer back to Table 3.1 for a brief summary of each of these controls.

When You Want	Use
A set of options from which the user can pick only one	Option buttons
A set of options from which the user can pick more than one	Check boxes
A scrollable list of options from which the user can pick	List boxes
A condition whereby users can pick from a list of options or type in their response	Combo boxes
A range of options corresponding to a numeric scale	Horizontal or vertical scroll bars

3.9. INDIVIDUAL OPTIONS WITH CHECK BOXES

Check boxes give users a yes/no or true/false option from which to choose. A number of check boxes can be set to ON at the same time since they work independently of one another. See, for example, Figure 3.6, an application in which the text that the user has entered has been changed to both bold and italic styles. Table 3.4 summarizes objects properties determined by the code segments shown and explained in the following paragraphs.

Note that the settings in Table 3.3 follow the format conventions mentioned previously in Table 3.2.

Remember that we are working here with event-driven programming. This means that immediately on checking a box or option, the indicated action will take place. In this program, when you type any text into the text box and then check one or

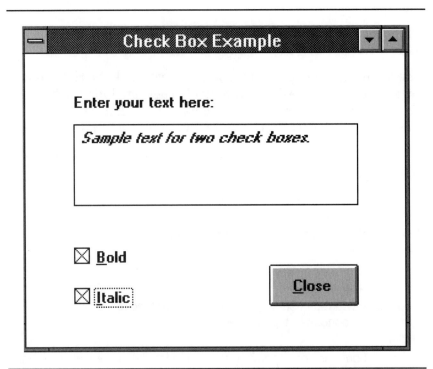

Figure 3.6.   Check box result.

Table 3.4.   Check box example settings.

Object	Property	Setting
Form	Name	frmCheck
	Caption	Check Box Example
Text box	Name	txtDisplay
	Text	(nothing)
Check box	Name	chkBold
	Caption	Bold
Check box	Name	chkItalic
	Caption	Italic

both check boxes, the text will change immediately to the style(s) you have checked (yes/true = 1 in the code).

At the program's beginning, the check boxes' Value properties are set to FALSE. When you then check Bold or Italic, the corresponding Value changes to TRUE for each respective check box. As shown in the following code, the Click event procedure for each check box tests to see if you clicked on either box. If so the text is converted to bold or italic (or both) when the FontBold or FontItalic property is set to TRUE.

```
Sub ChkBold_Click()
    If ChkBold.Value = 1 Then    'Is bold box checked?
        txtDisplay.FontBold = True
    Else                         'If not checked do this.
        txtDisplay.FontBold = False
    End If
End Sub


Sub ChkItalic_Click()
    If ChkItalic.Value = 1 Then   'Is italic box checked?
        txtDisplay.FontItalic = True
    Else                          'If not checked do this.
        txtDisplay.FontItalic = False
    End If
End Sub
```

3.10. GROUPING OPTION BUTTONS

Option buttons also present a set of choices to the user, and usually work in a group. Figure 3.7 illustrates what is called a *frame* around the option buttons used to select either portrait or landscape orientation. Options like this present only a single choice. If you click on one of these option buttons, the other button(s) is cleared, so only one option can be selected at a time.

If option buttons are placed directly on the main form or window with which you are working but are not in their own frame or picture box, they still represent a group. The difference is that they belong to the main form, though they act as if they had their own unique frame around them—in other words you can still pick only one of the options.

All option buttons in a frame constitute a separate group, as do option buttons inside a picture box. A separate frame such as was shown in Figure 3.7 provides a visual and functional grouping technique for controls. Frames are commonly used to group both check boxes and option buttons.

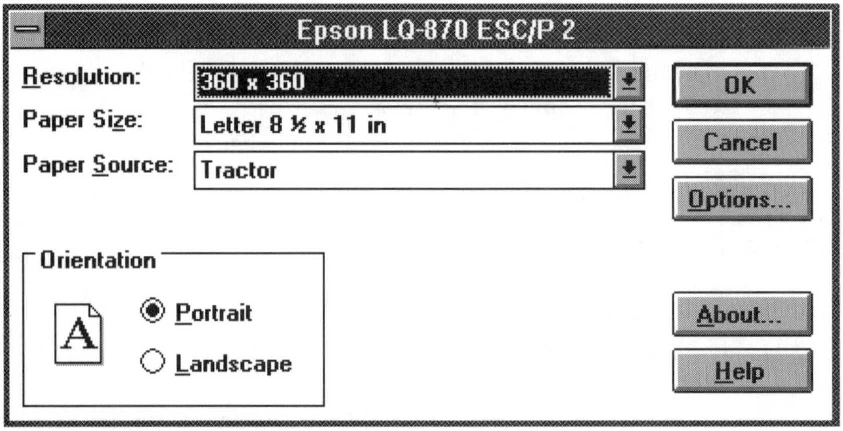

Figure 3.7. Option button group.

3.10.1. How to Group Controls in Frames

To group controls in a frame you must first choose the frame icon from the Toolbox (see Table 2.1) and draw the frame with your mouse. Then you must put your controls (e.g.: options buttons) in the frame.

> *Tip:* Always draw the frame first, *not* the controls. By doing so you may profit from the convenience of moving the frame and controls as one entity should you wish to for cosmetic reasons. It is easier to move the frame and controls as one entity rather than separately.

3.10.2. Selecting Option Buttons

The various ways to select an option button are:

- Tab to the option button group and use your arrow keys to select a button.
- Click the button with your mouse.
- Set the button's Value property to TRUE in the code (e.g.: Option3.Value = True).
- Assign a shortcut key in the caption of a label in which one of the letters is underlined. The option is chosen by pressing ALT + the underlined character.

If at a particular point in your program you wish to impede the user from selecting a certain option button, you can disable the button. To do so, set its enabled property to FALSE. This will set the button to a gray color and prevent the button from performing when it is clicked on by the user.

Figure 3.8 shows an example using option buttons to convert a number input by the user into one of three number systems: octal, decimal, or hexadecimal. In the figure, 10 was initially entered into the text box. As you see, when "Use Octal" was clicked, the value in the text box turned to 12, the equivalent in octal of the number 10 in base ten notation. The Change event for the text box reads in the number input by the user and stores it in a form level numeric variable called CurrentNum. The Click event procedures

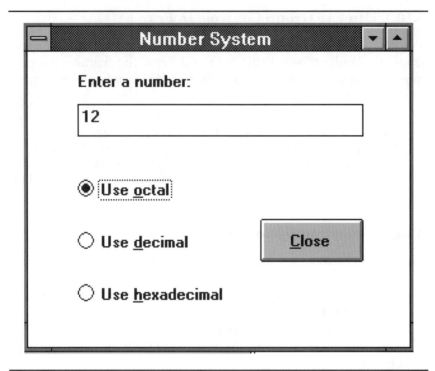

Figure 3.8. Three number systems.

for the three buttons use the Oct, Hex, and Format (default base 10) functions to display CurrentNum in the user-chosen number system:

```
Sub optHexButton_Click ()
  txtNumber.Text = Hex(CurrentNum)
End Sub

Sub optDecButton_Click ()
  txtNumber.Text = Format(CurrentNum)
End Sub

Sub optOctButton_Click ()
  txtNumber.Text = Oct(CurrentNum)
End Sub
```

3.11. COMBO BOXES AND LIST BOXES

Combo and *list boxes* give the user a list of choices. They are usually formatted in a single, vertical column. Multiple columns can also be set up, as will be seen shortly, though their use is more specialized. Figure 3.9 shows an example of a single-column list box. In this case the number of items exceeds what can be shown simultaneously in the box, so scroll bars automatically become part of the control. Note that the scroll bars are *not* coded in. Combo boxes combine the features of text and list boxes, allowing the user either to select from a list of choices or to enter a value not contained in the list.

3.11.1. Combo Box Styles

The three types of combo boxes described in the following sections each provide to the user a slightly different style and function.

3.11.1.1. Drop-down combo box (Style 0). Figure 3.10 shows this style of combo box, the default. In actual design, the arrow is slightly separated from the box as shown in the name Baud Rate. Clicking on the arrow opens a list of choices. Picking one of these options places that choice in the text portion at the top of the box. Alternatively, the user can type a new choice not in the list in the top line. If the control is highlighted you can also use ALT + DOWN arrow to open the list.

Figure 3.9. Single-column list box.

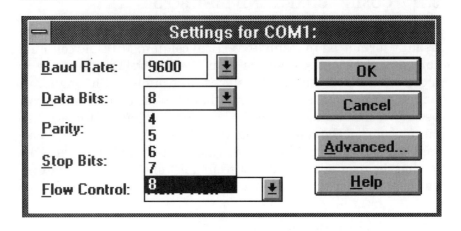

Figure 3.10. Drop-down combo box (Style 0).

3.11.1.2. Simple combo box (Style 1). Figure 3.11 shows a combo box whose Style property has been set to 1. This format displays the list all the time and so is used for relatively short lists. If you do not draw the box large enough to contain all the listed items a vertical scroll bar will automatically be inserted. As with Style 0 above, the user can enter in the text area a different item from those listed in the box.

3.11.1.3. Drop-down list box (Style 2). Figure 3.12 illustrates a combo box with a Style property of 2. The arrow must be clicked on to see the choices. Only one option can be picked, and the user is not permitted to type in a choice not contained in the list. In the figure only one of the two choices shown can be selected for "List Files of Type."

3.11.2. Putting Items in a List

The AddItem method is used to put items in a list or combo box. The syntax is

```
box.AddItem item[,index]
```

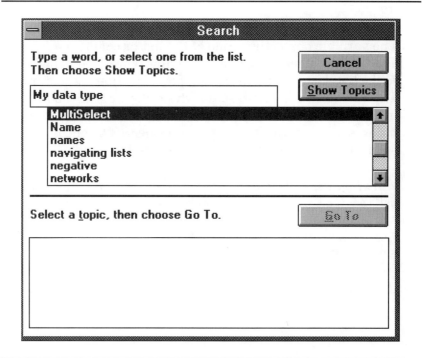

Figure 3.11. Simple combo box (Style 1).

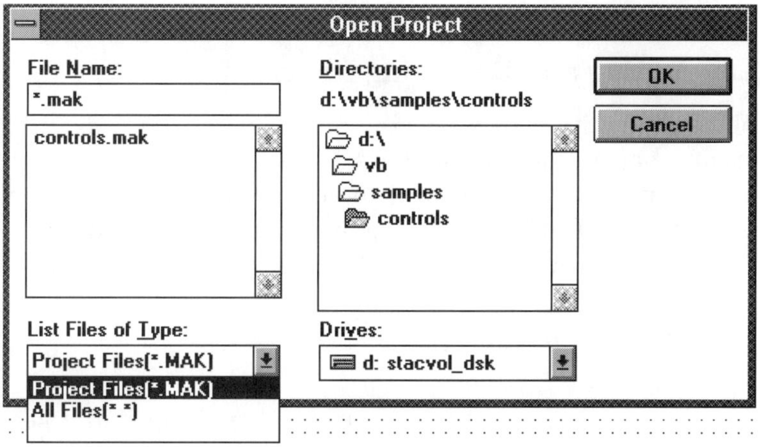

Figure 3.12. Drop-down list box (Style 2).

where:

- The variable *box* is the name of the list or combo box.
- The variable *item* is the value or string expression to be added to the list. Use quotation marks if this is a literal constant.
- The variable *index* represents where the item will be placed in the list. A zero indicates the first position. If the value of index is omitted, the item is placed either at the end of the list or in the correct sorted order within the list.

   Warning: Regardless of the order in which you enter items into a list, the items will be sorted alphabetically if no index is supplied and the property Sorted is set to TRUE. Further, be aware that specifying an index when using AddItem may lead to unpredictable results if the property Sorted is set to TRUE.

The following sample code puts "Notebook," "Laptop," "Desktop PC," and "Tower PC" into a list box named List1.

```
Sub Form9_Load()
   List1.AddItem = "Notebook"
   List1.AddItem = "Laptop"
   List1.AddItem = "Desktop PC"
   List1.AddItem = "Tower PC"
End Sub
```

3.11.3. Adding and Removing Items

To place a new item in a specific position in a list box, add an index number at the end of the AddItem line. Indexes start at position 0, not 1, so if you want to add the item "Mainframe" to the sample code at the end of the preceding section and make it the first item in the list, you must write the following code line:

```
List1.AddItem "Mainframe",0
```

This will move "Notebook" to position 1, making it the second item in the list.

RemoveItem and Clear are the two methods used to delete items from a list or combo box. RemoveItem deletes one item from the list. The item removed depends on the index number used. The code line

```
List1.RemoveItem 0
```

removes the item "Mainframe" from the sample list just described. To remove all items in this list use the code line

```
List1.Clear
```

3.11.4. Getting a List Value with the *Text* Property

Generally, the best way to structure an application to accept the value of a selected item input by the user is to employ the *Text property*. In combo boxes, the Text property corresponds to whatever is entered in the text-box part of the control. This will be either text that the user has typed into the box or an item from a list that the user has clicked on to select. Thus the Text property for list boxes is always whatever item the user selected, usually by clicking it with the mouse.

In the following code, the Text property contains the chosen item from the List9 list box. This routine checks whether "Printer" was chosen, and if so, displays a message in a Text box to tell the user to turn on the printer.

```
Sub List9_Click()
  If List9.Text = "Printer" Then
    Text1.Text = "Please Turn On Your Printer."
  End If
End Sub
```

3.11.5. Getting a List Value with the *List* Property

To access any item in a list, the *List property* is used. This property uses an array to access the different items in the list using the syntax

```
control.List(index)
```

where *control* is a reference to a combo box or list box, and *index* is the relative position of the target item in the array of items stored in the list. The following example code gets the seventh value string from the List5 list box and puts that string value into a text box.

```
Text1.Text = List5.List(6)
```

3.11.6. Total Number of Items

Figure 3.13 shows the total number of items in a list. Here, two names were added to the list by using the Add button after each name was entered into the Name to add text box. The ListCount property is used to find out how many items are in a list box or combo box. For example, to put the total number of items in a list into text box Text1 you would use ListCount as follows:

```
Text1.Text = "There are" & List1.ListCount & " items in
the list."
```

3.11.7. Multiple-Column List Boxes

The application in Figure 3.14 contains a multiple-column list box with two columns. The user can pick (click on) multiple items in the box and then click on the Transfer command button to copy all selected items to the bottom list box.

The Columns and MultiSelect properties in a list box control how many columns the box will contain and whether or not the user will be permitted to make multiple selections.

The *Columns property* is where you specify the number of columns in a list box. This property can have the following values:

Value	List Box Description
0	Usual, single-column box with vertical scrolling
1	Single-column box with horizontal scrolling
>1	Multiple-column with horizontal scrolling

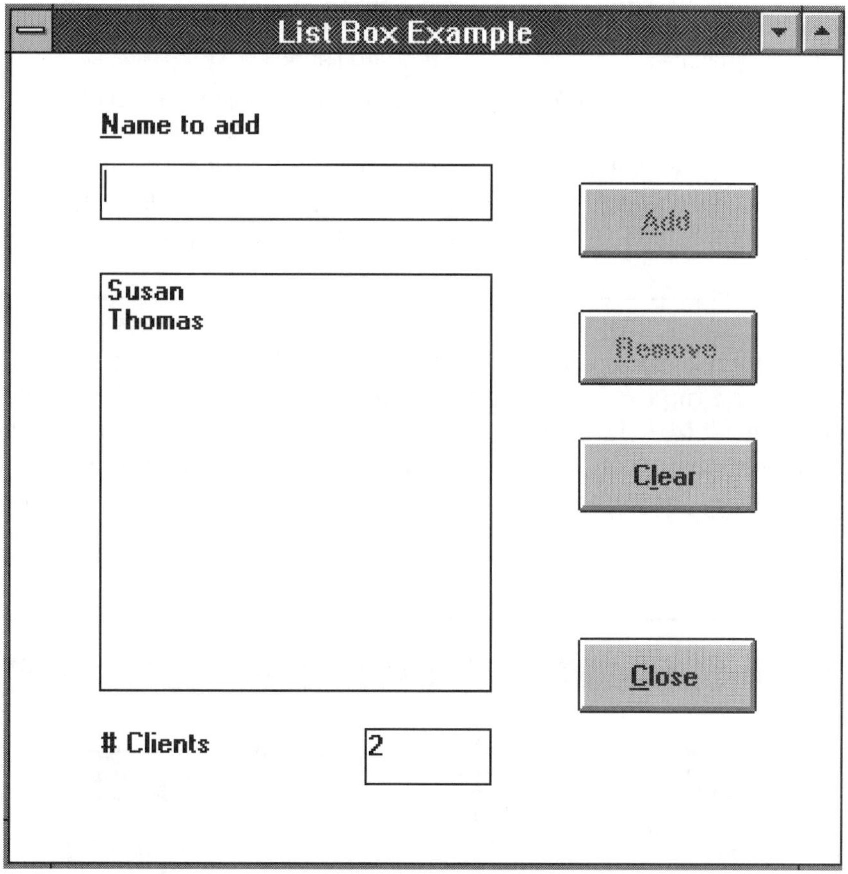

Figure 3.13. List box total example.

Visual Basic automatically wraps list items to the next line, adding a horizontal scroll bar to the list if needed. Wrapping to the next column is also automatic. Be aware, however, that if a list box entry is wider than the width of the column, the text will be truncated.

To allow users to select multiple items from a list, the list box property *MultiSelect* is used. MultiSelect can have the following values:

Value	Selection Type	Description
0	None	Standard list box
1	Simple multiple selection	Mouse dragging selects or deselects additional items in the list
2	Extended multiple selection	SHIFT+CLICK or SHIFT+an arrow key extends selection to include all items between current and previous selections

You must set both the Columns and MultiSelect properties to create the top list box shown in Figure 3.14. There, both properties are set to 2. This application also uses the Selected property, a boolean array containing the selection status of the top list box, to determine which items were selected by the user. Every entry

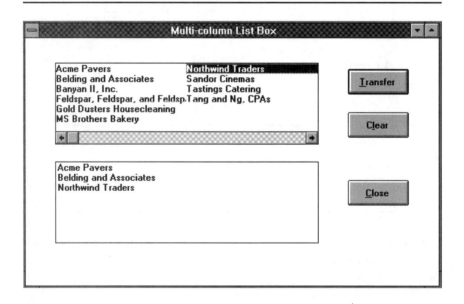

Figure 3.14. Multiple column list box.

in the array is set to TRUE if selected, or FALSE if not selected. After the user has selected all the desired items and clicked on the Transfer command button, each TRUE item is added to the second list box and displayed. The following code shows the loop that checks each item in the top box for a TRUE condition and then transfers such items down to the bottom list box when the user clicks the Transfer button.

```
Sub cmdTransfer_Click()
    For n = 0 to (1stTop.ListCount - 1)
      If 1st.Selected(n) = True Then
        1st.Bottom.AddItem  1stTop.List(n)
      End If
    Next
End Sub
```

3.12. SCROLL BARS AS AN INPUT SOURCE

Even though you may think of scroll bars as something you only see attached to windows and text boxes, they can also be used as input mechanisms. Depending on the position where you place the scroll bar, it will return different numeric values to your program. These values can be used for such varied purposes as setting color schemes or setting tone controls for a musical application. With the Toolbox you can create your own vertical or horizontal scroll bars as shown in Figure 3.15. Depending on where you set the three scroll boxes you can see different color results of the combinations in the text box.

The property Value is the integer value of the scroll box's position in reference to the minimum and maximum values in the area that the scroll box can travel. Min and Max are the properties whose values represent the minimum and maximum values, respectively, that the scroll bar can have and return back to the application. In the application illustrated in Figure 3.15, all three scroll bars are limited to return values between 0 and 255. The following list details these and other properties for the top scroll bar in the figure.

Object	Property	Setting
Top Scroll bar	Name	hsbRed
	Max	255
	Min	0
	LargeChange	30
	SmallChange	5

3.13.   SETTING FOCUS AND TAB ORDER

Focus and tab order relate to how the user navigates around a form that may contain many objects.

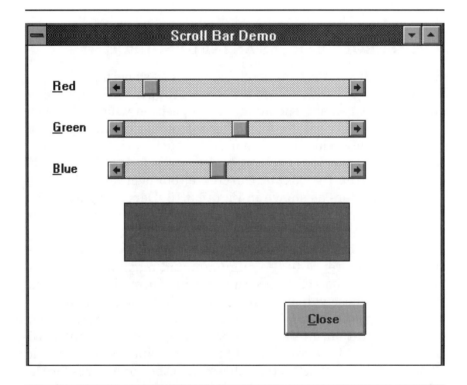

Figure 3.15.   Scroll bar inputs example.

3.13.1. Focus

The term *focus* refers to which object or control is active, that is, able to receive input from the user. Whichever control can respond to a user action is said to have the focus. For instance, when you are inputting text into a text box, that particular control—the text box—has the focus. Only one object at a time can have the focus. Two events happen when an object receives or loses the focus: GotFocus and LostFocus. The GotFocus event happens when an object receives focus. The LostFocus event happens when it loses focus. Clearly, the user of an application can make these events happen by navigating about a given form. You can also use the SetFocus method in code. An object can only receive focus when its Enabled and Visible properties are set to TRUE. *Enabled* means the object can respond to user input, and *Visible* determines if the object is visible or not on the form.

> *Note:* Timers, frames, menus, lines, labels, shapes, and images cannot receive focus. A form can receive focus only if it contains no controls.

3.13.2. Tab Order

The *tab order* is the order in which the controls move when the user presses the TAB button. Usually, this order is the same as the order in which they were created. However, you can change the tab order in the code by using the TabIndex property for controls. For example, if your form contained a Command1 button which was the last created control, located at the bottom of the form, it would normally be the last button to receive the focus as the user pressed TAB. To change this so that the Command1 button is the first in the tab order, use code statement

```
Command1.TabIndex = 0
```

The TabIndex values for all other controls on the form are automatically adjusted in such cases to compensate for the new order. To remove a control from the tab order, use the TabStop property. When this property is set to FALSE for a given control, that control is skipped when the user presses the TAB key. Set the

TabStop property back to TRUE when you wish to restore normal tab order conditions.

3.14. CONTROL STATE

You may change the state of a control by using code. For instance, the three actions listed here change the state of a command button:

Action	Technique	Purpose
Disable	Set Enabled property to FALSE	Stops user from choosing the command
Enable	Set Enabled property to TRUE	Allows user to pick the command again
Make Invisible	Set Visible property to FALSE	Removes the button from the visible form and disables the control

All controls have the Enabled property except for the frame, shape, line, and label controls.

3.15. CONTROL ARRAYS

Controls that share the same name and type and are organized in a group are called *control arrays*. A control array can contain between 1 and 254 elements. Some uses for control arrays are option button groupings and menu controls.

Control arrays are useful whenever you want many controls to share code. For instance, if four buttons are designed as a control array then the same code is executed for all four buttons. Without control arrays you could not create new controls at runtime. With control arrays you can do so since each new control inherits the common event procedures already written for the array. For example, if you have a form with multiple text boxes that all need a customer part number, a control array can be used to check that the entered value is a valid number for all of these text boxes. This saves a considerable number of code lines because a routine need only be written once to cover multiple instances.

Figure 3.16 uses two control arrays: one for the numbers 0 to 9, and another for the mathematical operator buttons. You can find this program in your Visual Basic subdirectory under \samples\calc.

3.15.1. Making a Control Array at Design Time

There are three methods you can use to set up a control array during design time. First you can set the Index property to non-null. Second, you may copy an existing control. Third, you may assign the same name to more than one control object. All three methods are described in detail in the following sections.

3.15.1.1. Set Index property. The Calculator example in Figure 3.16 uses a control array in which each control is referred to by

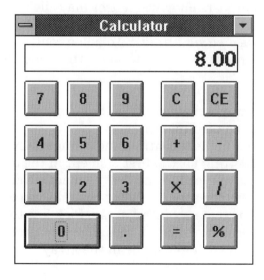

Figure 3.16. Calculator using control arrays.

the syntax *controlname(index)*. Here you must specify the index of each control when you create it. Specifying any index for a control at design time makes that control part of an array. The Index property distinguishes one element from another in the control array. As soon as any control in the array recognizes an event, Visual Basic calls a common event procedure and passes an argument—the Index property—to determine which control really recognizes the event.

To clarify this further using the Calculator example, assume that for the first two numbers on the calculator's numeric keyboard side the control array values are 0 = Number(0) and 1 = Number(1). Next, look at the first line of code for the Number_ Click event procedure for this program

```
Sub Number_Click (Index As Integer)
```

If Number(0) recognizes the event—that is, if the user clicked on the number zero—Visual Basic passes 0 as the Index argument. This is the only variable condition in the event procedure. The rest of the procedure Number_Click executes in the same way for all ten (0–9) numbers on which a user may click.

3.15.1.2. Assign same name. To add a control array element by assigning the same name to more than one control, do the following:

- Draw all controls that are of the same type. Then decide which control will be the first element.
- Pick another of these controls and change its Name setting to the Name setting for the first element in the array.
- After you have typed in the first element's Name for the second control in the array, a dialog box asks you to confirm that you want to create a control array. Pick Yes to continue. Repeat this procedure for all remaining controls of the same type that you wish to include in the array.

Controls added in this way share only their Name property and control type. Their other properties remain the same as when they were originally set and drawn.

3.15.1.3. Copying an existing control. To add a control array element by copying an existing control use the following procedure:

- Draw the initial control for the control array.
- Making sure that this control has the focus, choose Copy from the Edit menu.
- Pick Paste from the Edit menu options. Confirm that you want to create a control array with a Yes response.

The copied control is then assigned an index value of 1, while the original control drawn has an index value of 0.

3.15.2. Expanding a Control Array at Runtime

You can change an array by adding or removing controls at runtime with the Load and Unload code statements.

> *Tip:* The control to be added must be of the same type as the elements of an existing control array.

Use the following syntax for Load and Unload statements:

```
Load control(index)
Unload control(index)
```

When you load a new element, most of the properties from the lowest index level (usually 0) are copied to the new element. The properties not copied are Visible, TabIndex, and Index.

You can only unload (delete) those elements made with Load statements. Consider as an example Figure 3.17, which has three option buttons. Assume that when this program was first started only the top two buttons existed and that the user clicked on the command button Add and produced the third button with a Load statement. This means the user can only successfully use the command button Delete on the third button at this point. The user cannot unload (delete) the top two Option buttons since they were not made with a Load statement, whereas the third was made with a Load statement.

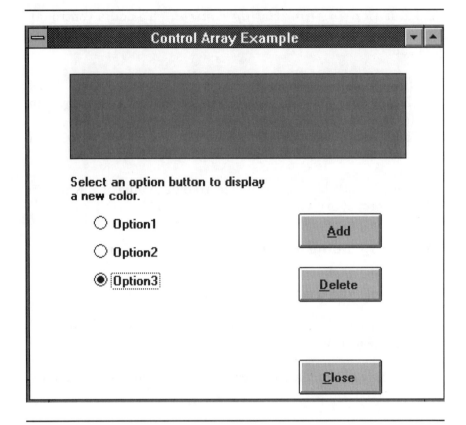

Figure 3.17. Control array for colors.

To give you an idea of the code involved, the following code is used to delete option buttons created by Load statements when the user clicks on the Delete command button.

```
Sub cmdDelete_Click()
   If MaxId = 1 then Exit Sub      'keep first 2 buttons
   Unload OptButton(Maxid)         'delete last button
   MaxId = MaxId - 1               'button count now 1 less
   OptButton(0).SetFocus           'reset button selection
End Sub
```

4

Menu and Dialog Box Usage

4.1. INTRODUCTION TO MENUS

So far the way to select what to do and when has been through controls such as command buttons and option buttons. If there are few options from which to choose on a form these formats may be sufficient. However, the device used most frequently in window applications to select which action to perform is the menu, as shown in Figure 4.1.

Menus save space because menu items drop down only when an option is clicked on. Also, menus are virtually an expected standard in window applications. These two considerations alone make learning how to create menus in Visual Basic as important to you as to your programs' endusers.

Figure 4.1 shows two menu titles: File and Country. Each of these titles has its own subset of menu items as shown in Figure 4.2.

In accordance with generally accepted guidelines, you should create and group menu titles and the items they contain according to function. For instance, it is generally understood that any program requiring file manipulation will have a menu title called File as its first menu title. The grouping of items under a menu title should also follow certain informal guidelines. Note in Fig-

This application has two menus on its menu bar: File and Country.
The commands on the menus remain hidden until the menu is selected.

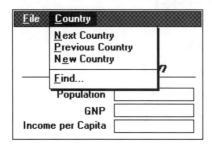

Figure 4.1. Menu example.

ure 4.2 that the items available under Country pertain only to
that main subject. You would not put a menu item called, for
example, Save Changes here. Because Save Changes pertains to
files, you would instead put it under the File heading.

4.1.1. What Menus Do

Some menu items when clicked present a *dialog box*, a window
that requires the user to enter information or choose one or more
options. Closing a project, for example, may involve naming the
file to which you wish to save your project or accepting a default

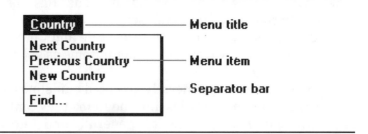

Figure 4.2. Submenu example.

name given for you to use. The application often obtains this information by means of a dialog box. Other menu items, such as Start under the Run menu option of Visual Basic, will perform an action immediately.

4.2. THE MENU DESIGN WINDOW

To create menus, use the Menu Design Window shown in Figure 4.3. You may add menu items to a menu or change existing items by creating menu controls and their properties during design time. To call up the Menu Design Window, either choose Menu design from the Windows menu, or click on the Menu Design Window icon in the Toolbar (see Table 2.1). The Menu Design Window has two main areas: the Menu control properties at the top, and the Menu control list box at the bottom, from the arrows and command buttons in the shaded area to the bottom of the window.

You design menus for your forms in the Menu Design window.

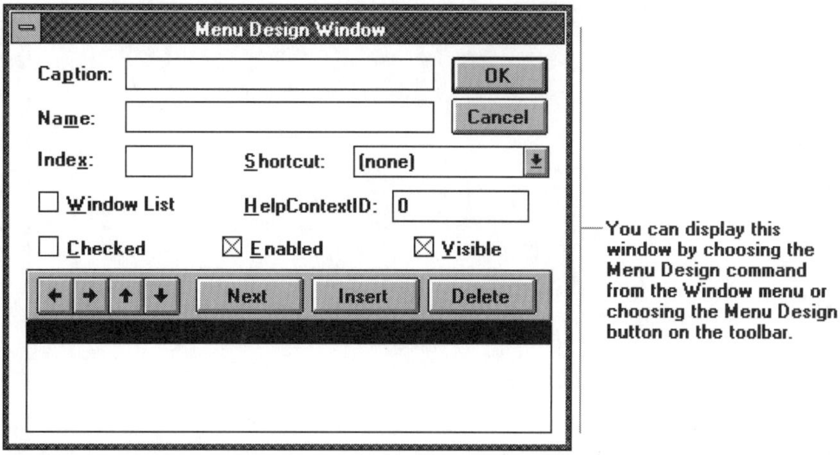

Figure 4.3.   Menu design window.

4.2.1. Menu Control Properties

Two of the most important areas in the Menu control properties portion are "Caption" and "Name." *Caption* is the text that appears on the control that the user sees, for example, Open, Save, or Quit. *Name* is the name used to reference that control in your code statements.

For the most part, the design of the menu system shown in Figure 4.4 will be the focus of this chapter. This application is a simple Windows text editor made with Visual Basic. If you have Visual Basic, I suggest that you load this application, TEXTEDIT.MAK, located in the directory \vb\samples\menus.

4.2.2. Menu Control List Box

The menu control list box in the Menu Design Window lists all the controls for the form that has the current focus. Typing in an

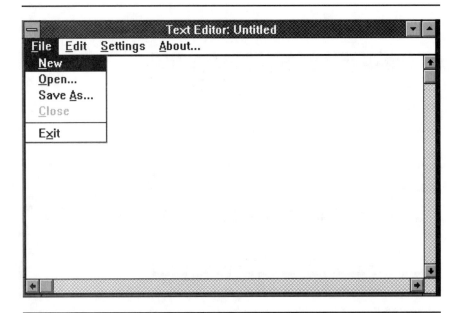

Figure 4.4. Text editor using menus.

item in the Caption box causes that same name to appear in the menu control list box. Clicking on any existing control from the list box allows you to edit the properties of that control. Figure 4.5 shows the &File item and its properties.

Note: Any time the & character appears at the beginning of an item's name or within it, it means that the item may be accessed during runtime using the keys "ALT+character after the &." Thus

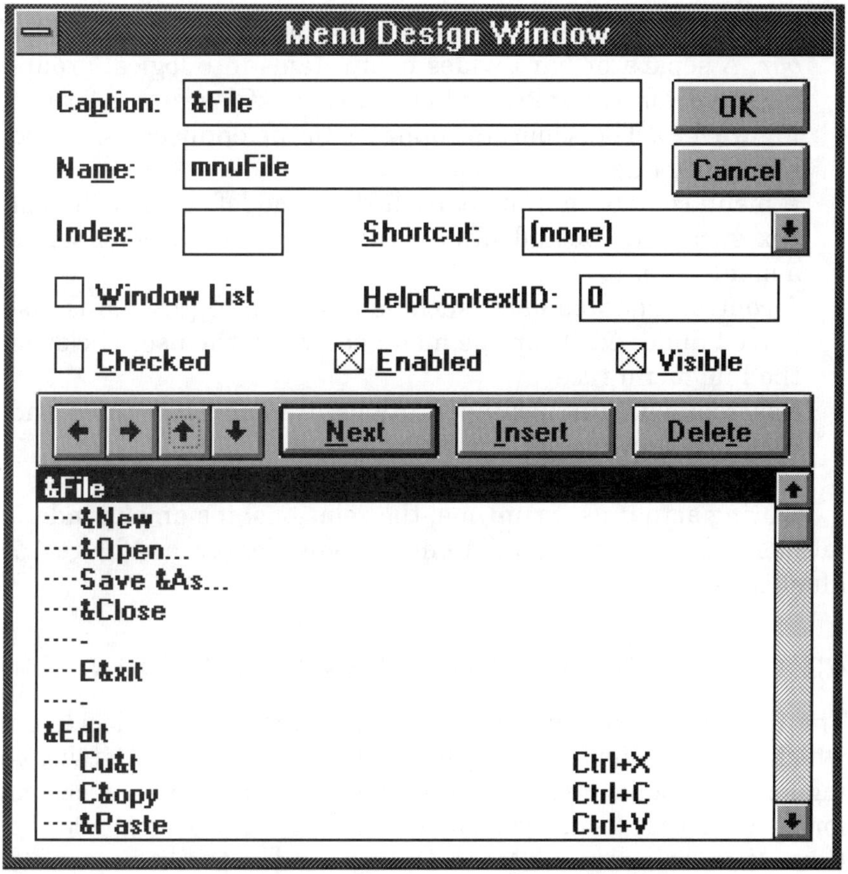

Figure 4.5.   Menu control list box.

in the &File case, the user may either click on the name &File
with the mouse or press ALT+F to activate this item during
runtime.

4.2.3.   Menu Control List Box Positions

The menu controls listed in the menu control list box are position
dependent. Each control's position depends on whether it is a
menu title, a menu item, a submenu title, or a submenu item.
You may determine a control's function by its position according
to the following rules of thumb:

- A line with a hyphen as its Caption property is a *separator
  bar*. A separator bar divides menu items into logical groupings (see, for example, the line between &Close and E&xit in
  Figure 4.5). The separator appears to the enduser as a solid
  horizontal line.
- A menu control that appears flush to the left side of the list
  box, such as &File and &Edit, is displayed on the menu bar as
  a menu title.
- A control indented once, such as &New in Figure 4.5 is displayed under &File on the menu bar when the user clicks on
  the File menu title.
- Controls with further indentations are submenu titles and
  items, as shown in Figure 4.6.

During actual user runtime, the relationships among indentations, submenu titles, and items become clearer, as Figure 4.7
illustrates.

4.3.   CREATING A MENU FOR AN APPLICATION

The first step in building an application's menu is to decide on
which form the menu will appear. Usually, this is the first working form that a user will see after any introductory and welcome
forms. Give that form the focus by clicking anywhere inside the
form. Next, bring up the Menu Design window by clicking on its
Toolbar icon (see Table 2.1) or choosing the Menu Design option

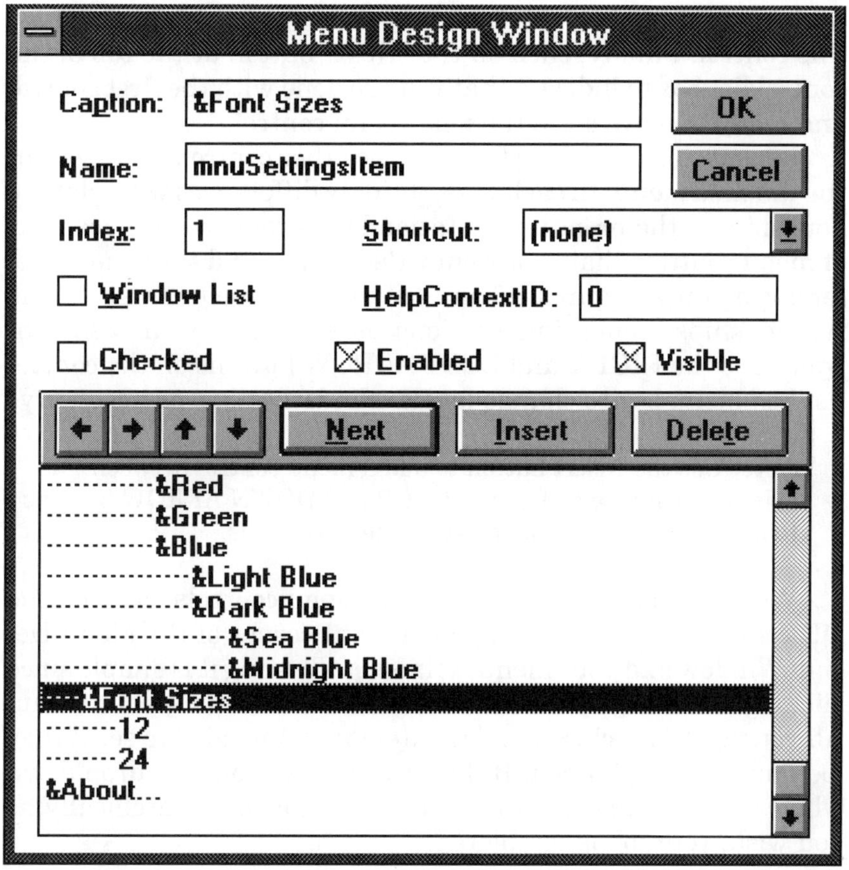

Figure 4.6.   Submenu &Font Sizes design.

from the Window menu. You may now add the items you want to include in your menu.

Begin by typing the text for the name of the first menu title in the Caption text box as you wish the user to see it in the finished menu and, if wanted, an access key &, which will be automatically changed to an underscore. (For example, &FILE will show as FILE and can be accessed with ALT+F) Then, in the Name text box, enter the name you will use in code statements to refer to this menu control. Next, set any other properties desired for this control. Finally, click on the "Next" button at the top of the control list box to indicate that you are done with the first control and ready to move on to the next menu control.

Repeat this procedure for all of the other controls to appear in the finished menu. In each case, the only differences will relate to determining the proper indentation levels for correct placement of menu controls that represent titles, items, and submenus. Referring again to Figures 4.6 and 4.7 will help you understand the relationships among indentations as you enter your own controls. Use the RIGHT and LEFT ARROW buttons on the control list box menu bar to change levels of indentations as necessary.

> *Note:* Use the Insert button to add a menu control between existing menu controls, and the UP and DOWN ARROW buttons to move a control among existing menu controls.

When you have inserted all your menu controls, click on the OK command button in the upper right corner of the Menu Design Window and your menu is finished. Testing it is simple since clicking OK brings you back to the form containing your menu. All you need do is click on all the items you included to see if they look and act as planned. If, for example, all controls drop down when you expected them to and are arranged hierarchically as you wish, your job is completed.

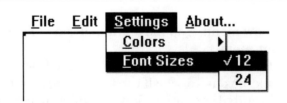

Figure 4.7. Submenu &Font sizes at runtime.

4.3.1. Menus and Control Arrays

In Chapter 3, control arrays were presented and used in a simple Calculator program. One control array was designed for the set of numbers (0–9) that the user might punch in, and another for the mathematical operators (+, ., −, *, and so forth). Each array helped avoid writing many unnecessary code statements since it could share a common routine designed to do different operations. For example, rather than six separate calculation procedures, only one was needed.

Menus can also use control arrays. A menu control array is a set of menu items that share the same name and event procedures. You may use a menu control array to create a new menu item at runtime or to simplify your code, since common code blocks can be used for all menu items.

4.3.1.1. Index values. Each menu control array element is identified by its own index number. This number appears in the Menu Design Window's properties area in the box labeled "Index," directly under the Name property.

When a member of a control array recognizes an event, Visual Basic passes its Index property value to the event procedure. The event procedure must include the code needed to check the value of this Index and perform the appropriate action accordingly.

4.3.2. Creating a Menu Control Array

The Menu Design window is needed to create the array, so again, either choose Menu Design from the Window menu or click on the appropriate icon from the Toolbar.

Begin by creating the menu item that will be the first element in the array and set the Caption and Name properties. Set the Index property to 0 to ensure that this item will be the first element in the array. Repeat this procedure for each item, being sure to use the same indentation level and to increase by one the Index property for each new item. Click on OK when finished and your control array is now set up.

*4.3.2.1. **Example control array.*** The Text Editor application uses the menu items under the menu title &Edit in a control array. See the list box in Figure 4.5 for the items under &Edit (the last items in the figure's list box). Cut, Copy, and Paste are set up as a control array with these property settings:

Caption	Name	Index
Cu&t	mnuEditItem	0
C&opy	mnuEditItem	1
&Paste	mnuEditItem	2

Since this book is a primer, again the meaning and reasoning behind these property settings will be explained. The reason the Name is the same for all three items is that mnuEditItem is an *array*—the way to access the Caption name routines is to refer to the array by the INDEX number. If you want to Cut during an Edit, refer to the index of Cut, in this case 0. As such, the Cut reference in your code statements must be mnuEditItem(0). For Copy it must be mnuEditItem(1), and for Paste use mnuEditItem(2).

4.4.   CODE REQUIREMENTS FOR MENU CONTROLS

Since a Click event occurs when you choose a menu control such as Cu&t, a Click event procedure must be written to cause the menu control to do what its name implies it will do. The index value of the clicked item is passed to the event procedure. By using If...Then or Select Case statements, you can make the routine go to the correct part of the procedure's code for that unique index number. In the following code, if the user clicks on C&opy then the index going to the procedure is 1. This satisfies the Select Case for 'Case 1', causing only the code under Case 1 (2 statements) to be executed, since that is where the actual work required to do a C&opy is located. If the user clicks on &Paste, the statements under 'Case 2' are executed. Do not be concerned if you do not understand all the code statement functions at this time. The purpose here is to show, in general, how a menu control array is executed.

```
Sub mnuEditItem_Click(Index As Integer)
  Select Case Index
    Case 0                              'Cut chosen
      Clipboard.Clear
      Clipboard.SetText txtEdit.SelText
      txtEdit.SelText = ""
    Case 1                              'Copy chosen
      Clipboard.Clear
      Clipboard.SetText txtEdit.SelText
    Case 2
      txtEdit.SelText = Clipboard.GetText()  'Paste
  End Select
End Sub
```

4.5.   SUBMENUS

A *Submenu* branches off another menu to display its own menu items, as shown in Figure 4.7. Here, both menu items, Colors and Font Sizes, branch into submenus (12 and 24 for Font Sizes). Note that all menu controls that have submenus have an arrowhead symbol on their right-hand side, as shown for Colors in the figure. If Font Sizes did not have the focus, you would see an arrowhead related to it as well. A menu can have up to four levels of submenus.

Use a submenu when the menu bar is full or when you have an item that is seldom used or changed. Most programs use only one level of submenus because accessing many levels of submenus can be confusing to the user when a dialog box could be used instead to better effect.

4.5.1.   Creating a Submenu

Create the menu item that will be the submenu title (e.g.: Font Sizes), indented at least one level from the left. To indent an item one level, press the RIGHT ARROW key; to delete an indent, use the LEFT ARROW. Each indent level shows up as four dots, so an item indented three levels would have twelve dots followed by its Caption name in the menu control list box line. The final steps in creating a submenu are to fill in the items that will appear under its title (e.g.,: 12 and 24 for Font Sizes), all indented one level more than the submenu title.

4.5.1.1. Creating menu separators. A separator bar, displayed as a horizontal bar between items, is a visual aid to the enduser, dividing menu items into logical item groups. These groups are created in the Menu Design Window. First, decide between which two items you wish to insert a separator bar. Click on the second of these items in the list box and press the INS key. If need be, use the RIGHT ARROW button to indent to the same level as the items with which you are working. In the Caption property box insert a hyphen, set the Name property, and finally click on the OK command button. You now have a separator bar between the two items.

> ***Note:*** Even though you built the separator as a regular menu item with a Name property, that Name property cannot be accessed by code statements. Furthermore, separators do not recognize the Click event.

4.6.   ACCESS AND SHORTCUT KEYS

People using only a keyboard, without a mouse, could not choose the actions required to run an application without using access keys. Shortcut keys are also handy because they execute a menu item immediately when pressed from a keyboard.

4.6.1.   Access Keys

Access keys allow the user to open menus by pressing ALT + some letter. Once the menu is open users can activate the menu items by pressing one key. In Figure 4.4 File can be opened by pressing ALT+F and the New can then be chosen by pressing only the letter N. This example illustrates an access key combination (ALT+F) and a one-letter access key (N).

To assign an access key to an item, put an & in front of the letter in the item name that you want as the access key. For example, to assign N as the access key for New place & in front of N (&New) in this item's Caption property box.

4.6.2. Shortcut Keys

Shortcut keys can include both control key and function key combinations (e.g.: ALT+F, F10+E). Note, however, that they may not include one-letter key designations such as the access key N for New described above.

Figure 4.5 shows the completed shortcut key setup for the Cut, Copy, and Paste menu items. Here, for instance, CTRL+X executes the menu item Cut.

To assign a shortcut key, open the Menu Design Window, select a menu item, and choose a function or control key combination in the Shortcut combo box. If you later wish to remove the shortcut key combination, repeat this procedure but pick none from the top of the combo box list.

4.7. RUNTIME CONTROL OF MENUS

Menus created at design time can also be changed dynamically during runtime. For example, menu items could be disabled under certain file conditions. If no files were open, for instance, you could disable the Close menu item—you can't close something that isn't open. The ability to control menus at runtime helps the user understand the application better and can prevent user input errors.

4.7.1. Enabling and Disabling Items and Making Items Invisible

All menu controls have an Enabled property. When set to FALSE in a code statement such as

```
mnuFileItem.Enabled(3) = False
```

the Close menu item is disabled and shown in gray as in Figure 4.4. If you want to disable the entire menu called File, use the statement

```
mnuFile.Enabled = False
```

Making an item or control invisible differs from disabling it. When a control is invisible, the rest of the controls move up to fill the empty space. An item that has been made invisible does not appear in gray; instead, it is not even seen by the user. The item can be reset and made visible again; it is not destroyed. To make New invisible under the File head, use the code statement

```
mnuFileArray(0).Visible = False
```

To make it visible again, use the code

```
mnuFileArray(0).Visible = True
```

4.8.   DIALOG BOXES

Dialog boxes are used to display information or to prompt a user to enter needed information. They can be likened to the forms where you have been putting your controls. In fact, a dialog box has the same file extension name (.frm) as normal frames. The text editor application Project dialog box in Figure 4.8 shows the About dialog box, ABOUT.FRM. During runtime, when the user clicks on the About menu title on the title bar, this dialog box is displayed.

> **Note:** Dialog boxes are either modal or modeless. If a dialog box is modal, you must close it before continuing on with any other operation in your application. Conversely, if the dialog box is modeless, you need not close it until a more convenient time and you may still execute other procedures in the application.

4.8.1.   Predefined Dialog Boxes

Predefined dialog boxes are the quickest, least complicated way to add a dialog box to your routine. Predefined means that they are defined in the Visual Basic language. As such, you do not have to load, unload, or design them. These boxes will be set up automatically for you—all you do is add your own specifics, such

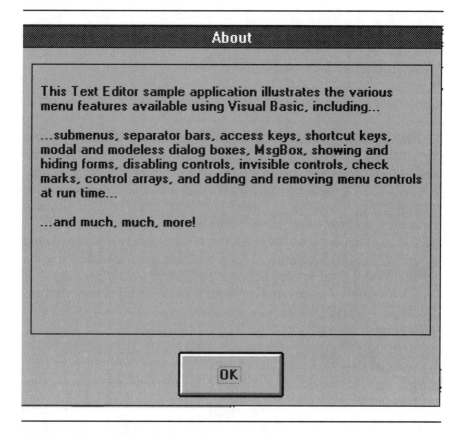

Figure 4.8.   'About' dialog box.

as the message text or title bar text. There are three classes of predefined dialog boxes: two for MsgBox (a statement and a function ability) and one for InputBox, which is used to return text from a user. All predefined dialog boxes are modal.

4.8.1.1. MsgBox.   The Msgbox keyword can be used either as a function or a statement. In either case, it displays a message, then waits for the user to choose a button before the application continues. The function returns a value indicating which button was chosen; the MsgBox statement does not.

The MsgBox Statement. The syntax for a MsgBox statement is

```
MsgBox msg [,[type][title] ].
```

To generate the message displayed in Figure 4.9, the statement needed is

```
MsgBox "File doesn't exist.",48,"MENU"
```

The parameter *Type* in the general syntax statement means the same to both statements and functions of MsgBox. The *type* numeric value is the sum of values specifying the number and type of buttons to display, the icon style to use, and more. For almost all normal applications the value 48 is appropriate for both MsgBox statement and function usage. The value 48 means that both an icon of an exclamation mark and an OK button will be displayed as in Figure 4.9. The many other possible combinations can be found in the Visual Basic language *Reference Manual*.

The MsgBox Function. The syntax for a MsgBox function is

```
MsgBox( msg [,[type][title] ]).
```

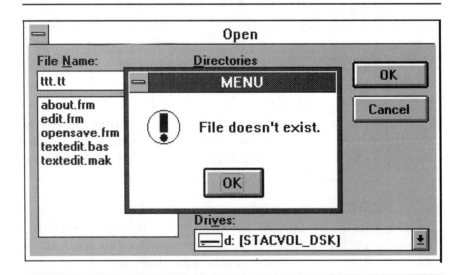

Figure 4.9.   MsgBox example.

For Figure 4.9 the function call could be

```
Response = MsgBox("File doesn't exist.",48,"MENU")
```

If Response returns a value of 1, then the OK button has been selected. Below are the other possibilities:

2 means the Cancel button has been selected.

3 means the Abort button has been selected.

4 means the Retry button has been selected.

5 means the Ignore button has been selected.

6 means the Yes button has been selected.

7 means the No button has been selected.

As previously mentioned, *type* in the syntax statement is the same in the MsgBox Statement section that immediately preceded this section.

4.8.1.2. InputBox. The InputBox function is used to receive text information from the user. It displays a modal dialog box and asks for a string value—a text string also called a variant. Figure 4.10 shows a called InputBox that asks you to enter a file name in the text box, then click on OK when you are done.

The only statement needed in the calling procedure to produce this box was

```
FileName = InputBox("Enter File Name:", "Enter File")
```

This statement has two parameters: the text instruction line (Enter File Name:) and what the dialogs form title will be (Enter File). See Figure 4.11 for the full procedure code. In this case the procedure Form_Load is executed as soon as the form is loaded at runtime, causing Figure 4.10 to appear.

4.8.2. Custom Dialog Boxes

Because this is a somewhat advanced topic, in keeping with the purpose of this book only the basics will be explained here. Usu-

Figure 4.10.   Enter file InputBox.

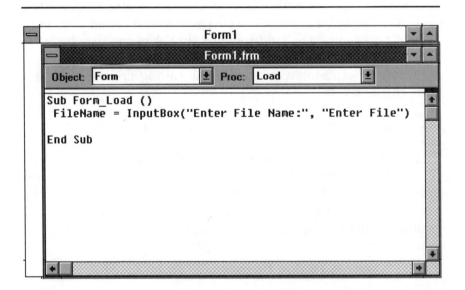

Figure 4.11.   InputBox code.

ally you can use predefined dialog boxes for most tasks. However, for the rare occasion when you may need them, this section explains how to create and use basic custom dialog boxes. Unlike predefined dialog boxes, a custom dialog box is a form that *you* create, containing controls such as command buttons and text boxes. Property values and the code needed to display the dialog box must also be done or chosen, usually at design time. Custom dialog boxes are most useful when it is necessary to give more information to or receive more information from a user than predefined dialog boxes can provide.

The easiest way to make a custom dialog box is to modify an existing form. To do this, pick Add Form from the File menu and select an existing form, choose Save As from the File menu, give the form a name, customize the form, and customize the event procedures in the Code Window.

The other way to make a custom dialog box is to create one from scratch. To do this, pick New Form from the File menu (or click on the New Form icon in the Toolbar), customize the form, and customize event procedures in the Code Window.

4.8.2.1 Custom dialog command buttons.

Modal dialog boxes *must*, by any design standards, have at least one command button to exit the dialog box and signal the application to continue. You needn't concern yourself with this when using predefined dialog boxes, but you must when creating your own custom dialog boxes. Without at least one Exit, OK, or Cancel button, your application remains stopped and cannot continue as the user expects it to after, for example, clicking on a control such as a command button.

A minimum of two command buttons is considered adequate. Use one to close the box and one to continue the application without making changes, such as OK and Cancel buttons, respectively.

A menu or command button in one dialog box can also call and display another dialog box. For example, clicking the Add command button, from the Edit Watch dialog box displays the dialog box Add Watch, shown in Figure 4.12.

4.8.2.2. Default and Cancel properties.

The Default property gives one command button the focus in a given window when

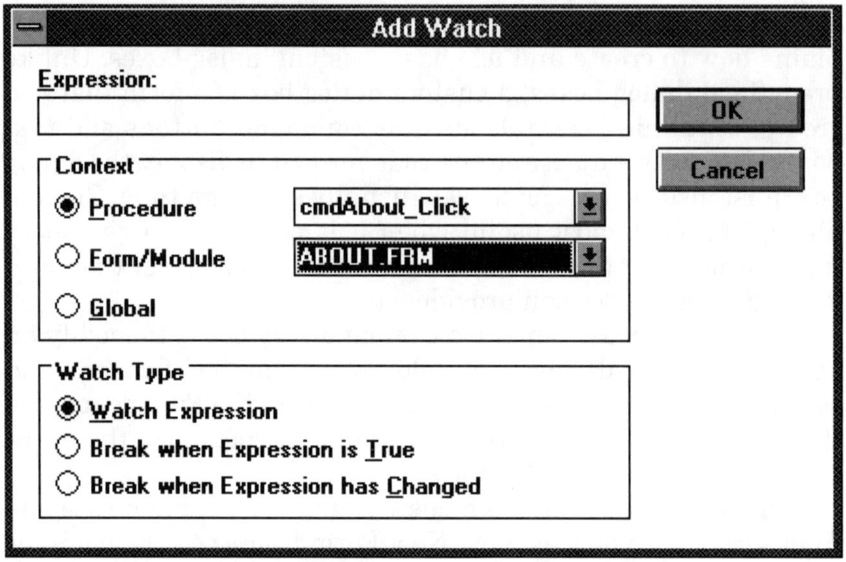

Figure 4.12. Add Watch dialog box.

the window is first displayed. To activate the default button, click on it or press ENTER. In Figure 4.12, OK is the Default button—you can tell which is the default since the control has a 3D darker color around it. To make a button the default command button, set the button's Default property to TRUE.

The Cancel button in Figure 4.12 is selected at runtime by either pressing your ESC key, or clicking on the button. Only one button per form or dialog box can have its Cancel property set to TRUE. Use the Cancel button for a quick user response. Pressing ESC is much faster than using the mouse or some other means to cancel a dialog box.

4.8.2.3. Disabling controls. Disabling a control, usually temporarily, means the user is unable to choose it. Figure 4.13 shows five command buttons, three disabled and two enabled. Note that the text in the disabled buttons is gray and dimmer than its

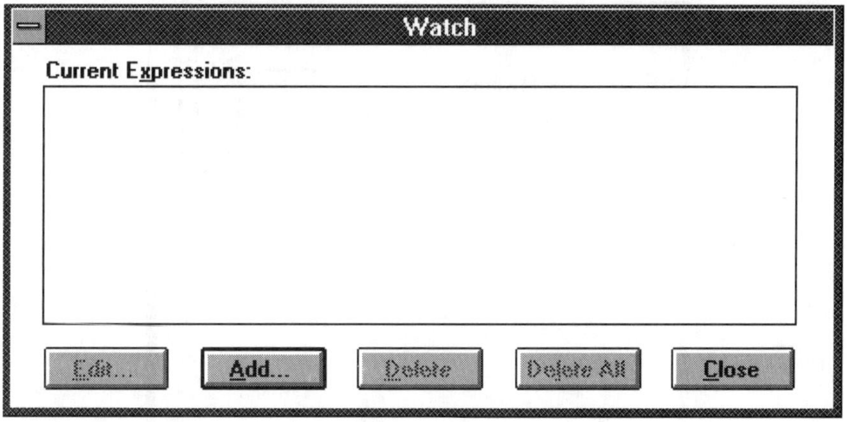

Figure 4.13.   Disabled controls example.

enabled counterparts. Use this feature to help the user tell which options are not relevant to processing *at this point*. This can change as the program progresses, so that at one point few, if any, options apply, whereas later it may be possible to access all the options. In Figure 4.13, since no expressions are current, the only logical options are either to Add expressions or to close the dialog box.

To disable a control, set its Enabled property to FALSE, as in

```
cmdAddItem.Enabled = False
```

Later, if you wish to enable the control, set the expression to TRUE as in

```
cmdAddItem.Enabled = True
```

4.8.2.4. *Displaying a custom dialog box.*   In the Text editor application, choosing Open from the File menu calls the dialog box in Figure 4.14. You display a custom dialog box in the same way as any other form. The first form one sees in an application

Figure 4.14.   File Open custom dialog box.

is loaded automatically, but all others must be coded if they are to be loaded and viewed in procedures. The following skeleton code shows the single statement that loads and displays the custom dialog box that appears as shown in Figure 4.14 when the Open option is chosen in the Text editor program.

```
Sub mnuFileItem_Click (Index As Integer)
  Select Case Index
    .
    .
  Case 1
      .
      .
      frmOpenSave.Show 1         'Load and display
                                 'OPEN form
    .
    .
  End Select
End Sub
```

Table 4.1.   Display tasks.

Form Display Task	Use
Load and display a modal form	Show method and style=1
Load and display a modeless form	Show method
Load a form without displaying it	Load statement or reference a control or property on the form
Display a loaded form	Set Visible property to TRUE or use Show
Hide a form from view	Set Visible property to FALSE or use Hide
Hide and unload a form from memory	Unload statement

4.8.2.5. Display options.   The code used for dialog boxes establishes how the dialog boxes will be displayed and loaded into memory. Table 4.1. shows a task and what code format you must use to execute it.

Some discussion about Unload and Hide is necessary here. When Unload is used, the form and its controls are unloaded from memory. You lose all settings that may be needed again sometime later in the program. Unless you are low on memory, it is safer and more efficient to use Hide rather than Unload. Hide removes the dialog box from view, setting the Visible property to FALSE, but keeps any data or settings attached to it. These include property values and dynamically created controls. Your code can therefore still refer to form item values that are hidden but not to those that have been unloaded.

5

Managing Projects and Creating Executables

5.1. INTRODUCTION TO PROJECTS AND EXECUTABLES

To create applications in Visual Basic, you make *projects*. A project basically equates to an application. Projects are used to manage the files you create for an application.

An *executable* is any file with the extension .EXE. In terms of your applications, an executable is in a form that does not need the Visual Basic environment to run in. It may be called and run from Windows 3.X just as any other program, such as a Windows spread sheet or database application. The executable may also be called by double-clicking on an icon that calls and loads the application.

5.2. PROJECT COMPONENTS

A project is made up of these files:

1. A file for each form
2. A file for each code module, if any
3. A file for each custom control, if any
4. A project file (.MAK)

Other files may also be included in a project, but these are the principal types of files used in most development work.

The *project file* contains only a list of the files needed for the application, along with environment options. It is made and updated as you work with and save your application. After you have made all the files for your application, you can convert it into an executable file. Table 5.1 shows the relationships between your files and an executable.

5.2.1.   What a Project Can Include

Three types of files can be included in a project: forms, modules, and custom controls.

Forms (files with .frm extensions) have been used in this book from the beginning to interface with the user.

Modules (files with .bas extensions) contain code statements and global or module-level declarations of types, variables, constants, and global or external procedures. Chapter 6 will examine and explain modules and related terminology in depth.

Custom controls (files with .vbx extensions) were examined in Chapter 3. They contain the data needed for using add-in controls that provide and add additional functions for the developer.

5.2.2.   The Project Window

Figure 5.1 shows a project window with a project file named PROG1.MAK. As files are created and added to or removed from a project, these changes are shown in the project window's list of files.

Certain default files are added to every new project. These are usually custom controls and their number varies depending on whether you are using Standard or Professional Visual Basic. Many more default files are added automatically for the Professional Version as shown in Figure 5.1.

5.2.3.   The Project File

A project file, which has the .MAK file extension, contains the same file list as seen in the project window. It also contains data about where these files can be found and how the environment

Table 5.1.   File relationships to an executable application.

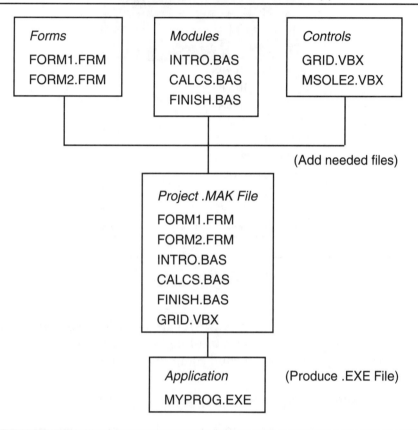

Forms	*Modules*	*Controls*
FORM1.FRM	INTRO.BAS	GRID.VBX
FORM2.FRM	CALCS.BAS	MSOLE2.VBX
	FINISH.BAS	

(Add needed files)

Project .MAK File
FORM1.FRM
FORM2.FRM
INTRO.BAS
CALCS.BAS
FINISH.BAS
GRID.VBX

Application   (Produce .EXE File)
MYPROG.EXE

looks to the user when a project is opened. Project files are saved in ASCII format, so the developer can display or change them with any text editor or from within Visual Basic. The project file is updated each time you save your project.

Upon first starting Visual Basic in normal design mode, you can start a project file by clicking on the Toolbar icon that opens project files and start the application by clicking on the start icon in the Toolbar (see Table 2.1).

To start a project from Windows 3.X, double-click on its icon.

To start a project from MS-DOS, use the syntax:

```
vb /run filename [/cmd commandline]
```

Figure 5.1. The Project Window.

The *filename* must include the .MAK extension. The *commandline* is used to send a list of command-line arguments to the application. In most programs the /cmd commandline option is not used.

5.3. NEW FORMS AND CODE MODULES

To create new forms and modules, click on the following menu options from the File menu or the equivalent Toolbar icons shown. Clicking on the Toolbar icon, when available, produces the same effect and is faster.

Menu Option	Icon Option	Result
New Form		Creates a new form, adds it to the project
New MDI Form	(N/A as an icon)	Creates a new MDI (Multiple Document Interface)
New Module		Creates a new code module, adds to project

5.4.   CREATE, OPEN, AND SAVE A PROJECT

You create, open, and save projects by clicking on the following menu options from the File menu or corresponding Toolbar icons. Again, clicking on the Toolbar icon produces the same effect and is faster.

Menu Option	Icon Option	Result
New Project	(N/A as an icon)	Closes the current project and creates a new project with the AUTOLOAD.MAK parameters
Open Project		Closes the current project and asks for an existing project name, which it then opens
Save Project		Updates current project file
Save Project As	(N/A as an icon)	Updates current project file, saving it under a file name you specify

5.5.   ACTIONS TO PERFORM WITH FILES

Menu Option	Result
Add File	Adds an existing form, module, or VBX to project
Remove File	Removes a form, module, or VBX from a project
Save File	Saves a form or module in a project under its current name
Save File As	Saves a form or module under a name you select, giving you a choice of binary or text format

Note: Modules are files that contain code statements.

Projects can share files with the same name (e.g.,: FORM1 .FRM). If FORM1.FRM contains common file functions, you can use the name FORM1.FRM for any projects that use these same file functions instead of rewriting the same code a number of times. However, you must take precautions with this approach, because if you change FORM1.FRM for use in a new project, then *all* other projects using the form will also be changed accordingly. This may not be what you want. To be safe *rename* the form for your new application before changing it. That will protect your older applications and allow you to change the renamed form safely to fit the new application's needs.

5.6.   TEXT AND BINARY FORMS AND MODULES

You can save your forms and code modules in either binary or text format. To make either of these options the default, use the Environment options dialog box (see Section 5.8). The default can be overridden by using options in the File menu, giving you a way to save some files in binary and some in text. Thus you can save all files in the format you want for your project.

If you save files in text format, you can easily make hard copies of textual representations of forms and code, use external tools to generate new files, and use program management systems on these files.

A variety of options exist for loading a file in text format into a project as code. You can replace the code of a module or form with the text file, merge it into existing code, or load the text file as a new module (see Section 5.6.1.4 for load details). Figure 5.2 shows these dialog box options.

5.6.1.   How to Create a Text File

The Save File As option in the File menu is used to create text files. The steps in the following sections are not necessary if the default under Environment is set to Text.

5.6.1.1. Saving a form or module as a text file.   Click or select the form or module you want converted to text format. Choose Save File As under the File menu, enter the name you want to assign to the file, select the Save as Text check box, and click on the OK command button.

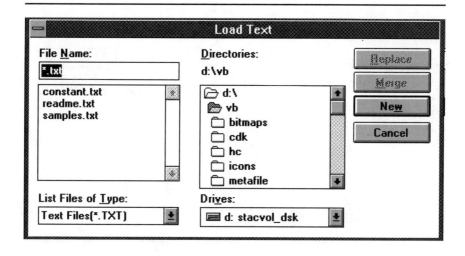

Figure 5.2.   Load text.

5.6.1.2. Saving code as a text file.   Select the form or module
containing the code, choose Save Text under the File menu to
open the dialog box in Figure 5.3, type in the desired file name,
and click on the OK command button.

5.6.1.3. Add a text file as a form or module.   Choose Add file
under the File menu to call the dialog box in Figure 5.4, select the
name of a text file, click on the Save as Text box, and then click on
the OK command button.

5.6.1.4. Load a text file as code.   Choose Load Text under the
File menu, select the name of a text file, and click on one of the
command buttons labeled Replace, Merge, or New (see Figure 5.2).

5.7.   MAKING AN EXECUTABLE FILE

You can make an executable file either from Visual Basic or from
a MS-DOS command line.

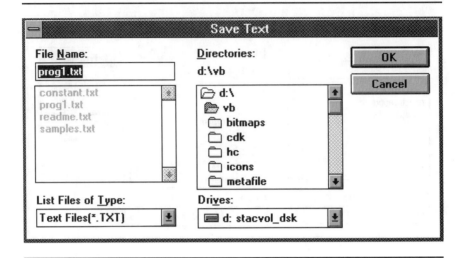

Figure 5.3. Save text.

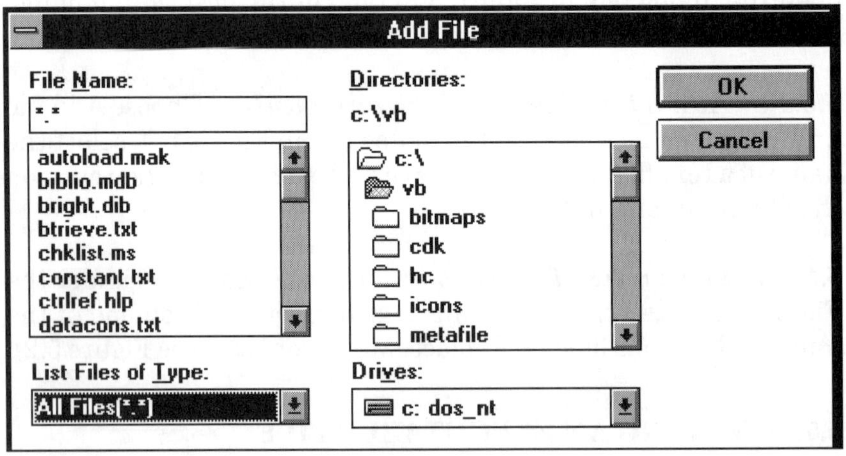

Figure 5.4. Add file.

5.7.1. Making an Executable from Visual Basic

Choose Make EXE File from under the File menu to bring up the dialog box shown in Figure 5.5, enter a file name, change the Use Icon From icon if desired, insert a new file name in Application Title that better suits the file's function, and click on the OK command button.

5.7.2. Making an Executable from MS-DOS

This method for making an executable may be the only way you can build the file if your application is large or you are low on system resources such as memory or disk space. The syntax line is

```
vb /make projectname[.MAK] [exename]
```

where *projectname* is the project name from which an .EXE will be made, and *exename* is an optional name you may assign to the file if you want the .EXE to be named differently from the default of projectname.exe. An example using this syntax is

```
vb /make proj1.mak sample1
```

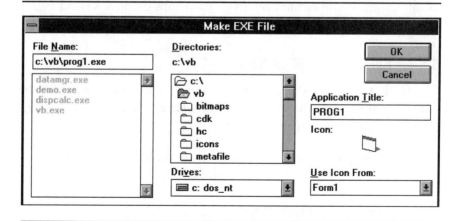

Figure 5.5. Make EXE file.

In this example, the files contained in the project file proj1.mak will be made into an executable file named sample1.exe.

5.7.3.   Custom Controls, Runtime File, and Executables

When using custom controls, other considerations must be taken into account in addition to those addressed in Sections 5.7.1 and 5.7.2. A custom control file is a DLL (Dynamic Link Library) used by Visual Basic. Running an executable containing a custom control requires that its .VBX file be on your systems path or in the same directory as the .EXE file. If you plan to sell or distribute an application, I recommend that the .VBX files be copied to the user's \windows\system directory.

Whether you sell or give away applications you make with Visual Basic Professional (see Section 5.11.), users will need copies of these files:

- Visual Basic runtime file (VBRUN300.DLL)
- All required .VBX files
- Required DLLs (e.g.: Graph control needs a DLL called GSWDLL.DLL)

One file you cannot give away with your application is VB.LIC. This file allows you to use the Professional Version of Visual Basic at design time and cannot be given to others using a Visual Basic application at runtime.

5.8.   ENVIRONMENT SETTINGS

Choose Environment under the Options menu (see Figure 5.6) to examine or change the environment settings. These settings are saved in the file VB.INI.

> *Note:* Here is where the option to save files in either binary or text format is stored and can be changed.

5.9.   PROJECT OPTIONS

Choose Project from the Options menu to examine or change the three lines, or options, shown in Figure 5.7. These settings are

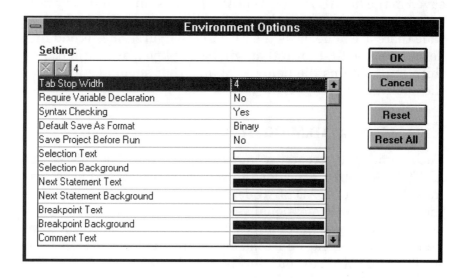

Figure 5.6. Environment options.

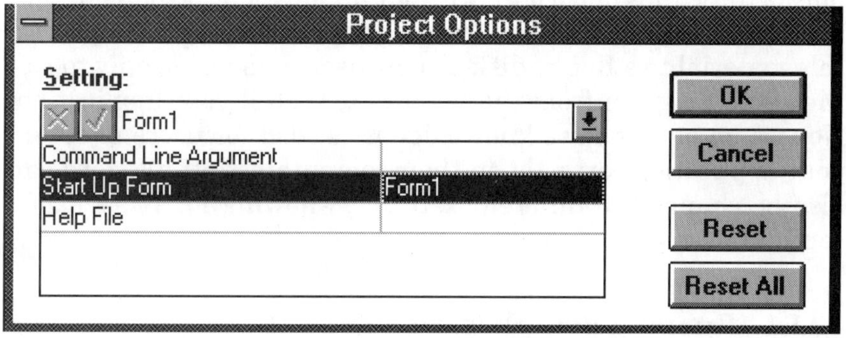

Figure 5.7. Project options.

saved in the file AUTOLOAD.MAK. The first line sends any necessary arguments when the application is started. Most of the time there are none, as is the case in the figure. The second line designates the first form that will be displayed at runtime. The third line contains the help file, if any, that should be linked to the application.

5.10. AUTOLOAD.MAK FILE

Each time you create a new project, the files listed in AUTOLOAD.MAK are added to your new project. What is contained in AUTOLOAD.MAK depends on whether you are using the Standard or Professional version of Visual Basic. It also depends on your system resources. For example, if you do not have Pen capabilities, no Pen controls or files will be loaded from AUTOLOAD.MAK to your new project file.

You can edit AUTOLOAD.MAK just as you edit a project file. To do so, choose Open Project under the File menu, select AUTOLOAD.MAK, click on OK, include file names that you want to add to new projects, set Environment options, and choose Save Project from the File menu.

5.11. SETUPWIZARD

The SetupWizard automates the tasks necessary for distributing your finished applications. It looks through your project and marks those files needed to run your application. It then builds a custom setup program, compresses all needed files, and copies all this material to a floppy disk. A new user then needs only to run the setup program from the floppies to install your application. No system or Windows knowledge is needed for users to set up your application correctly on their computers. SetupWizard can also be changed to different settings, allowing for more exotic configurations.

5.11.1. Running SetupWizard

Here are the six setup steps used to create the Master Distribution disk(s) for your Visual Basic applications.

Step 1: Double-click on the SetupWizard icon in Visual Basic's program group. When you see the first screen (Figure 5.8), click on the Select MAK File button. SetupWizard will ask for the location of your Visual Basic application's .MAK file. Instead of choosing the Select MAK File button, you can alternatively type in the full path to the MAK file. Click the NEXT button to continue.

SetupWizard will try to determine all files needed for distribution. Project files such as form files (.FRM) and code modules (.BAS) should be saved in ASCII format for SetupWizard to work optimally. SetupWizard will automatically build your Visual Basic application's executable if the executable specified cannot be found in the project file (.MAK) or if you check the Rebuild the project's EXE file check box.

Step 2: Check any features that your application supports. For instance, you may choose to have SetupWizard include support files such as Data Access and OLE Automation on the master disk(s). Click the Next button to continue to the next step. Click the Back button to return to Step 1.

Step 3: SetupWizard now collects Data Access information.

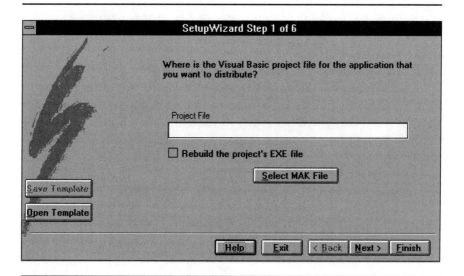

Figure 5.8. SetupWizard Step 1.

Select one or more of the non-native data formats that your application will support. For example, if your application uses FoxPro data files, then choose that format option from the list. Multiple selections are allowed in this list. Click the Next button to continue to Step 4. Click the Back button to go back to Step 2. Step 3 will be skipped if you do not check the Data Access choice box.

Step 4: SetupWizard also collects floppy disk and disk drive information. Select the disk drive and the disk type on which you wish to have SetupWizard create the Master Distribution disks. Click the Next button to continue on to Step 5. Click the Back button to go back to Step 3.

Step 5: SetupWizard allows you to add and remove files before building your master disks. Because SetupWizard sometimes cannot determine all files or special files required by your application, you will have the chance to add these files to the distribution list. Click the Add Files button to add the necessary files. These may be, for example, data files, bitmaps, or INI files. You can use multiple selection in the Add Files dialog box. Click the Remove Files button to remove any files that you do not want included on your distribution disks. Once again, you can use multiple selection in the Distribution file list box. Click the Next button to continue to Step 6. Click the BACK button to go back to Step 4.

Step 6: SetupWizard compresses files into a temporary directory, creates Disk Layouts, and will build SETUP.LST. SetupWizard will also create a SETUP1.EXE by modifying SETUP1A.MAK and SETUP1.FRM.

SetupWizard will then create the master disks, telling you the number of blank formatted disks needed. As it copies your application, SetupWizard will prompt you to insert each blank formatted disk required to contain the entire application. SetupWizard will notify you when the Master Distribution disks are completed. Use MS-DOS's DiskCopy or File Manager's Disk Copy Disk menu choice to make copies of your Master Distribution disks.

6

Visual Basic Programming Basics

6.1. INTRODUCTION TO LANGUAGE FUNDAMENTALS

Thus far, the approach this book has followed has been to proceed from the broadest, program-level concepts downward to the structural concepts and finally to the syntax required to support those concepts. In this top-down approach from, for instance, what code procedures are to what rules make a variable local, static, or global, I have basically sought to structure each chapter so that it leads logically and progressively to the next. For example, to discuss variables first and only then discuss the basics of procedures would be boring and in poor style. As much as possible, this book avoids that type of "cart before the horse" style of teaching. It is thus important that you read the whole book to enjoy the full benefit of learning all of the Professional Basic language—even those areas you think you may never use.

6.1.1. Language Overview

Both Standard and Professional Visual Basic are complete programming languages supporting structured programming concepts. This chapter covers the essential parts, or components, of the language used in both the Standard and the Professional versions.

As discussed in previous chapters, an application can contain forms (.FRM extensions), custom controls (.VBX extensions), and code modules (.BAS extensions). A form contains the visual parts seen by the enduser, such as controls, and also the code associated only with that form. Custom controls, as shown in past chapters, are referenced either in forms or in code modules. Thus in one sense, you do not make custom controls *in* your Visual Basic application. Instead, custom controls are *called in* to perform their function. They are precoded for your use and reference to them in your code only when they are needed. Code modules contain only code statements. You *must* have at least one form or code module to make an application. The default on starting a new project contains one form and two or more custom controls (.VBX file extensions). You add more forms, .VBX's, and code modules, as needed, while you are designing your application.

6.2. INTRODUCTION TO EVENT-DRIVEN PROGRAMMING

Event-driven programming requires a different way of looking at *how* you are going to program an application when compared with older, traditional Basic language dialects. In older Basic programs, execution of a program started at the top of a main module and continued sequentially from one code line to the next. The application called other routines as needed and jumped around at times with GO TO statements, until a STOP, END, or EXIT halted execution. In contrast, with event-driven programming as used in Visual Basic, a user action such as clicking on a button or a system event executes a procedure—a subroutine or function. In short, the user is in command of what happens and when, whereas in older versions of Basic, the user reacted to the code being processed.

6.2.1. Event-Driven Programming in Visual Basic

In event-driven programming, code is executed in response to an event. Every form and control has a predefined set of responses.

If an event occurs on a form or control, Visual Basic calls, or responds with, the associated event procedure. The event procedure is the code you have written. Every time the same event— for example, clicking on an OK button—occurs on the same form or control, that event procedure code is called in response to this action.

> *Note:* A couple of important points need to be understood by Basic and nonBasic programmers alike at this juncture if they are to understand more in-depth information on programming in Visual Basic. First, even though objects such as command buttons recognize a predefined set of events, *you* determine whether these events are to cause an effect, or call a procedure, in your application. Just because a control can recognize both a Change and a mouse Click event does not mean you need to write code for both events. If only one event is needed, then that is the event for which you write a code procedure. A Click may be the only event your application needs to continue normal processing. In that case, only a Click event procedure for that object should be written. You do not care that internally a Change event also occurred; you only care that the user clicked on an object and that something should happen in the form of executed code because of it.

Though many objects can recognize the same event, such as Click, the combination of each object's name and the event name makes a unique procedure name. The reason for this naming convention is to prevent a Click event, for example, from triggering multiple procedures. To illustrate this, if a user clicks on a command button the Command1_Click procedure is executed, but if the user clicks on a form then the Form1_Click procedure is executed. Both have recognition of the Click event in common but call different procedures as a result.

6.2.1.1. *Normal Event-Driven Scenario.* In the normal course of events, a Visual Basic program executes in accordance with the following steps.

1. The application is started and loads the startup form.
2. Either the form or a control receives an event. For instance, the user may click on a command button. An event can be

caused by the user, the system (e.g.: a timer event), or indirectly by code (e.g.: a Load event caused by the automatic loading of the startup form).

3. If a procedure is related to any of the preceding events, that procedure is executed.

4. The application stops until another event occurs.

5. Steps 2–5 are repeated until an event occurs that terminates the application.

6.2.2. Application Startup Code Options

The first form in your application is called the *startup form*. Visual Basic's default option is to load and show that form as soon as you start the application. If you have written code for this event, it will be in procedure Form1_Load and will execute when the application starts. As discussed before, you do not *have to* have program code in Form1_Load. You need only generate event procedures that make your application do the tasks it is designed for. In this case, nothing else may be required other than loading and showing the startup form. Just because the form loads doesn't mean you want other actions to take place that would require placing code in the procedure Form1_Load. On the other hand, you may want to open certain files every time the form is loaded. In that case you would put the code to open those files in the Form1_Load procedure.

While in design mode you choose to make a different form your startup form. To change to the new form, first choose Project from the Options menu, then choose the Start Up Form option. In the list box select the form you wish to be your new startup form.

You can also dynamically choose which form will be the startup form, and/or execute code before any form is shown to the user. To do this, make a Sub (subroutine) called Main in a code module that is not in, or part of, a form. In other words, put Main in a separate *.bas file. In the subroutine called Main you can include code statements that open files, check file status, and so forth before the statements that will load your first form.

Using Main defeats the auto load of a startup form, so you must code statements to load whatever form you want the user to see first. The final step is to select Sub Main from the Start Up Form option in the Project Options dialog box.

6.2.3.   Quitting Your Application Safely

The only completely safe way to stop, or quit, a Visual Basic application is by using the End statement in one of your procedures. If you do not, the program may seem to have terminated but in fact still be running. This would be the case if there were a hidden form in use. From the user's standpoint if a form has a command button labeled 'Quit Application' and the user clicks on this button, he or she will consider the application closed and all system resources given back to the computer. However, if the event code in the button only closes the visible form and nothing else, the application will appear to terminate but still be running due to the hidden form. In contrast, the End statement stops all execution of code and closes any open files, thus affording a "clean" stop to an application. Therefore, to avoid possible confusion on this point, you should add the statement End as the last line in any event code labeled "Quit Application."

6.3.   TYPES AND USE OF MODULES

A *module* is a unit with a .bas file extension containing code and possibly declaration statements. As your command of Visual Basic grows, you may find yourself writing the same procedures repeatedly for a number of your forms. You cannot call one form's procedure from another. Form procedures are local, meaning that they cannot be called or used from another form. To overcome the inconvenience of rewriting the same code for multiple forms, use a separate module containing this common code. Each form can then call or use this module as needed, and you only need to code one module.

A code module or form module can contain declarations, event procedures, or general procedures. Declarations are statements such as *constants* and *type* (Ex. Global) that declare an object or variable to be of some particular class. Such statements must be placed before the first procedure in the file; that is, they must be at the module level—the first statements in the file. Event and general procedures are discussed in the next two sections.

6.3.1. Event Procedures

When an object (i.e.: form or control) recognizes that an event such as a Click event has occured, that object calls the *event procedure* with the name corresponding to the event. Event procedures are basically used only on forms and controls.

The name of an event procedure for a control combines the control's Name property with the event name (e.g.: cmdOkButton_Click); form procedure names combine the word Form with the event name (e.g.: Form_Click).

6.3.2. General Procedures

Any procedure that is not called in response to an event is called a *general procedure*. General procedures must be called from within other procedures such as the statement block of an event or form procedure. A statement block is the body of code between the first and last lines of a procedure.

One reason to use general procedures is to reduce an application's total number of code statements. If a procedure used in multiple forms serves the same function, you can code one general procedure for the task, versus having each form contain a duplicate task procedure. Note that if a general procedure is to be called from anywhere in an application, it must be put in a code module (file with .bas extension) rather than in a form module. If a general procedure is put in a form module, it can be called only from the event procedures in that particular form.

6.3.3. Managing Procedures

To construct a general procedure, make the Code window active and choose New Procedure from the View menu. You can also enter a procedure heading in the Code window and press ENTER. The procedure heading can be a Sub or Function followed by the name you want the routine to be called, as in "Sub CloseAll ()" or "Function ReadMouse ()."

Table 6.1.   Procedure tasks.

Management Task	Do This
Delete a procedure from a module	Select the procedure in the Code window; select Cut from the Edit menu.
List all procedures in the application	Choose Procedures from the Window menu.
Edit a procedure in another module	Choose Procedures from the Window menu; select the module and procedure wanted; click on OK.
Copy or move a procedure from one module to another	Select the procedure in the Code window; select Cut or Copy from the Edit menu; click the destination module; and pick Paste from the Edit menu.

To edit a general procedure, select "general" from the Object box in the Code window, and select the routine you want to edit in the Procedure box.

Visual Basic offers other ways to manage procedures, as well. Table 6.1. summarizes commonly performed tasks related to procedures and explains how to do each task.

6.4.   TYPES OF PROCEDURES

There are two types of procedures: Sub and Function. Sub (subroutine) procedures do not return a value when called, whereas Function procedures do return a value.

6.4.1.   Sub Procedures

The syntax for a Sub procedure is

```
Sub ProcedureName (arglist)
   'code statements'
End Sub
```

ProcedureName is the name you wish to call the Sub. Arglist is a list of arguments. Each argument looks like a variable declaration and acts like a variable in the procedure. The syntax for each argument is

```
[ByVal] variablename [()] [As type].
```

The ByVal option will be explained in Chapter 7. Type can be any data type such as Integer, Long, Double, String, or Currency, user-defined, or object (see Section 6.6 and Chapter 7). To make this more understandable, you only need the variable name part of the preceding syntax statement. Adding parentheses after a variable name signifies that the variable is an array. This automatically makes the variable what is called a variant type. Because a variant can contain almost all basic data types, explicitly using the "As type" portion of an argument is often unnecessary.

Every time a procedure is called the statements between Sub and End Sub are executed. When you call your own general procedures you must supply the necessary arguments. With event procedures Visual Basic supplies values for each argument if needed. For example, suppose that the following code block is defined as a general procedure called LoopDoLoop

```
Sub LoopDoLoop (NTimes)   'Ntimes is a VARIANT
Dim K
Dim Dummy
    For k = 1 to Ntimes
        Dummy = k
    Next k
End Sub
```

The statement LoopDoLoop 7 calls LoopDoLoop with an argument of 7. The integer 7 is substituted for NTimes, causing the For Loop to execute seven times, end the procedure, and go back to the code that called the Sub. The next code statement to be executed will be the line following the line that called LoopDoLoop.

You can also use the statement Call LoopDoLoop (7) to accomplish the same thing as LoopDoLoop 7. Using the Call parameter in front of the Sub name makes it clear to all that this is a subroutine made by a programmer, not a built-in routine of the language.

6.4.2. Function Procedures

The syntax of a Function procedure is

```
Function ProcedureName (arglist) [As type]
   'code statements'
End Function
```

ProcedureName, arglist, and type are the same as their equivalents in Sub procedures (see Section 6.4.1.). There are three differences between a Sub and a Function. In the case of a Function:

- Parentheses are always used around arguments when a function is called;
- Like variables, arguments have data types ([As type]). The information provided here determines the type of the return value. If you do not specify As type, variant type will be used;
- A value is returned to the calling routine by assigning it to the ProcedureName in the code statements.

In the following example, a function finds the square root after multiplying two numbers.

```
Function SqrMult (X, Y)
   SqrMult = sqr(X * Y)
End Function
```

Using this function is the same as using other, built-in Visual Basic functions such as:

```
A = 1.11
B = 2.22
Z = SqrMult (A, B)
```

6.4.3. Public vs. Private Procedures

As mentioned before, procedures in a form are private to that form. You can call them within that form, but code in other forms or code modules cannot call or use them. Procedures in code modules, on the other hand, are public. They can be used and called anywhere in your program.

To make a code procedure private even though it is in a code module, use the keyword Private. This keyword can be applied either to a Sub or to a Function, as in the following statements:

```
Private Sub MySecret ()
```

or

```
Private Function MySecret (A,B).
```

There is no way to make a procedure in a form public other than to move it out of the form and into a code module.

6.5. CODE STATEMENTS IN PROCEDURES

If some of the code and terms you have seen so far have been confusing, this section is intended as an attempt to clear up some areas of doubt. It is difficult to present and analyze code using variables, constants, data types, and so forth without explaining these also. I hope that the examples given so far have been simple enough to understand without insight into these other areas. Chapter 7 will deal with these topics in detail, clarify what has been presented regarding them thus far, and pave the way for the information presented in subsequent chapters.

6.5.1. Comments, Numbers, and Code Statements

In many code examples you have seen the comment symbol ('). When Visual Basic sees this symbol in a code statement, it ignores any words that follow it. The main reason for comments is to help you, and future programmers dealing with your code, understand why a code statement was placed in a procedure, what it accomplishes, and how it works. A comment can take up a whole line or part of a line as shown below:

```
'This comment takes up the whole line, but executes nothing
'Following comments tell about a change made to X
X = Sqr(A) 'Take Square Root of Total for Task B.1.A
           'Modification Done By: Tom Torgerson (12/1/99)
```

Code statements are usually limited to one per line, but you can have more than one if you use a colon to separate them as in

```
X = 1.23 : Y = 3.14
```

This statement assigns the value 1.23 to variable X and 3.14 to variable Y.

Numbers are usually expressed in base ten, the decimal system. But you can use other number systems also. Octal (base eight) and hexadecimal (base sixteen) are the most common. Octal numbers have &O in front of their value, and hexadecimal numbers are preceded by &H. As an example, the equivalents of decimal 15 would be &O17 in octal, and &HF in hexadecimal.

6.5.2. Naming Rules

Names of variables, procedures, and constants used in your code must follow these rules:

- They must start with a letter.
- They may not be longer than 40 characters.
- They may contain only letters, numbers, and underscores.
- They may not be a reserved word.

A *reserved word* is a word that is part of Visual Basic's language. Such words include, among many others, If, Or, Sqr, and Loop. The complete list can be found in the Visual Basic Language *Reference Manual* or under "Reserved words" in the Help menu.

Note: Forms and controls *can* have names that use reserved words if brackets surround any such word used, as shown in the following example:

```
'[For].Visible = False'
```

This approach is not recommended. I show it here only so that if you see this type of code statement you will understand why it is permissible.

6.5.3. Assignment and Retrieval Properties

The equal sign is used in assignment statements of the type

```
destination = source
```

Such statements assign a value to the property reference or variable by copying data from source to destination. The destination must be a reference to a property or a variable. The source can be any valid expression and may contain calculations. Assignment statements can set or retrieve the value of a property, and store or retrieve data in a variable.

To set the value of a property, place a reference to the property, in the syntax format object.property, on the left side of your assignment statement, as in:

```
Text1.Text = "Social Security Number"
```

The object here is Text1 and the property is Text, so this statement puts the text "Social Security Number" in the text box Text1.

When coding form properties and referring to a form property for that form, you can omit the name of the form, as in:

```
Sub Form_Click ()
  Caption = "No reference to the FORM to change this Caption"
End Sub
```

To retrieve the value of a property and store it in another property or variable, place the reference to the property on the right-hand side of the expression, as in:

```
X = Text1.Text
Text3.Text = Text4.Text
```

6.5.3.1. *Controls and Properties on Other Forms.* When referencing properties and controls on one form through code in another form or code module, you must specify the form name when referring to a form property, as shown below:

```
Form1.Caption = "Here's a new caption for Form1"
```

When referencing a control on one form through code in another form or code module, the name of the form that contains that control must also be specified. Form and control references are separated by using the ! operator as shown below:

```
Form1!Text1.Text = "Social Security Number"
```

6.5.4. Value of a Control

All controls (e.g.: Text box) have a property whereby you can refer to the control and, without using a property name, set its default property. This default property is usually the most common property of the control. In the case of the control Label, the default property is the Caption. Thus if you use the statement

```
Label1 = "This becomes the caption for control Label1"
```

this text string becomes the Caption property for control Label1. Although this approach causes the code to execute a bit faster, its drawback is that it makes the code less readable and thus harder to maintain. I therefore recommend that you not use default control properties in this way. Keeping the same syntax for control properties may make life much easier if, 3 years from now, you or someone else must change the application. For this reason, I suggest that instead of using the shortcut for Label1, you use

```
Label1.Caption = "Here is Label1's Caption"
```

6.6.   OVERVIEW OF VARIABLES

A *variable* stores data. Without variables one cannot do calculations, print output, or save data. Variables have a name and a type. The *name* is what you use to refer to the value the variable contains. The data *type* determines what kind of data the variable can store: numbers or alphabetic characters.

6.6.1.   Data Types

When the data type is not explicitly defined, the default type is *variant*. A variant can store most data types such as numeric, alphanumeric strings, and dates or times. Converting between data types is handled automatically by Visual Basic. For instance, if a variable is set to a numeric value (A = 3.14) and later reset to a string data type (A = "Hello") this is perfectly acceptable with a variant. It would *not* be acceptable if A were assigned the data type Integer. In this case, resetting A to a string type would cause systems errors, or at best a value of A other than what was intended. If you know what type of data a variable is supposed to contain, declare its variable type. (Details on procedures for declaring variable types are given in Chapter 7.) If you are not sure what type of data the variable may contain, use the variant default type.

6.6.2.   Declaring Variables

As discussed above you do not have to declare your variables explicitly. If you do not, they become variant type. It is still good style to declare your variables at the top of your modules so you don't get any surprises such as a variable you forgot about causing problems in, for instance, a formula. Grouping the variable declarations also makes it easier to add or delete variables without fear of affecting program logic.

To ensure that you declare all your variables, you can specify that variable declarations are required, using the Environment Options dialog box option.

To declare a variable, use the Dim statement. The syntax is

```
Dim variablename
```

or

```
dim variablename As datatype
```

For example,

```
Dim X
Dim Y As Integer
```

In this example the declared variable X is still a variant type since no data type was assigned to it.

6.6.2.1. Introduction to Variable Lifetimes. When a variable is declared in a procedure with the Dim statement as shown in the preceding section, its lifetime is only as long as the procedure is running. After the procedure has finished the value the variable had is gone. In addition, you cannot access that variable from another procedure in the code module. In Chapter 7 you will learn how to change these constraints and how to preserve variable values globally by using a different declaration.

6.7.   CONTROL STRUCTURES

Control structures are the statements that control loops and decisions. They are similar to other Basic, C, and Pascal control structures and include

- If/Then
- If/Then/Else
- Select Case
- Do loops
- For loops.

The first three of these structures are called *decision structures*, since they have statements that may or may not be executed depending on a condition and decision. The last two are loop structures that repeatedly execute one or more code statements.

6.7.1.   Decision Structures

Decision structures test a condition or conditions, and based on the result, execute corresponding code statement blocks. A code statement block can contain one or more code statements.

6.7.1.1. If/Then.   An If/Then block is used to execute one or more statements based on a condition. Two different If/Then syntax formats can be used:

```
If condition Then statement
```

or

```
If condition Then
    statement block
End If
```

For example,

```
If answer = "YES" Then result = True
```

```
If answer = "YES" Then
    result = True
End If
```

Both examples accomplish the same thing.

6.7.1.2. If/Then/Else.   An If/Then/Else block is used to define multiple blocks of statements, only one of which will be executed. In the example that follows the syntax, note that the Else option section (statementblockN) will execute if NONE of the above conditions is true.

```
If condition1 Then
   [statementblock1]
[ElseIf condition2 Then
   [statementblock2]]...
[Else
   [statementblockN]]
End If
```

Example

```
Sub List1_Click ()
    If List1.Text = "Screen" Then
      A = True
    ElseIf List1.Text = "Printer" Then
      B = True
    ElseIf List1.Text = "Modem" Then
      C = True
    Else
      D = True
    End If
End Sub
```

6.7.1.3. Select Case. A Select Case block is a more efficient and easily understood alternative to using If statements with multiple Else conditions. The syntax is

```
Select Case testexpression
  [Case expressionlist1
     [statementblock1]]
  [Case expressionlist2
     [statementblock2]]...
  [Case Else
     [statementblockN]]
End Select
```

Now consider the following example.

```
Select Case Index
  Case 1
     A = True
```

```
Case 2
    B = True
Case 3
    C = True
Case Else
    D = True
End Select
```

Here, if Index has a value of 1, 2, or 3 then either A, B, or C will be set to True. If the Index value is any other value, D will be set to True.

6.7.2.   Loop Structures

Loop structures allow the execution of one or more statements repeatedly. The two types of loops are Do/Loop and For/Next.

6.7.2.1. Do/Loop.   A Do/Loop is used to execute a statement block an unspecified number of times. Though Do/Loops have many forms, they all check a numeric condition to resolve whether processing should continue. The numeric condition checked must be an expression or value that equates to either False (zero), or True (nonzero), just as the If/Then structure requires.

One form of the Do/Loop's syntax is

```
Do While condition
  statements
Loop
```

An example is

```
I = 1
Do While I < 10
  Print I
  I = I + 1
Loop
A = "Start here after the Do loop finishes."
```

> ***Note:*** In real life the condition would more likely be on the order of I < XYZ, where XYZ is a variable given different values as the

program uses this Do/Loop structure time after time. If statements are always to use a constant value such as 10, a For/Next structure is more appropriate and faster than a Do/Loop.

Referring to the syntax, this example Do loop first tests the condition, I < 10. When the condition is True, or nonzero, the statements are executed and the routine goes back to the condition to see if the loop should still continue. If the condition happens to be False, or zero, the routine skips past the statements and stops the loop structure. Program execution continues at the code statement that immediately follows the line containing the word Loop.

The statements will never be executed if the condition is initially False. This feature can protect your variables from unintentional changes, since nothing is executed until the condition is checked. This would be the case if, instead of I = 1, the first line were I = 100.

In the example, the nine numbers 1–9 will be printed. When I reaches 10 (due to I = I + 1) the condition will be 10 < 10, which is False; ten is not less than ten. The False condition causes the loop to cease, and execution resumes at the string assignment of variable A.

A variation of this Do/Loop is Do/Loop While. The syntax and an example are given below. The main difference in this variation is that there will be at least one execution of statements. The statements are executed first, then the condition is checked.

Syntax:

```
Do
   statements
Loop While condition
```

Example:

```
X = 9
I = 0
Do
   I = I + 1
   Print I
Loop While I < X
```

Two other variations, similar to the two you have seen, loop as long as the condition is FALSE. Their syntax is as follows:

```
Do Until condition
   statements
Loop

Do
   statements
Loop Until condition
```

6.7.2.2. For/Next. When you know the number of times a statement block will be executed, the For/Next structure is a more efficient code alternative than Do/Loop. The For loop utilizes a counter variable that increases or decreases in value each time the loop is repeated. This counter has a built-in ability to use step increments that Do loops do not have. The default step increment adds 1 to the previous counter value (e.g.: 1, 2, 3, 4, 5), but you can increment by any number using the Step increment option. If you want all odd numbers starting from 1, set the Step increment to 2, resulting in the numbers 1, 3, 5, 7, 9, and so forth being used by the counter. This example shows use of a Step increment to print the numbers 1, 3, 5, 7, and 9:

```
For i = 1 To 9 Step 2
   Print i
Next i
```

The syntax for a For/Next structure is

```
For counter = start To end [Step increment]
   statements
Next [counter]
```

The argument *increment* can be either positive or negative. If it is negative, start must be greater than or equal to end. If no increment is set, the default is one.

The steps used to execute a For/Next are thus clear. First, set the counter (i) to start (1). A test then occurs on the counter to see if it is greater than the end (9). If it is, the loop quits; otherwise, the statements are executed. The counter is increased (or decreased) by one—or by whatever Step increment value you assigned. If the increment is 2, the counter i will have the value 3. Again, the statement Print i executes, and the process of incrementing and testing the counter continues until counter is 11. This figure is greater than the end, 9, so the For/Next structure is stopped and execution continues on the line following Next i.

Here is another example using a general procedure to print the square roots of the numbers 1–5.

```
Sub sqrtprint ()
Dim i
   For i = 1 to 5
     Print sqr(i)
   Next i
End Sub
```

6.7.3. Nesting Control Structures

You can put control structures within each other to form a nested structure. For instance, you may put an If/Then inside a For/Loop structure, or use multiple levels of the same control structure, as shown in the following example using two For/Next structures:

```
Sub dblesqr ()
Dim i, j
   For i = 1 to 5
     For j = 6 to 10
       Print sqr(i), sqr(j)
     Next j
   Next i
End Sub
```

Though the Next [counter] statement does not require using the counter name, doing so makes code much easier to read, especially when For loops are nested.

6.7.4. Exiting Control Structures and Procedures

An Exit statement in the appropriate place can make your application run much faster particularly if the application contains large or numerous Do or For loops. Thus we will now examine control and procedure Exits.

6.7.4.1. Exit Control Structures. Exiting from a Do or For loop before its normal looping time would end can speed up loop processing and your application. The syntax is simply Exit For or Exit Do, depending on whether you want to exit prematurely from a For loop or a Do loop. The exit statement can occur as many times as wanted, and be placed anywhere between the first and last statement of a For or Do loop control block.

Here is an example of exiting from a control structure.

```
Dim Count
For i = 1 to A
    For j = 1 to B
        If j > i Then
            Print "Error ", i
            Exit For                'Exit inner For loop
        Else Count = Count + 1
        End If
    Next j
Next i
```

If j is greater than i, then this structure exits the nearest inner loop, in this case, For j = 1 to B. This approach eliminates any more unnecessary looping with j. It causes i to increase by 1 and continues the checking process. This admittedly nonuseful routine does serve the purpose of showing you how to use an Exit statement, where to place it, and what happens as a result of using an Exit For statement. If the routine consisted of Do loops, the check would still incorporate an If clause, but with an Exit Do statement instead of an Exit For.

6.7.4.2. Exit Sub and Exit Function Procedures. To exit from a Sub or Function procedure, use the statement Exit Sub or

Exit Function. Here, too, the Exit statement can occur a number of times, and be placed anywhere in the body of a Sub or Function. Again, the reason the exit procedure is important is that you can skip all further statements when Exit is called and immediately get back to the calling routine. The following example illustrates the use of Exit Sub:

```
Sub checkij ()
Dim Count
For i = 1 to A
   For j = 1 to B
       If j > i Then
           Print "Error ", i
           Exit Sub                 'Exit Sub checkij ()
         Else Count = Count + 1
       End If
     Next j
Next i
End Sub
```

This is similar to the example code in Section 6.7.4.1 except for the use of Exit Sub rather than Exit For. Note also that in this code, the first time j becomes larger than i, an error is printed, and instead of going to the next i counter, the whole routine stops and control goes back to whatever code called this Sub.

7

Variables and Data Types

7.1. INTRODUCTION TO VARIABLES AND DATA TYPES

This chapter looks at how your application stores and retrieves data. Managing how, when, and where your program's data changes, or ensuring that it stays the same, is what programming is really about. The more you understand the concepts of variables and data types, the easier it will be to program an application.

Variables are names you supply to hold data. That data can have many data types. *Data types* tell a variable what type of data can be stored in it. Some variables are used to hold only numeric values, or alphanumeric values, or date or time values, or user defined types. Variables can also have different lifetime and scope properties. This means that some variables are available to an application during its whole lifetime, and some for only a very short time. Some variables can be used in other code modules and others cannot. You will learn about these issues, and many others, in this chapter.

Many of the examples presented thus far have used the default *variant* data type for variables. The reason for this is that you need not declare variables nor define their type. The system takes care of that for you. However, good programming practice dictates that using the variant type for all your program variables is not a good idea, since doing so makes the program harder to debug, maintain, and follow.

7.2. DECLARATION OF VARIABLES

As shown in Chapter 6, the syntax for declaring a variable in a procedure is

```
Dim variablename [As type]
```

The rules for making up a variablename are that a variable's name must begin with a letter, cannot be over 40 characters long, must contain only letters, numbers, and underscores (_), and cannot be a reserved word such as Integer. The type defaults to variant if the [As type] option is not used.

7.2.1. Implicit Declaration

Implicit declaration occurs when you do not declare a variable in your procedure. If the program encounters an undeclared variable, it will automatically make one of the type variant for you. The problem with this approach is that it is more prone to programmer code errors—especially spelling errors. If a frequently used variable in your procedure is misspelled anywhere, a new variable will be created with the misspelled name. As a consequence, your calculations may not be what you expected. However, no error message will be given, and you will be stuck trying to figure out why your application is not giving correct results.

7.2.2. Explicit Declaration

To avoid the problems implicit in using variant variables you can force each variable you use to have an explicit declaration. Doing this will cause the system to give you an error message each time it encounters a variable that is unknown to the code or form procedure. You can do this in two ways. The first method works only on the code or form procedure in which you are working. It consists of inserting the statement Option Explicit in your Declarations section as the first declaration and the second line in your code. The second approach makes you declare your variables not only in one form or procedure, but in all form and code modules in your application. To accomplish this you set an environment option as follows:

- Choose Environment from the Options menu.
- Select the Require Variable Declaration option.
- Type Yes in the Settings box or in the Settings list box.

> *Note:* The Declaration section of a module consists of the statements that precede your first Sub or Function statement line. Consider:

```
Option Explicit      -
Global A             -
'End Declarations    -
Function sqrt(xyz)   ──────────→ Module ABC.BAS
  A - abs(xyz)       -
  sqrt = sqr(A)      -
End Function         -
```

Here in module ABC.BAS, the Declaration section consists only of the two top lines. Actually the Declaration section can be of any size from no Declarations to a large number of needed Declaration statements.

7.3. SCOPE AND LIFETIMES OF VARIABLES

Scope can be viewed as the range in which a variable can be accessed by other variables and modules. Some variables can only be accessed within one procedure, while others can accessed from anywhere in the application.

Lifetime refers to how long the variable is available to the application before the system reclaims the variable, and the space it once took up in system memory. If the variable is needed again, the system must reallocate space and its default value.

7.3.1. Scope of Variables

How a variable is declared determines its scope. The following list shows the various scope options and how to declare each.

Local	->	Dim, Static, or ReDim; within a procedure
Module	->	Dim; in Declaration section of code or form module
Global	->	Global; in Declaration section of module

For instance, if you want a variable to be scope Module, use the Dim statement in the Declaration section of your code or form module.

7.3.1.1. *Local variables.*

Local variables are only recognized by other variables and statements within their procedure. They lose their scope and value when the procedure is done. There is one exception: local Static. If a variable is declared Static, no other procedure can use or access it, but it retains its value when it leaves its procedure. This makes local variables good for such things as keeping totals or counts of items, since when their procedure is called again, they retain the old value assigned to them.

7.3.1.2. *Module level variables.*

Module level variables can only share their values with other procedures in their module. You create them with the Dim statement in the Declaration section of the module.

> *Note:* These variables remain in existence for the whole application. The variables in a form module keep their value even when the form is unloaded. However, to use them again after leaving their module, you must return to the original module or form in which these variables were first declared and reference them from there.

7.3.1.3. *Global variables.*

Global variables, which have the largest scope of all variables, are available in every form and module in an application. Using the Global statement, put global variables in the Declaration section of a module. You cannot put

Globals in a form module. Globals exist and retain their value for the lifetime of your application.

For the sake of clarity, use one module to declare all your Global variables. In this way they will be easy to find, change, and maintain.

7.3.2. Lifetime and Static Variables

Variables have various lifetimes in an application, depending mostly on how and where they are declared. Local variables have a lifetime limited to the procedure in which they are found. When the procedure is finished, so are they and their values. However, you can prevent local variables from vanishing by using the keyword Static. Use Static in the same way as the Dim statement (e.g.: Static ATotal) inside a procedure. Using Static will preserve the value of the variable when the procedure is finished. The following code keeps a total count of the records in a database, updating the total each time the procedure is called.

```
Function DBRecordTotal (n)
   Static SaveOldRecNum
   SaveOldRecNum = SaveOldRecNum + n
   DBRecordTotal = SaveOldRecNum
End Function
```

7.4. FUNDAMENTAL DATA TYPES

When you declare a variable in, for example, a Dim statement, you can also assign it a data type. The data type determines what kind of data can be stored in that variable. If you want to store a text line in a variable, use a data type that permits storing text, a string data type. Among the fundamental data types are String, Integer, Variant, and Currency. If you do not specify a data type, the defaults type is Variant.

7.4.1. Variant Type

The variant data type has the ability to store many different forms of data: numbers, text, dates, and times. One advantage of using the variant data type is that you need not convert one type to another type when the kind of information you wish to access or use changes. The following example shows that initially the variant variable X stored a text or string value; however after the second line, it will then store the numeric value 6.

```
X = "2"      'Put string value into X
X = X + 4    'X now is numeric 6
```

7.4.1.1. VarType. Most of the time you need not be concerned with the particular data type a variant variable is, but if want to know what type of data is currently stored in a variant you can use the VarType function. In Visual Basic Version 2.00 nine return values are available for VarType, but when writing your code, to be safe, allow for the possibility of more return values in newer Visual Basic versions. Below are the current nine return values and what each return value represents.

0—Empty	5—Double
1—Null	6—Currency
2—Integer	7—Date/Time
3—Long	8—String
4—Single	

One occasion when you may want to know for sure what data type is in your variant is when prompting the user for a Date or Time value. If the user inputs a wrong data type, the variables' values will be useless to your program. Checking the user input with a statement such as

```
If VarType(X) = 7 Then Exit Sub
```

to make sure the user entered a valid response will bulletproof this section of your code.

7.4.1.2. IsNumeric and other functions. The numbers stored in a variant variable take on the most compact form possible for representing the number. For instance, if the number stored is 123 and it has no decimal value, it will be stored as an Integer data type.

Numbers used in currency calculations must be used in such a way that round-off errors do not occur. To solve this problem, use the CCur (Change to Currency) function with your variants. The statement

```
PayOut = CCur((hrs * hr_rate) + OverTimePay)
```

Makes the PayOut figure a currency data type.

An Error message will result if you try to do a math calculation involving a variant variable such as a String that does not have a value that can be considered a number. To get around this problem, use the IsNumeric function as shown:

```
Do
   X = InputBox ("Please enter a Numeric Value:")
Loop Until IsNumeric (X)
MsgBox "The Number Squared Is: " & (X * X)
```

Visual Basic will automatically assign a variant that contains a string variable ("17") to a number (17) for you. But to convert a number explicitly to a string, use the CStr function

```
String_Var = CStr (17)
```

Use the Format function to convert a number explicitly to a string that includes formatting options such as thousands separators, currency symbols, and other useful options for making your data look presentable in reports and printouts.

7.4.1.3. Concatenation and addition.   In variant variables a problem can occur when using the + operator. If both variants contain numbers, the + produces numeric addition. However, if both contain strings, concatenation occurs. The problem arises when one variant is numeric and one is string. When this happens you cannot be sure what the result will be. To avoid this, if you want concatenation, use the & operator instead of the + op-

erator. If you want addition, make sure both variants are numeric by using the IsNumeric function discussed previously. Consider the ramifications of the following example.

```
X = "2"
Y = "3"
Print X + Y, X & Y
' Above will print 23   23
Y = 3
Print X + Y, X & Y
' Above will now print 5   23
```

The need for awareness about the data types your application will manipulate should now be more apparent.

7.4.1.4. Date/Time variant example. Variant variables are handy and quick to set up when using the Time/Date data type. In the following example, one variable is set to the time, while other built-in functions extract the hour and minute from it.

```
Sub Form1_Click
   Dim Current_Time
   Current_Time = Now  'Return the current time
   Print Hour(Current_Time)     'print the hour
   Print Minute(Current_Time)    'print the minute
End Sub
```

The range of dates that can be stored in a variant variable is from January 1, 0000 to December 31, 9999. Date and time can be enclosed in # signs for comparison checks such as

```
If Contract_End < #3/1/98# Then Exit Sub.
```

A variety of ways exists to set up a date and time as shown here:

```
SaveDate = #April 1, 1998 3:30pm#
SaveDate = #May-23-1997#
SaveDate = #14 July 1999#
```

If you do not insert a time, Visual Basic sets the time to midnight. If you do not insert the date, Visual Basic sets the date to 12/30/1999.

If you are not sure whether the user has entered a legal date or time text value for a variant you can use the IsDate function to check it as follows:

```
If IsDate(User_Input) Then Exit Function
```

Here, if the user input is a valid date the Function will be exited. In actual code, if User_Input is a valid date or time value, the next step is to convert that text into a valid date with the CVDate function as shown here:

```
If IsDate(User_Input) Then User_Date = CVDate(User_Input)
```

7.4.1.5. *Empty value.* A variant has the Empty value before it is assigned a value. This Empty value is different from zero, null value, and a zero-length string (""). Use the IsEmpty function to test for an Empty value, as in

```
If IsEmpty(A) Then A = "Not Empty Now!"
```

7.4.1.6. *Null value.* The variant data type can also have the special value Null. Because of its special characteristics, Null is commonly used in database applications to flag missing or unknown data.

If any part of an expression evaluates to Null, the entire expression evaluates to Null in a process referred to as *propagating*. Passing Null or an expression that evaluates to Null as an argument to most functions will cause the function to return Null.

You can assign a variable the Null value with the Null keyword as in

```
X = Null
```

To check whether a variable is Null, use the IsNull function as in

```
If IsNull(X) Then Y = Null.
```

If you assign Null to a nonvariant variable, an error will occur. If you have not explicitly set any variants to Null in your application, you need not check for such an error because the system never sets a variant or statement to Null unless your program has explicitly set statements to Null.

7.4.2. Other Data Types

Though the variant data type is very important to Visual Basic, the other data types are equally or more important to creating professional looking and acting applications. By using the following data types you can create smaller executables, and faster applications. For instance, by always using the variant data type for small, nondecimal numbers you are wasting considerably more memory area than if you declared these smaller numbers to be of the data type Integer. The more code in your application, the more this becomes a factor.

The seven fundamental data types are shown in Table 7.1, which gives the type declaration character, name and allowable ranges.

When using data types other than Variant you must ensure that the Dim, Static, or Global declaration is followed by an As type clause, as these examples show:

```
Dim Xyz As Integer
Static X As Double
Global Name_It As String
```

When using Dim, you can include multiple declarations in a single statement, as in

```
Dim X As Integer, Y As String
```

However, note that the As type clause must be used for every variable thus declared and typed. In the statement

```
Dim I, J As Integer
```

I will default to the variant type, since As type was not used for variable I.

Table 7.1. Visual Basic fundamental data types.

Character	Type Name	Allowable Ranges
%	Integer	−32,768 to 32,767
&	Long	−2,147,483,648 to 2,147,483,647
!	Single	−3.402823E38 to −1.401298E−45 [Negative numbers] 1.401298E-45 to 3.402823E38 [Positive numbers]
#	Double	−1.79769313486232D308 to −4.94065645841247D−324 [Negative numbers] 4.94065645841247D−324 to 1.79769313486232D308 [Positive numbers]
@	Currency	−922337203685477.5808 to 922337203685477.5807
$	String	0 to about 65,500
(N/A)	Variant	Date Values: 1/1/0000 to 12/31/9999 Numeric: same as double String: same as regular String

7.4.2.1. Type declaration character. For compatibility with older versions of BASIC, instead of using As type you can use a Type declaration character. To do so, simply add the appropriate character from Table 7.1 to the end of the variable name (Ex. Dim X%). The As type examples from the preceding section would result in these statements using this method:

```
Dim Xyz%
Static X#
Global Name_It$
```

7.4.2.2. Numeric variables. If you know that certain variables will only contain small whole numbers, use the Integer rather than the default Variant type. Integer will use less memory, and in the case of For/Loops will increase execution speed. If decimals are involved, use Single, Double, or Currency data types. Using the right data types makes your application much more efficient and maintainable.

7.4.2.3. *Strings.* When a variable will be used only for text data, use the String data type as follows:

```
Dim A As String
```

This makes assigning and manipulating text strings easier.

```
A = "This is a Message String"  'assign A a text string
L = Len(A) 'find the length of string A
```

A string data type will expand and shrink as the program gives it new text values. To make the variable accept only a pre-set maximum number of characters, use a fixed-length string, with the syntax String * size. Size is the number of characters that the variable will use in references from this point of declaration. The following code declares a string of 35 characters to Name_Enter. It also shows that truncation occurs if you try to put a larger string into a smaller one.

```
Dim X As String * 10
Dim Name_Enter As String * 35
'                          10        20         30    35 characters
Name_Enter = "12345678901234567890123456789012345"
X = Name_Enter
'   X now contains the first 10 text numbers
```

String comparisons such as

```
If Name_Enter = X Then Exit Sub
```

default to case-sensitive. This would make

```
If "Abc" = "ABC"...
```

false. Using the statement Option Compare Text in the declaration section changes this comparison to true. The declaration statement makes comparisons case-insensitive.

7.4.3.   Argument Types

Although by default the arguments for procedures are Variant, most of the time it is better to declare the data types explicitly. The following Sub accepts a string and an integer for its arguments.

```
Sub PrintNletters (A As String, ByVal i As Integer)
   'Print the first i letters in string A
   Dim j As Integer
   '
   If i > Len(A) Then i = Len(A)    'i can CHANGE value
   '
   For j = 1 to i
      Print A(j)
   Next j
End Sub
```

> *Note:* If a procedure has specific data types for its arguments, you cannot use the Variant type to utilize or call this procedure. You must call it with the same type of arguments as the procedure is built upon.

As the preceding note states, one must pass a value of the appropriate type to argument-specific procedures. One way to work around this—not usually recommended—is by passing an expression for an argument. You do this by surrounding the variant and any other variable(s), with parentheses as shown here:

```
Dim C                   'data type of C is Variant
Dim D As Integer
C = "ABCDEFG"
D = 3
PrintNletters((C), D)   'now variant C will work
```

7.4.4.   Argument by Value

Another way to pass a variant to procedures that have specific argument data types is to declare the arguments with the ByVal keyword (see the Sub statement in Section 7.4.3). Using ByVal allows you to call the second argument with a Variant data type as in:

```
Dim C                   'data type of C is Variant
Dim D                   'data type of D is Variant
C = "ABCDEFG"
D = "3"                 'Variant string
PrintNletters((C), D)   'variant C and D works
```

ByVal enables other data types to be passed to an argument of a specified data type. It also ensures that values are passed to an argument by value, not by reference.

If a variable is passed as an argument to a procedure by reference, the variable's value can be changed during the procedure. When a variable is passed by value, only a copy is passed to the procedure. This makes changing the original value in the procedure impossible. Only the copy can be changed, and the copy disappears after the procedure is finished.

7.4.5. Function Data Types

Functions return a value when their code finishes executing. This return value is by default a Variant data type with the 'Empty' value. As with variables, you can make the function return the data type you wish. For example:

```
Function CountLetters (A As String) As Integer
```

will return an integer value.

Since Variants are so diversified in what they can handle, it is not always necessary to declare a function data type, but Visual Basic works more efficiently if you do.

7.5. ARRAYS

An *array* is a set of variables using a common name and an integer index number to reference each variable in the set. As an example, Dim xyz(3) is a set of four variables using the name xyz and an index that can be from 0 to 3. The variables are xyz(0), xyz(1), xyz(2), and xyz(3). By using the same name and a different integer to reference each variable, arrays are perfect for tasks such as finding matches using For/Next loops:

```
For I = 0 to 3
  If(xyz(I) = "Torgerson") Then Print "Match Found: " & I
Next I
```

You can declare an array to be of any fundamental data type. Most of the time it is of one data type, such as String or Integer. If the Variant type is used, each variable in the array can be of a different data type.

Arrays can be fixed or dynamic in size. *Fixed* means you have set an integer limit to the size, as in xyz(3) where the integer limit is 3. Dynamic will be covered in Section 7.5.2.

There are three ways to declare an array, each giving the array a different scope. For a local array, the Static statement must be used. Local fixed-sized arrays must be static (e.g.: Static xyz(3) As String). Module-level arrays use the Dim statement in the Declarations section of a code or form module (e.g.: Dim xyz(3) As String). Global arrays use the Global statement in the Declarations section of a code or form module (e.g.: Global xyz(3) As String).

When you declare an array, the number in the parentheses must be between the values –32,768 and 32,767. For array indexes greater than 999, do not use commas in the statement; instead of Dim xyz(1,500), you must use Dim xyz(1500).

If you do not want to use the indexing method of 0 to N, you can change it to 1 to N. To do this, use the Option Base statement, Option Base 1, in the Declarations section.

7.5.1. Multidimensional Arrays

Arrays can have a maximum of 60 dimensions. For example, Static Dble_Array(4, 9) As Integer is a two-dimensional array with a maximum total of 5 times 10, or 50, elements belonging to Dble_Array. A three-dimensional array example is Dim Tri (4, 9, 19).

> *Note:* Both single and multidimensional arrays can use the keyword To for setting arrays that involve indexing a range of values. For instance, the example Dim Add_Them (130 To 200) As Integer only allows indexing between 130 and 200 for referencing values in the Add_Them array.

The efficiency of multidimensional arrays again is shown best in For/Next loops. The following code initializes or reinitializes the complete array to zero to make sure no forgotten value in the array remains to invalidate future calculations with the array.

```
Dim A As Integer, B As Integer
Static Num(9, 9) As Integer
For A = 0 To 8
   For B = 0 To 8
      Num(A, B) = 0
   Next B
Next A
```

7.5.2. Dynamic Arrays

One of the most versatile features of arrays is the ability to use *dynamic arrays*. Instead of the fixed indexes you have seen so far, you can use variable indexes to make the array exactly the correct size for your application without the additional overhead caused by loading values you do not need from the full, fixed-sized array. If you have an array of 500 items, but many times need only 50 of those 500 items, you are wasting memory and usually sacrificing execution speed.

You declare a dynamic array in the same way that you declare a fixed-sized array, except that you do not put a number inside the parentheses, as in 'Dim xyz().'

To allocate the array to a certain number of items in the array, use the ReDim statement. To allocate 10 elements for array xyz, you would use ReDim xyz(9). Alternatively, you could set a variable to 9 (e.g.: i = 9) and use that variable in ReDim xyz(i). The ReDim statement can be used multiple times in a procedure or application. What makes this feature powerful is that you can change the size of your array as the application dictates. This affords much better procedural efficiency on many arrays than being confined to fixed-sized arrays only.

The one drawback to using a ReDim code statement is that the variables' information is lost after the ReDim statement is used. When a ReDim statement is used, Visual Basic sets:

- Variant elements to the Empty value
- Numeric elements to zero
- Strings to a zero length string
- Objects to the Nothing value.

> **Note:** *Objects* in this case are variables that represent objects such as forms.

If you want to change the size of your array without losing your data, you can accomplish this by using the Preserve keyword. Single-dimension arrays can be increased easily, as shown in the following code where the elements in the array are increased by ten:

```
Redim Preserve Single_Array(UBound(Single_Array) + 10)
```

In changing and preserving multidimensional array data, you must follow one very important rule. Only the upper boundary of the *last* dimension can be changed using the Preserve statement. If you try to change any other dimensions, an error will occur. The following statement is fine:

```
Redim Preserve Dble(9, UBound(Dble,2) + 10)
```

However, this statement is not acceptable:

```
Redim Preserve Dble(UBound(Dble,1) +10), 9).
```

Since Dble has two dimensions, only the second, or last, dimension can be changed.

7.5.3. Huge Arrays

Huge arrays—arrays greater than 64K—are created automatically for you, so there are no keywords to be concerned with. The 64K value here does *not* mean arrays whose elements are greater than 64K (e.g.: Dim A(66000) As Integer). Instead, 64K is a total figure—the total of the array's number of elements times the size of each element. An integer array with 5000 elements (Dim x(5000) As Integer), represents a total of 5000 times 2 (each integer uses 2 bytes), or 10,000. Thus the size of array x would be about 10K, far less than 64K,so this array would not be termed a huge array. If the number of array elements were some 40,000 (Dim x(40000) As Integer), it would be a huge array: 40,000 * 2 = 80,000, or about 80K.

> *Note:* The preceding example using an index of 40,000 would, in actual programming practice, be illegal. Each index has to be in the range of –32,768 to 32,767. To get around this limitation, use multidimensional arrays such as x(2, 20000).

The restrictions on making huge arrays are: (1) they cannot be created on variable length strings: (2) they take some additional overhead in memory space other than the element size times byte size, and (3) they cannot be made of object variables.

7.6. USER-DEFINED DATA TYPES

User-defined data types are variables that represent multiple related data items. They resemble classes in C++, and the Struct in regular C. User-defined types are placed in the Declarations section and use the keyword Type. They are always global, and as such they cannot be created in forms. The variables declared in a user-defined type can be local, module-level, or global in code modules. The following code creates a user-defined data type called Emp_DP, for employees in a data processing department.

```
Type Emp_DP
    Emp_Name As String
    Emp_ID As Integer
    Manager As String
    Languages(15) As String
    Date_Hired As Variant
End Type
```

Once you have created a user-defined data type, you declare local, module, or global variables of that type.

```
Global CPU_Persons As Emp_DP, ALL_Emp As Emp_DP
```

Assigning and retrieving variables in the user-defined data type is done in the same way as for other variables.

```
CPU_Persons.Emp_Name = "Thomas W. Torgerson"
CPU_Persons.Date_Hired = #12/01/97#
```

If two variables are of the same user-defined type, you can assign one to another, and ALL elements will be copied to the other variable as in

```
ALL_Emp = CPU_Persons
```

This one statement will make ALL_Emp.Emp_Name equal to Thomas W. Torgerson and ALL_Emp.Date_Hired equal to 12/01/97.

Note that Languages(15) As String is a regular, fixed-sized array and is thus legal. Dynamic arrays are *not* allowed. So that there are no questions as to what this statement does, it allows you to enter up to sixteen languages for each person. Most persons will not know that many, but you have space to enter them if they do. The first and second languages would be assigned as follows:

```
CPU_Persons.Languages(0) = "Visual Basic"
CPU_Persons.Languages(1) = "C++"
```

User-defined types can also be used as arguments in procedures:

```
Sub Fill_Name(New_Person As Emp_DP, NameS As String)
   New_Person.Emp_Name = NameS
End Sub
```

Arrays of user-defined data types are allowable and very useful in structuring your data. For example:

```
Dim Sorted_DP(1000) As Emp_Name
```

7.7. CONSTANTS

Values that are used many times in an application and do not change are best put in the form of a *symbolic constant*. These constants are basically used and declared in the same way as regular variables, the main difference being that you cannot change their value. Once such constants are declared and assigned a value, that value stays the same for the whole application. Examples of common constants are:

```
Global Const PI = 3.14
Const FILE = "myfile.txt"
Global SquareNs = 4
```

Note that it is common practice to capitalize constants. It is also a good idea to put all global constants in one file for easier maintenance and debugging.

8

Files, Databases, and Reports

8.1. INTRODUCTION

This chapter first looks at creating and using data files, then at database access, and finally at report capabilities in Windows Visual Basic 3.0 applications.

8.2. TYPES OF FILES

The three types of file access you can use for your data files are: random, sequential, and binary. Each type will be discussed separately in the following sections.

8.2.1. Random Access Files

A *random access file* is a series of records all of the same length. A record is of a single data type, but since that type can be user-defined, the record usually consists of multiple fields. The length of a record is specified on use in the Open statement. If no record length is given, a default of 128 bytes is used. The length is used by the system to count how many bytes on the disk are used before another record is positioned for processing. Without a specific length, the system would not know how to calculate the position of each record in the data file. The position is known as the record number. To access any record you need only provide the record number wanted. Using the record length and number, the system will calculate the record's position and go to that record. One disadvantage to using random access records is that since all fields and records are of fixed length, if fields do not require all the space allocated to them you will have wasted disk space.

Figure 8.1 shows a record editor program that uses random access as the method of storing, adding, and editing employee information. Code examples will be shown in Section 8.3 so that you will understand the basics of how an editor like this is constructed. If you have the Visual Basic package, you can run this applica-

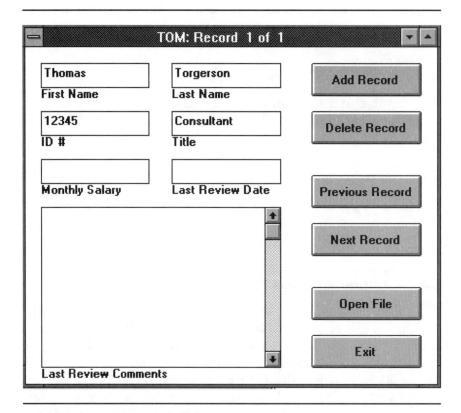

Figure 8.1. Record editor.

tion by loading RECEDIT.MAK from the vb\samples\files subdirectory.

8.2.2. Sequential Files

Text-only data typically is organized in *sequential access* files. Sequential access lets you program procedures especially designed for reading and writing lines and strings of text information. Sequential access data is not split into a series of records. A screen editor is perfect for this type of file handling, since each character in the editor is text or a format sequence such as the new-line character.

Sequential access is not well suited for number storage. For example, the number 1,234 would require four bytes of disk storage, one character for each digit. If stored as an integer value, the same number would require only two bytes, thereby saving half the disk space. If most of the file consisted of integers, and the number of integers were fairly large, you would be wasting considerable disk space.

Sequential access is also not recommended unless you always start reading your data file from the beginning. After opening a sequential file, unlike other types of files, you cannot go directly to a certain line in the file. Instead, you must read from the beginning of all the records or lines, until you reach the one you want.

Figure 8.2 shows the text editor we have discussed briefly in previous chapters. More details on how it is constructed will be covered in Section 8.4. If you have Visual Basic, this program can be run from TEXTEDIT.MAK in the \menus subdirectory.

8.2.3. Binary Files

Binary access gives you the greatest flexibility in storing data. You can use variable length records that waste absolutely no disk space, a concern that may be of extreme importance if you are designing a large database application.

You can store data records in whatever way you want, without using a fixed record length. Though this is fine for outputting data, it causes overhead when retrieving the records and their fields. You must keep track of exactly how the data was written;

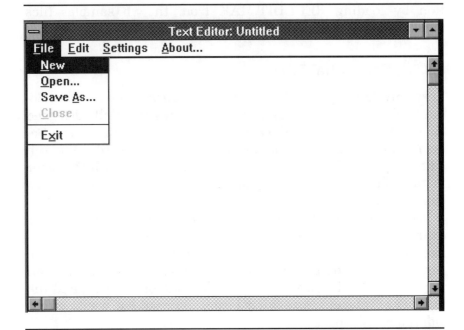

Figure 8.2. Text editor.

otherwise, you will not be able to read your records back as they were written.

8.3. USING RANDOM ACCESS FILES

In random access files each record contains one or more fields and has the same length as any other record, as shown in the following list.

Record 1		Record 2	
12345678901234567890 ← Number of bytes →		12345678901234567890	
Torgerson	44B21	Johnson	185C3
Last_Name	ID_Code	Last_Name	ID_Code
Field 1	Field 2	Field 1	Field 2

In the list are two records, each with two fields. Field one uses 15 bytes and is called Last_Name. Field two uses 5 bytes and is called ID_Code. This makes each record 20 bytes long. To read the information in record two, you must skip 20 bytes and starting retrieving data from byte 21. All records must relate to one type. In the preceding list, it is a user-defined type called Name_ID. The code to make this user-defined type follows.

```
Type Name_ID
    Last_Name   As String * 15
    ID_Code     As String *  5
End Type
```

8.3.1. Functions and Statements

The functions associated with random access files are: Dir, Dir$, EOF, FileCopy, FileDateTime, FileLen, FreeFile, GetAttr, Loc, LOF, Seek, and SetAttr.

The statements associated with random access files are: Open, Close, Get, Put, and Type . . . End Type.

8.3.2. Defining the Data Type

As discussed earlier in Section 8.3, before you can work with a random access file using multi-field records, you need to declare a user-defined type. The type used in the record editor example of Figure 8.1 uses the following code to declare the type Person:

```
Type Person
    ID              As Integer
    MonthlySalary   As Double
    LastReviewDate  As Long
    FirstName       As String * 15
    LastName        As String * 15
    Title           As String * 15
    ReviewComments  As String * 150
End Type
```

Note that the fields listed in this code can all be found on the left-hand side of the form as text boxes.

8.3.3. Variables for Random Access

When using random access, you must declare the needed variables for opening and using a random access file. This is done right after declaring the user-defined type, in this case the type Person. In Record Editor, the variables are Employee, Position, and LastRecord.

```
Global Employee As Person       'A data record will be a
                                'variable called Employee

Global Position As Long         'Use variable Position to
                                'track the current record

Global LastRecord As Long       'Store the last record
                                'number of the data file
```

8.3.4. Opening Random Access Files

The syntax for the Open statement for random access files is:

```
Open file For Random As filenumber Len = recordLen
```

Where *file* is the random access file name you wish to open, *filenumber* is a system reference number, and *recordLen* is the size in bytes of each record.

The following code is an example of how you can open a random access file.

```
'Begin Declaration Section
Dim FileN As Integer            'see above for filenumber
Dim Record_Length As Long       'see above for recordLen
'End of Declaration Section

Record_Length = Len(Employee) 'find the length of records

FileN = FreeFile 'find the next available file number
                 'from function FreeFile
```

```
''''''''''''''''''''''''''''''''''''''''''''''''''''''
Open "TOM.FIL" For Random As FileN Len = Record_Length
''''''''''''''''''''''''''''''''''''''''''''''''''''''
```

Since random access is the default file mode you could have used:

```
Open "TOM.FIL" As FileN Len = Record_Length
```

but the code is easier to understand using the previous Open statement.

8.3.5. Editing Random Access Files

To edit random access files, insert file records into variables, have the user change the variable values, and copy the variables back to the file by overwriting the old records.

8.3.5.1. Get statement. Use the Get statement to insert a record's data into variables that your application can use and manipulate. The Get statement can be used in the Record Editor program to retrieve a record and place the data into the Employee variable:

```
Get FileN, Position, Employee
```

FileN contains the file number from the Open statement. Position is the record number of the record just read, and Employee (declared as type Person) contains the data of the record.

8.3.5.2. Editing data. When a record has been retrieved, the fields can be placed on a form where each field can be edited or simply viewed. In the Record Editor program, the fields are contained in a control array of text boxes.

8.3.6. Writing Random Access Files

Random access files use the Put statement to write records into a file. Record Editor uses Put when replacing (editing), adding, and deleting records.

8.3.6.1. *Replacing records.* To replace records, use the following statement:

```
Put FileN, Position, Employee
```

Position in this case is the record number you want to overwrite with new field information contained in Employee.

8.3.6.2. *Adding records.* Adding records in Record Editor means adding a record to the end of the file. This means LastRecord must be incremented by 1 before the data is written to the file. The following code shows how this is done and adds the new record to the end of the file.

```
LastRecord = LastRecord + 1
Put FileN, LastRecord, Employee
Close FileN
```

8.3.6.3. *Deleting records.* The easiest way to delete a record is to blank out the record's variables. That creates problems because the record is still there taking up disk space. The more records this is done to, the more disk space is wasted, slowing down file operations. A more efficient way to delete records is to move up by one each record following the record to be deleted. This overwrites the record you want deleted with a good record, leaving no holes in the data file. The following code shows how this can be done.

```
Dim Temp_Variable As Person
Dim Indx As Integer
     .
     .
For Indx = Position To LastRecord -1   'start loop at the
                                       'record to be deleted

   Get FileN, Indx + 1, Temp_Variable  'get a good record

   Put FileN, Indx, Temp_Variable      'overwrite unwanted
                                       'record with good one
```

```
Next Indx

Close                                    'close all files
```

Upon closer examination, you will see that a duplicate of the last record will remain when the For/Next loop is finished. To remove this duplicate record:

- Create a new random access type file.
- Copy all wanted records to the new file, except the last record.
- Close and Kill (e.g.: Kill OldFile) the original file so the file is now deleted.
- Use Name statement to rename the new file with the name of the original file.

8.4. USING SEQUENTIAL ACCESS FILES

Sequential access files are best suited to tasks such as the text editor in Figure 8.2. Since text files are usually not structured in the manner of fixed-field variables, they are better suited to the sequential access method.

8.4.1. Functions and Statements

The functions associated with sequential access files are: Dir, Dir$, EOF, FileCopy, FileDateTime, FileLen, GetAttr, Loc, LOF, Seek, and SetAttr.

The statements associated with sequential access files are: Open, Close, Input$, Input #, Line Input #, and Write #.

8.4.2. Opening Sequential Access Files

You open a sequential access file for one of three uses:

1. Input—to input characters from a file, which must already exist
2. Output—to output characters to a file
3. Append—to append (add to the end) characters to a file.

If the file does not exist when using Output or Append, the file will be created and opened with the file name used in the Open statement.

The syntax to open a sequential access file is:

```
Open file For [Input | Output | Append] As fileNum Len =
Buffersize
```

Where *file* is the desired filename, *fileNum* is an integer or integer variable designating a free system file number, and *Buffersize* specifies the number of characters to be loaded into the buffer before the buffer is written to or read from the disk. The default for *Buffersize* is 512 bytes.

> *Note:* A *buffer* is a temporary holding area that acts as a buffer between the instructions that tell the computer to retrieve or write data and the actual physical device (here, the disk drive). Using a buffer helps speed operations between the computer and the physical device by cutting down the times a physical device is called. For example, 512 character strings could require accessing the device 512 times, but using a buffer could result in calling the device only once. External devices such as the disk drive are the slowest parts of your computer. If you cut down the amount of times you need to access them, you speed up your application's processing capability.

8.4.3. Editing and Reading Files

To edit a sequential access file, read the file into variable(s), change the variable(s) as wanted, and copy the variable(s) back into the file. The steps for editing, writing, and reading files will be discussed here and in the next few sections.

To read a sequential access file one line at a time, use the Line Input # statement. The following sample code shows the basic loop for reading a file in this manner until the End Of File (EOF) occurs. Line Input # recognizes a carriage return-linefeed in the file, and on finding one puts the text line into the variable Text_Line. Note, however, that the carriage return-linefeed is *not* read into the Text_Line variable. To keep the carriage returns and linefeeds, you must manually code them back into the variable after the line is read from the file as shown here.

```
Do Until EOF(FileN)
 Line Input #FileN, Text_Line
 Text_Line = Text_Line & Chr(13) & Chr(10)
 .
 .
 .
Loop
```

The Input$ statement can be used to read the whole file, or a specified number of characters, into a string or variant variable. If the text file is not very large (e.g.: less than 32K), this is very useful, since everything is done in one statement:

```
All_Lines_In_File = Input$(LOF(FileN), FileN)
```

where LOF stands for Length Of File.

If your file was written by using the Write # statement, use the Input # statement to read it back.

Make sure to use the Close statement (e.g.: Close filenumber) when you have finished your file operations.

8.4.4. Text Boxes and Files

The Text box control is a near perfect place to display your text files. The Text Editor in Figure 8.2 uses a Text box to display its text information. Using this type of display limits the length of any file to be shown to a little under 32K. This is usually not a problem, since 32K of text at a time is more than adequate for most applications. You do need to check that the file is under this limit before reading the file into the Text box, as is done here, checking for 30K maximum:

```
If(LOF(FileN) > 60000 Then    '30K times 2 bytes = 60K
  Msg = "File too large to use for editing..."
  MsgBox Msg, 16, "File exceeds limits"  'inform user
   Exit Sub                               'leave sub
End If
```

Using LOF statement requires that the file be opened. Use the FileLen function if you do not want to be required to have the file open to determine its length.

8.4.5. Placing Strings into Files

To output data to a sequential access file, open the file as Output or Append, then use the Print # or Write # statement. The following code shows how one line can copy all the data in the Text box to a file.

```
Print #FileN, TextBox3.Text
```

The Write # statement is best for writing a list of string and numeric expressions into a file. It separates each expression with a comma and puts quotation marks around any string expression. The following example will make this clear:

```
Dim A_String As String
Dim N_Number As Integer
'
A_String = "This is a string."
N_Number = 23
'
Write #FileN, A_String, N_Number
```

The result of this write statement to the file is to put the two variables in the following format on the disk.

```
"This is a string.",23
```

The line written to the disk file will contain the quote marks as shown. Any string will be surrounded by quote marks in this way.

8.5. USING BINARY ACCESS FILES

Of the three types of file access methods, the binary method gives you the largest flexibility in file usage. The bytes in a binary access file can represent any type of data. Binary access files are also a good choice when you are concerned with keeping your data files as small as possible.

8.5.1. Functions and Statements

The functions associated with binary access files are: Dir, Dir$, EOF, FileCopy, FileDateTime, FileLen, FreeFile, GetAttr, Loc, LOF, Seek, and SetAttr.

The statements associated with binary access files are: Open, Close, Get, Put, Input, and Input$.

8.5.2. Opening a Binary Access File

The syntax for opening a binary access file is:

```
Open file For Binary As filenumber
```

An example open statement is:

```
Open "EMPLOYEE.FIL" For Binary As #1
```

8.5.3. Records and Fields in Binary Access Files

The Record Editor program in Figure 8.1, which uses fixed-length random access records, uses the following user-defined Type statement to store information about Employees.

```
Type Person
    ID              As Integer
    MonthlySalary   As Double
    LastReviewDate  As Long
    FirstName       As String * 15
    LastName        As String * 15
    Title           As String * 15
    ReviewComments  As String * 150
End Type
```

A problem with this setup is that the string information limits may be too small in some cases, and too large for effective disk usage in other cases. If the review comment is "Ok Job", there will be many unnecessary blanks in the field to fill all 150 characters. This waste of space can be avoided by using binary access. Instead of strings with fixed-length parameters, you can use variable-length string fields. Using binary access, the preceding Type section can become:

```
Type Person
    ID              As Integer
    MonthlySalary   As Double
    LastReviewDate  As Long
    FirstName       As String
    LastName        As String
    Title           As String
    ReviewComments  As String
End Type
'
''''''''''''''''''''''''''''''''''''''''''''''''''''''''
Dim Emp As Person   'define Emp as a record of Type Person
''''''''''''''''''''''''''''''''''''''''''''''''''''''''
```

Now the string fields can expand or shrink to fit exactly the size of the string assigned to them in various parts of the application.

8.5.4.   File Output

The main problem with using variable-length strings is that they can change in size. Thus the way you write them out to a file also changes, making for a problem in calculating record lengths. One way to solve this problem is to write an integer out to the file just before the actual string. The integer represents how many characters long the string will be. This must be done for each variable-length value: a number followed by the actual string; another number and another string; and so on. Fields such as Integers do not need this number prior to the actual value, since fixed-length Types like integers always take the same amount of space in storage. The following sample code writes out the variable Emp, as defined in the Type definition in Section 8.5.3 with all of its fields, some of fixed length and others of variable length. Note that though binary access gives you more flexibility, it requires more code than other access methods.

```
Sub Write_Emp_Record (Position_To_Start_Writing As Long)
   Dim String_Len As Integer
    '
    'open file number #1 in another Sub
    '
    'Position_To_Start_Writing is the byte position where
    'writing out of the record will begin
    '
    '...............................................
   Put #1, Position_To_Start_Writing, Emp.ID  'fixed size
   Put #1, , Emp.MonthlySalary                'fixed size
   Put #1, , Emp.LastReviewDate               'fixed size
    '...............................................
    '
    ''''''''''VARIABLE-LENGTH FIELDS''''''''''''''''''
    ''''''WRITE OUT EACH LENGTH, THEN THE STRING DATA''''''
    '...............................................
    '
   String_Len = Len(Emp.FirstName)
   Put #1, , String_Len
   Put #1, , Emp.FirstName
    '
   String_Len = Len(Emp.LastName)
   Put #1, , String_Len
   Put #1, , Emp.Last_Name
    '
    '
   String_Len = Len(Emp.Title)
   Put #1, , String_Len
   Put #1, , Emp.Title
    '
    '
   String_Len = Len(Emp.ReviewComments)
   Put #1, , String_Len
   Put #1, , Emp.ReviewComments
```

```
    '
    '
End Sub
```

8.5.5.   File Input

The Get statement is one way to read binary access files. It
knows the length of fixed-length variables such as Integers, but
not the length of variable-length variables. Thus it must read in
the String-Len (string length) variable and use this value to determine the length of the variable-length string that will be read
in next. The following code uses this method to read a record
made in Section 8.5.4. The String$ function uses what was called
String_Len to set the variable field (e.g.: Emp.LastName) to the
correct size needed so that the variable-length field data string to
be read in next will fit.

```
Sub Read_Emp_Record (Position_To_Start_Reading As Long)
   Dim String_Len As Integer
'
''''''''''''''''''''''''''''''''''''''''''''''''''''''''''''
   Get #1, Position_To_Start_Reading, Emp.ID   'fixed size
   Get #1, , Emp.MonthlySalary                 'fixed size
   Get #1, , Emp.LastReviewDate                'fixed size
''''''''''''''''''''''''''''''''''''''''''''''''''''''''''''
   '

   '
'''''''''''VARIABLE-LENGTH FIELDS'''''''''''''''''''''
'''''''READ IN EACH LENGTH, THEN THE STRING DATA'''''''
''''''''''''''''''''''''''''''''''''''''''''''''''''''''''''
   '
'Read FirstName
   Get #1, , String_Len                      'get size
   Emp.FirstName = String$(StrSize, " ") 'set field size
   Get #1, , Emp.FirstName                   'read data field
   '
'Read LastName
   Get #1, , String_Len                      'get size
   Emp.LastName = String$(StrSize, " ") 'set field size
   Get #1, , Emp.LastName                    'read data field
```

```
'
'Read Title
   Get #1, , String_Len                    'get size
   Emp.Title = String$(StrSize, " ")       'set field size
   Get #1, , Emp.Title                      'read data field
'
'Read ReviewComments
   Get #1, , String_Len                         'get size
   Emp.ReviewComments = String$(StrSize, " ") 'set field
size
   Get #1, , Emp.ReviewComments                 'read data
'
....................................................
' Get and save present file position to Global variable
....................................................

   Position = Seek (#1)
'
End Sub
'————————!END OF SUB  Read_Emp_Record!————
```

8.5.6.   Input$ Statement

Another way to read the variables in a binary access file is to use
the Input$ statement, which requires a little less code than the
Get statement.

```
Sub Read_Emp_Record (Position_To_Start_Reading As Long)
   Dim String_Len As Integer
'
....................................................
Get #1, Position_To_Start_Reading, Emp. ID    'fixed size
Get #1, , Emp.Monthly Salary                  'fixed size
Get #1, , Emp.LastReviewDate                  'fixed size
....................................................
'
'
''''''''''VARIABLE-LENGTH FIELDS - USE INPUT$''''''''''''
'
Get #1, , String_Len
Emp.FirstName = Input$(String_Len, #1)
```

```
'
'
Get #1, , String_Len
Emp.LastName = Input$(String_Len, #1)
'
'
Get #1, , String_Len
Emp.Title = Input$(String_Len, #1)
'
'
Get #1, , String_Len
Emp.ReviewComments = Input$(String_Len, #1)
'
'
''''''''''''''''''''''''''''''''''''''''''''''''''''
' Get and save present file position to Global variable
''''''''''''''''''''''''''''''''''''''''''''''''''''

   Position = Seek (#1)
'
End Sub
'————————!END OF Read_Emp_Record!————————
```

8.6. TRACKING RECORD LOCATIONS

Finding records in a file can be a major problem of data file usage. The reason you use a data file is so you can get information out of it when you want it. If you must search every record from beginning to end to find a match for, say, a certain ID number, your application becomes frustrating, and sometimes even unusable. Anything that can be done to speed up access times to wanted records must be done.

Random access has an edge on resolving this problem since it keeps track of the location of records. The problem with random access is that it only tracks the record number. If you need to find records based on an ID number instead of the record number, you must build this ability into your application.

With sequential access files, this problem is generally not a concern, since these files are not usually organized around a record-based format. Instead, they are usually strings of text, not organized in any particular order.

Binary access files present even more of a problem than random access files, since they are based on variable-length string records whereas random access files have fixed-length strings and records.

One way to solve the access problem with random or binary access files is to make a form of index file called a *file allocation table*. For instance, if you want fast access by ID number in the Record Editor application, make a file allocation table containing the position and ID number for each record in the main data file. This will create an index into the file for each ID number, giving direct access to the record with the desired ID number.

To accomplish this, first decide for which field you want to search—the ID number in this case—and then make a new data type and a table for the maximum number of records in the main file (TOM.FIL).

Below is the file allocation table that will contain all the positions and ID numbers in the TOM.FIL for a maximum of 500 records.

```
Type Record_Table
    Dim ID As Integer
    Dim File_Location As Long
End Type
Const TABLESIZE = 500
Dim Emp_Table(1 To TABLESIZE) As Record_Table
```

The next step is to write the Sub that fills the table with the current data file information for ID and its respective location in the file. You then call this Sub every time you start an application that searches for records by ID number. Once this Sub has been executed, you have an index and position, allowing you to go directly to any record in your data file.

```
Sub Make_Emp_Table()
   Dim i As Integer
   '
   Open "TOM.FIL" For Binary As #1          'date file
   Position = 1                             'start at record 1
   For i = 1 to TABLESIZE                    'do until EOF
      '                                      'or = 500
```

```
   IF EOF(#1) = True Then
     Emp_Table(i).ID = "END_OF_RECORDS"  'flag EOF
     Exit Sub                            'exit routine
   End If
   '
   Emp_Table(i).File_Location = Position 'save location
   Read_Emp_Record(Position)             'read a record
   Emp_Table(i).ID = Emp_ID              'save ID #
 Next i
 '

End Sub
```

8.7. MICROSOFT ACCESS 1.1 ENGINE INTRODUCTION

Visual Basic 3.0 includes the database engine from MS Access 1.1. This allows you to access data stored in MS FoxPro, MS Access, dBASE, Paradox, Btrieve, SQL Server, and Oracle.

A couple of years ago, companies frequently used C and dBASE for their application work, dBASE for making custom databases and C for making custom applications. The drawback of such an arrangement was the lack of common ground between the two. If a project had two areas to it, the C programs and the dBASE databases, if one area got ahead of or behind the other, it affected the whole project. One part could cause a complete stoppage of work on the other part, until the first part caught up to the second.

Today, with Visual Basic and MS Access, this problem should not occur because both use the same database engine and the same language system. There is now that common ground with Visual Basic and MS Access that has been missing in database and application environments. Since Visual Basic 3.0 includes the MS Access 1.1 engine, you have everything you need to make applications ranging from daily automated business reports to network utilities.

8.7.1. True Transaction Processing

True transaction processing is very important for critical business applications. One very important feature of transaction processing is that operations can be cancelled before actually changing the database data. This feature is available in MS Access and any ODBC (Object Database Connectivity) form that supports transactions. A transaction can be thought of as a group of related operations all done at once to a database, rather than as a series of single operations such as an edit being done one at a time.

8.7.2. SQL

You may use the optimizing query engine in MS Access to parse the SQL statement, or pass the SQL statement through to the back end by ODBC, letting the back end (as SQL Server or Oracle) parse the statement. This allows you to use Visual Basic 3.0 to execute SQL Server stored procedures or other features of any back end.

8.7.3. Multiuser

Both Standard and Professional editions support multiuser data access. Locks with read-only access are supported, as are explicit record and table lock commands. You can use optimistic and pessimistic locking or a default lock mode. Update notification is given if two users are trying to edit the same record.

8.7.4. Security

Visual Basic knows the difference between read/write security, obeys field-level privileges, and can display the correct log-in dialogs automatically. You can set User and Password information, and finally, encrypted databases are supported.

8.7.5. Programmatic Objects

The programmatic data-access object layer (the use of program statements) has eight objects that provide coverage on manipulating a database. The following eight sections provide an explanation of these objects. To avoid confusing users of older Visual Basic versions, objects can now be declared as different database types, such as Database or Table. Objects are no longer limited to data types such as Integer or Currency. For example:

```
Dim My_db As Database
Dim My_Table As Table
```

8.7.5.1. *Database objects*. The OpenDatabase function is used to create the database object. For instance, the following code opens an MS Access database:

```
Dim My_db As Database
Set My_db = OpenDatabase("c:\vb\biblio.mdb")
```

8.7.5.2. *Table Object*. The Table object (OpenTable function) gives you the ability to manipulate the data stored in tables. This code opens the Authors table:

```
Dim My_db As Database
Dim t_author As Table
Set My_db = OpenDatabase("c:\vb\biblio.mdb")
Set t_author = My_db.OpenTable("Authors")
```

8.7.5.3. *TableDef Object*. The TableDef object defines a table. The following example adds a field to the Authors table:

```
Dim fNew As New Field
fNew.Name = "Worst Book"
fNew.Type = 10      '10 field type means a text field
fNew.Size = 40      '40 character field length
My_db.TableDefs("Authors").fields.append fNew
```

8.7.5.4. *Dynaset object*. A Dynaset object allows you to access the results of a query. These objects can be created using a SQL statement, a table name, or a stored query name if MS Access is used. The following code shows how a Dynaset can be created using a table name:

```
Dim d As Dynaset
Set d = My_db.CreateDynaset("Authors")
```

8.7.5.5. *Snapshot object*. A Snapshot object is a read-only Dynaset optimized for speed in processing.

8.7.5.6. QueryDef object. A QueryDef object allows you to define or modify a query stored in a MS Access database for later reference.

8.7.5.7. Field object. A Field object defines a field. Table, TableDef, Dynaset, and Snapshot all have a field object for every field in the table or query. The following code returns the value of the AU_ID (Author's Id) column in the first record of the Authors table:

```
Dim My_db As Database
Dim t As Table
Set My_db = OpenDatabase("c:\vb\biblio.mdb")
Set t = My_db.OpenTable("Authors")
Print t("Authors")
```

8.7.5.8. Index object. The Index object defines an index. The TableDef object has a collection of Index objects, one for each table. The following code deletes the AU_ID index from the Authors table:

```
My_db.TableDefs("Authors").Index.Delete AU_ID
```

8.7.6. Data Control Use

The Data control used in Section 8.8.1 acts like a visual Dynaset object. This control accepts any query and allows you to navigate through the query with the arrow keys.

Use the DatabaseName property to pick a database. The RecordSource property is used to define the source of the control's records. The RecordSource may be a SQL statement, a stored query name, or a table name. The Connect property is used to set the user name and password, or to access databases other than MS Access.

8.7.7 Data-aware Controls—Visual Layer

Data-aware controls can be set to a Data control without writing any code statements. Data-aware controls are used in the sample application in Section 8.8.

The following controls are all Data-aware: Label, Text box, Check box, Picture, Image, Masked edit field, 3D Check box, and 3D Panel. All of these have two new properties: DataSource, which defines the Data control to which the control is set, and DataField, which defines the field to which the control is set.

The following list summarizes the steps for setting up a sample data-aware control.

1. Put a data control on a form.
2. Put a Text box on the form.
3. Set the data control's DatabaseName to "c:\vb\biblio.mdb".
4. Set the data control's RecordSource to "Authors".
5. Set the text box's DataSource to "Data1".
6. Set the text box's DataField to "Author".
7. Run application (F5).

At present, the Grid is not data-aware, but third-party companies will soon be selling data-aware grids and spreadsheets, according to Microsoft.

8.8.   A DATA CONTROL SAMPLE APPLICATION

The next few sections will describe, in general, how an application can work as a front-end to an employee database. Data-aware controls will be used so you can see their function.

For these sections a third-party control will be needed. If you were developing this application, you would need to install a Calendar control. You would select File | Add and add MHGCAL.VBX from the \SYSTEM directory. Other controls such as MAPI, Pen, and Multimedia controls may also need installation. The Toolbox would look similar to that shown in Figure 8.3.

8.8.1.   Placing a Data Control

The Data Control is selected from the Toolbox and dragged to the position shown in Figure 8.4. This control will allow the enduser to step through the query. The data control will be used to define the query.

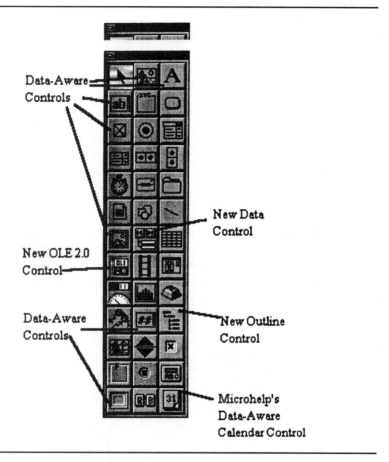

Figure 8.3. Toolbox controls.

8.8.2. Data Control Properties

A database needs to be chosen for the query to work on. This will be done in the properties for control Data1. Pressing F4 shows the property window. Click on the DatabaseName property as shown in Figure 8.5. Then click on the ellipse button to select a particular database to use. As shown in Figure 8.6, choose the database named SAMPLE.MDB. Click on OK to proceed.

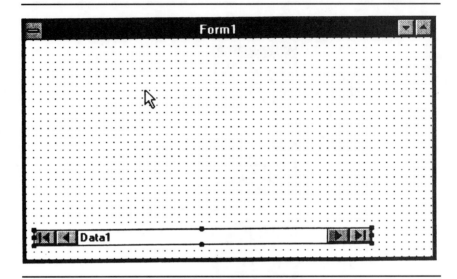

Figure 8.4. The new Data Control.

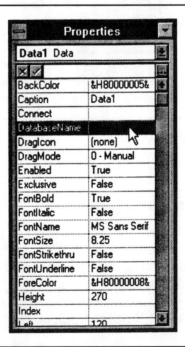

Figure 8.5. DatabaseName property.

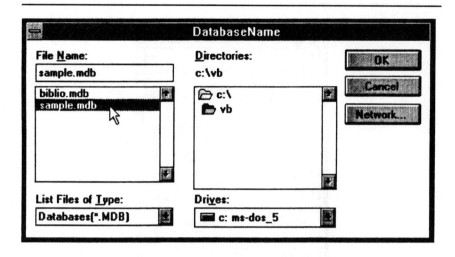

Figure 8.6. Picking the database.

8.8.3. Data Control Query

With the database chosen, the actual query can be defined. This is done with the RecordSource property of Data1. This property can be set to a SQL statement, a stored query, or a table name. Here a table called the Employees table is used. By clicking on the RecordSource property, then clicking on the combo-box down arrow, you can select the table from the list as shown in Figure 8.7.

The Data control (Data1) has other useful properties. For example, if you want to make sure no one changes the database, you can use the ReadOnly property. Using the Connect property sets a user name and password, or the ability to access other formats such as Paradox, FoxPro, ODBC, dBASE, and others.

8.8.4. Placement of Data-aware Controls

Two Text boxes, a Picture box, and the Calendar control must be placed on the form as shown in Figure 8.8. The Calendar's DividerStyle property is set to Lowered, and the form's BackColor property is set to gray.

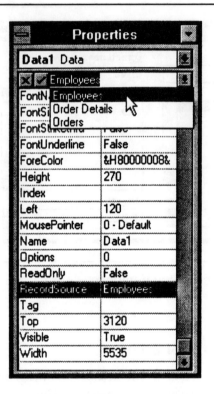

Figure 8.7. RecordSource property.

8.8.5. DataField and DataSource

Two new properties included in data-aware controls are Data Source and DataField. The DataSource property sets which Data control will be referenced. The DataField property sets the field to be referenced. The next two sections will make using these properties easier to understand.

8.8.5.1. Set DataSource property. All the data-aware controls are to be set to the Data1 control. You can use multiple selection to set all the controls at once to Data1, instead of setting each control separately. To do so, click on the upper left corner of the form, and drag until the selecting box includes all data-aware controls, but *not* the Data control itself. Press F4 to pop up the

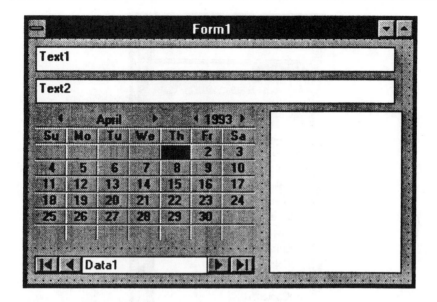

Figure 8.8.   Placement of data-aware controls.

properties window, and select the DataSource property. Then click on the combo-box down arrow, which gives you only one option: Data1. Click on Data1, to bring up the screen illustrated in Figure 8.9.

8.8.5.2. Set DataField Property.   Now it is time to set a field for each control in the properties window in Figure 8.9. Select the first Text box in the application's Form1 form—the top one. Set the DataField property to First Name with the ellipse button.

Now click on the second Text box to give it the focus, and activate the properties box (F4). Set the DataField to Last Name.

Use the same procedure for the other controls, selecting Photo for the Picture box, and Hire Date for the Calendar control.

8.8.6.   Execute Application

At this point the application can be run (see Figure 8.10) by clicking on the run button or pressing F5. If you edit a field, such as

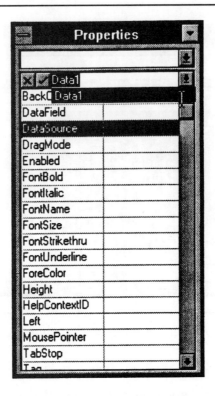

Figure 8.9. DataSource property setting.

the First Name field, and then later go back to it, note that the changes you made were already put into the database. There is no waiting nor pressing a Save Changes button to make the changes effective. The Hire Date can be changed by clicking on another date in the calendar. Use the Data1 arrow keys to go forward and backward in the database.

8.8.7. Validation

Validating data before it goes into a database is an important part of applications. The procedures illustrated in Figures 8.11 and 8.12 check whether the first name is a nonblank value. But first the program is stopped, using the Stop button on the Toolbar.

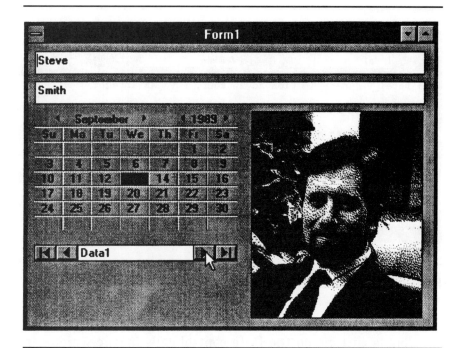

Figure 8.10.   Running sample application.

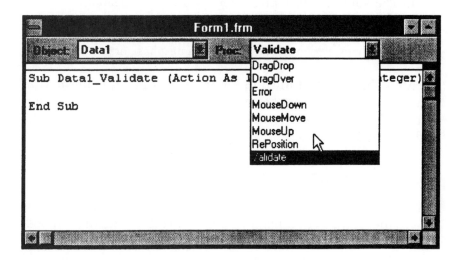

Figure 8.11.   Blank Validate code window.

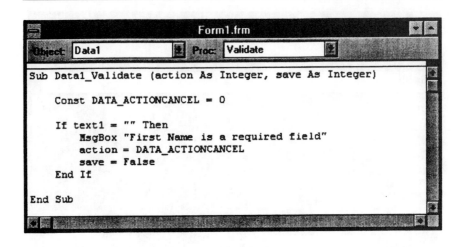

Figure 8.12.   Validate First Name code.

Double clicking on the Data control calls up the window in Figure 8.11. The Validate procedure template is now ready to be filled in.

Note: There are three new data events, or procedures:

1. The Validate,which fires before records are updated.
2. The Reposition, which fires every time the current position changes.
3. The Error, which fires every time a database error occurs.

After the code contained in Figure 8.12 is inserted in the window, the First name Text box value will be checked to see whether it is empty. If it is empty (blank), a message will flash and the update will be cancelled.

8.9.   CRYSTAL REPORTS

Crystal Reports 2.0 for Visual Basic uses the included MS Access 1.1 engine. It also contains a custom control for making embedded reports easier to insert in your applications. Crystal Reports can be called by selecting Report Writer from the Window menu, or double-clicking on its icon in the Program Manager.

8.9.1. Report Writer Design Environment

Crystal Reports allows you to design reports with WYSIWYG. After you have designed and tested your report, you can include it in any applications that you wish to distribute, with no royalty fees.

Crystal Reports 2.0 has features such as support for formulas, unlimited grouping, print-time customization of reports, standard Avery and custom mailing label formats, bitmaps, borders, lines, boxes, and more.

8.9.2. Report Writer Custom Control

The file for Crystal Reports 2.0 custom control is called CRYSTAL.VBX. It must be added to your project before you can access it using the icon shown below:

The report control allows you to set the number of copies, embed formulas, determine sort order and the destination of the report, and more.

8.9.3. Quick Start

To make a report quickly, follow these steps to set up and print a Crystal Reports report.

1. Start Crystal Reports by double clicking on the Crystal Reports icon located in Visual Basic's Program group.
2. Select New Report from the File menu.
3. When the Choose Database File dialog box appears, select the first database you want to activate from your report and Click OK when done.

    If you want to use data in a SQL table, click the SQL Server button, choose the server type in the SQL Server

Types dialog box when it appears, and Click OK. Select the database you want to activate in the SQL Server Login dialog box when it appears and Click OK, then choose the table of interest from the Choose SQL Table dialog box when it appears and Click OK when finished.

The Crystal Reports Report Editor appears with Page Header, Details, and Page Footer sections set up on your report template. The sections are initially all blank. You create your report by inserting and formatting items in each of these sections.

4. The Insert Database Field dialog box appears onscreen with the Report Editor. The Insert Database Field dialog box displays a list of all of the fields in the active database. To speed the entry of multiple fields, the box remains onscreen until you Click on the Done button. You can move the dialog box to a new location if you wish.

5. Select the first field you want to appear on the report. A rectangular placement cursor appears.

6. Position the cursor at the point in the Details section where you want your field to appear, and mouse click to enter it. Crystal Reports marks the field position with a rectangular box. The characters in the box indicate whether the field is text (XXX...), numbers (555,...), a dollar value ($555,...), a date (YYYY—M...), or a Boolean operator (T/F). The number of characters in the box indicates the number of characters allowed for the field in the database from which it came.

7. Repeat Steps 5 and 6 until you have placed all the fields you want to place.

8. To create a title, select Insert | Text Field, type in the information you want to appear, click Accept when finished, and position the field where you want it in the Page Header section. You can also insert database fields or special fields in the Page Header section from the Insert menu.

9. To see how your results will print, select Print To Window from the Print menu. Close the window when you are finished reviewing.

10. If you wish to change the placement or width of a field, format the field, insert a subtotal or grand total for a field, or delete a field, click the field box for that field. Black handles

appear on the right and left sides of the field box to indicate it has been selected.

To change the placement of the field, drag the field box to its new position using the mouse or the arrow keys. The arrow keys move the field box one grid position each time you press them. To change the width of the field, drag the right or left handle using your mouse. To format or subtotal the field, Click the right mouse button while the cursor is inside the field. A pop-up menu appears listing your various options.

To change the font, select Change Font and define your selection using the Font dialog box when it appears. To change the format (alignment within a field; number, currency, or date display; and so on), select Change Format and define your selection using the Field format dialog box when it appears. To insert a subtotal, select Insert Subtotal and define your selection using the Insert Subtotal dialog box when it appears. In this dialog box, you select the sort and group by field, the condition that triggers a new subtotal whenever the field's value changes, and the sort direction: ascending or descending.

Note: The program automatically sorts the data based on the field that triggers the subtotals before it subtotals. You don't have to enter a subtotal sort manually.

To insert a grand total (or a grand total average, a grand total count, and so forth), select Insert Grand Total. To delete the field, select Delete Field.

11. If you want to create a formula to make data calculations or comparisons, select Formula from the Insert menu. Enter a name for your formula in the Insert Formula dialog box, and enter the formula itself in the Formula Editor when it appears. Enter fields, operators, and functions by selecting them from their respective boxes. You can get complete information on each available Function and Operator via the Help button, and you can check your formula syntax via the Check button. Entering a Crystal Reports formula is similar to entering a formula in a spreadsheet cell. When finished

editing, click Accept and place the formula just as you do a database field.

12. To change the sort order, select Record Sort Order from the print menu. Select the field(s) you want Crystal Reports to use for sorting the report data.

13. To change the sort and group by field, select the Group Section from the Edit menu. Select the group section of interest from the list that appears in the Edit Group Section (sections) dialog box, and select the new trigger field from the Edit Group Section (edit) dialog box when it appears.

14. If you want to limit your report to specific records (for example, the records of California customers that have YTD sales greater than $10,000), click the first field on which you want your selection to be based (in this case, the State field) and choose Select Records from the Print menu or the right mouse button pop-up menu. Answer the questions that appear in the Select Records dialog box and click OK when finished. If your selection is based on more than one field, repeat the process with the remaining field(s) until you have completed entering your selection specifications.

15. When you are done, you can print your report by selecting Print To Printer from the Print menu.

9

Debugging and
Error Handling

9.1.   INTRODUCTION

Locating the source of errors in your application is called *debugging*. Handling errors that occur during your application's run-time so that the program can continue instead of crashing is called *error handling*.

Debugging as discussed here does not fix your errors but instead helps you find where they are. Visual Basic has numerous tools to aid in debugging applications. You can find out how, what, and where your variables and procedures are executing. You can stop the application at key areas and look at variable values, change values, and continue execution, or run an application one line at a time to check variables and program flow. Figure 9.1 shows the Debug options on the Menu bar and summarizes what they do.

Error handling is code you put in your application in anticipation of expected and unexpected problems. For instance, you know that at some time a disk will be filled and not accept any more data. By putting an error handling routine in your code to handle this possible situation you can avert an application crash or shutdown. Error handling is the process of anticipating un-

- **Debugging tools**

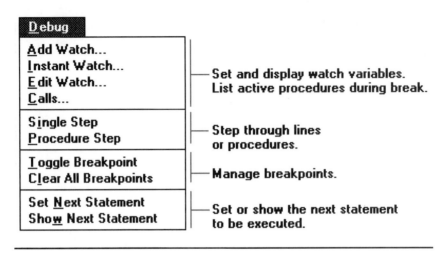

Figure 9.1. Debugging tools.

likely situations that could stop application processing and possibly damage data files.

9.2. TYPES OF DEBUGGING ERRORS

Visual Basic can present three types of errors: compile, runtime, and logic. Each are handled, or debugged, differently.

9.2.1. Compile Errors

Compile errors are usually caused by improper code statement syntax. Other causes include improper punctuation and keyword errors (such as SSub instead of Sub). When you try to compile your application, error messages are given. You can avoid waiting until compile time to receive these messages by having the syntax checked as you enter code lines. To activate this option, make sure the Syntax Checking option is set to "yes" in the Code window.

9.2.2. Runtime Errors

Runtime errors occur as you execute your application. The best example of this is the statement A = B/C in cases where the variable C becomes zero as the application runs. When compiled, this statement will not produce an error message because it is a legal statement. You will only receive an error message when the application is running and the value of C reaches zero. Error handling, or dealing with and trapping these types of errors, will be covered in Section 9.5.3.

9.2.3. Logic Errors

Logic errors occur mainly when you have programmed a section of code in such a way that its results are not what you intended. For instance, you may have used a variable that you thought was global in a calculation, when in fact you declared that variable as local in another procedure. Thus while you think the statements are correct and should work, that one variable that you are using as global will make your final results inaccurate.

9.3. TOOLBAR DEBUGGING TOOLS

Five buttons on the Toolbar provide functions that are helpful while debugging applications. Table 9.1 shows these icons, gives their names, and describes their functions.

9.4. DESIGN, RUN, AND BREAK TIME MODES

Design time is the period when you are entering code statements and creating items such as forms and procedures. Though you cannot execute code while in the design mode, you can set breakpoints and create watch expressions.

Runtime mode is the period when you execute the code as an enduser would. You can view code but you cannot change it in this mode. If you pick End from the Run menu or click on the End button, you will be switched back to design mode.

Break mode occurs when you pick Break from the Run menu, click on the Break button, or press CTRL+BREAK. If your pro-

Table 9.1.   Toolbar Debugging Tools.

Toolbar Icon	Name	Function
	Breakpoint	Defines the line in the Code window where execution breaks (suspends application execution)
	Instant Watch	Displays the value of an expression while in break mode
	Calls	While in break mode, shows all procedures that have been called but not yet fully completed
	Single Step	Executes the next line of code
	Procedure Step	Executes the next line of code but skips stepping in procedure calls

gram has code that executes when the application starts, press F8 or Single Step from the Debug menu to put the application in break mode on the first executable code statement. When you invoke break mode, execution is stopped so you can view and change code statements as needed. Many of Visual Basic's debugging tools work only in this mode.

9.4.1.   Changing Modes by the Toolbar

Three buttons on the Toolbar help you quickly change from one mode into another.

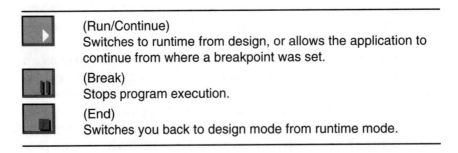

(Run/Continue)
Switches to runtime from design, or allows the application to continue from where a breakpoint was set.

(Break)
Stops program execution.

(End)
Switches you back to design mode from runtime mode.

9.5. BREAK MODE USE

Break mode stops your application and allows you to examine its status. You can find out what values your variables contain, what properties are set, and make changes to them. After examination and possible changes, you have the options of starting your application from the beginning or continuing on from the point where you stopped it.

While in break mode you can determine what procedures have been called, watch and change values of variables, run statements immediately, and control which statement the application should operate on next.

9.5.1. Breaking on Code Statements

There may be times when you suspect a certain code statement is the cause of your incorrect results. In such cases you may want to set up a breakpoint or a Stop code statement. A breakpoint defines a code statement or set of conditions at which the application stops running and enters the break mode. The program does not execute the statement that contains the breakpoint.

9.5.1.1. Break automatically. Your application will enter break mode automatically when an untrapped runtime error occurs, a breakpoint line is encountered, a Stop statement is reached, or a break expression changes or becomes true.

9.5.1.2. Break manually. Manual conditions can also cause your application to enter break mode. These include pressing the CTRL+BREAK keys, picking Break from the Run menu, or clicking on the Break button.

9.5.2 Break Variables

When your application enters break mode automatically, the Code window appears and shows the currently active module or form, the procedure that was executing, and the next statement to be executed.

When your application enters break mode manually the Debug window appears (see Section 9.7).

9.5.3. Runtime Errors and Debugging

Runtime errors are usually relatively easy to fix, since they are found by the system and give you a hint and highlighted area where the problem is located. The code

```
Sub Form_Load ()
Dim a As Integer
a == 3.14
End Sub
```

has two obvious errors. One is that == should be =, and the other is that 3.14 is not an Integer type. When you run this subroutine the first error message you will receive will concern the ==, which will have to be fixed before you can go on. As shown in Figure 9.2, you will be given ample information as to what and where the main problem is. All you must do is click on the highlighted area

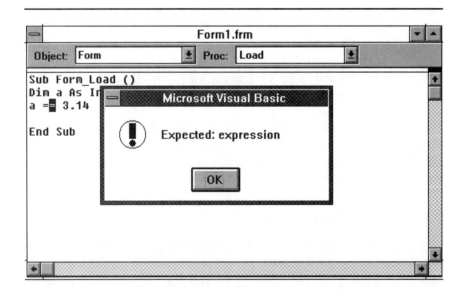

Figure 9.2.   Runtime error.

and delete one of the = signs to debug this error. Then click on the Run button on the Toolbar to continue.

9.5.4. Breaking at a Specific Point

A breakpoint tells your application to stop just before a certain line. When the breakpoint is encountered during runtime, the application switches to break mode. These breakpoints are set or removed at design time. To set or remove a breakpoint in the Code window, first click on a code line where you want the breakpoint to occur. To mark this point you can either press F9 (the quickest way), click on the Break button on the Toolbar, or pick Toggle Breakpoint from the Debug menu. Breakpoint lines are easily recognized since they are displayed in boldface and in color.

9.5.5. Examination at Breakpoint

Once break mode is in operation you can check the state of your application, moving easily between forms, the Code window, and the Debug window.

A breakpoint stops your execution just *before* executing the line that contains the breakpoint. This means that if you are interested in that breakpoint code line you must execute one more code line after the application stops. You may do this by using Single Step (see Section 9.6.1).

Since you are new to Visual Basic and possibly to programming in general, one issue about breakpoint values and debugging needs to be discussed here. Just because a statement is not acting as you think it should does not always mean that the problem is in the statement being examined. The problem could be the fault of a variable within the statement that was set previously in the procedure or even in another procedure. For example, what you think is a global value set to 3.14 may in fact have been set as an integer value of 3 when it was last set to a value. Thus your calculations using 3.14 will never give you the results expected in the code line you are examining. Not until the value of 3 is set to 3.14 will your calculations be as expected. The lesson here is that things are not always as they appear. Carefully examining each variable and not taking things for granted will help you resolve many bugs and logic errors.

9.5.6.   Stop Statement

You can put a Stop statement in your code to halt execution and enter break mode as follows:

```
Sub Abc ()
   Dim i As Integer
   i = 300
   Stop            'stop execution here and enter break mode
End Sub
```

Although you can leave breakpoints in an application and still make an executable file, you must remove Stop statements from your program to make an enduser executable application.

You may think using an End statement is like using a Stop statement, since both halt execution. This is false because a Stop statement only halts an application temporarily, whereas an End statement not only stops application but also brings you back to design mode, *not* break mode.

9.6.   EXECUTING ONLY SELECTED CODE AREAS

A breakpoint helps most when you are fairly sure that only select statements are causing you problems. Many times, though you cannot guess which lines are at fault, you will have a general idea which area is the trouble spot. In this case using a breakpoint and then single stepping and procedure stepping will pinpoint the exact problem.

9.6.1.   Single Stepping

Single stepping is executing an application one code statement at a time. The results can be seen in the application's forms or Debug window.

To use single stepping, press F8 (the quickest way), pick Single Step from the Debug menu, or click on the Single Step button.

9.6.2. Procedure Stepping

Procedure stepping, like single stepping, executes statements in a procedure one at a time. The main difference is that procedure stepping, when faced with a call to another procedure, will execute that procedure without using single stepping. It will execute the procedure in regular runtime mode and then return to the procedure that called it and resume single stepping. Conversely, single stepping follows calls to other procedures in single stepping mode. Because stepping only occurs in the procedure that called for procedure stepping, this approach can save time if you are interested in the values of only one procedure and not the associated ones that it calls or uses. If there are hundreds of statements to execute in these other procedures, you can spend many minutes single stepping through procedures that you do not care about before eventually returning to the original procedure that you do want to follow. Thus though using procedure stepping allows you to bypass what you do not want to follow, thereby saving considerable time, it should again be stressed that this approach gives you information *only* for the procedure set up for procedure stepping.

To use procedure stepping press SHIFT+F8, click on the Procedure Step button on the Toolbar, or pick Procedure Step from the Debug menu.

You can also SWITCH between single and procedure stepping. This gives you greater control over which areas to analyze and which areas to skip.

9.6.3. Set Next Line to Execute

While in the break mode, you can choose to skip code statements and instead continue execution at a statement you select. A good time to use this option is when you change a variable's value and wish to go back in the code to see the change's effect by comparing its results to the earlier results. Selecting the next line to execute allows you to do this without restarting the application. The only limitation to this option is that the statement you specify must be in the same procedure in which the break mode was activated.

To set the line, click on the line you want executed next, pick Set Next Statement from the Debug menu, and restart your application.

9.7. DEBUG WINDOW

While in break mode only, the Debug window allows you to check on variable values and expressions, and change them if need be, while stepping through your code statements. Figure 9.3 shows a typical Debug window.

The Debug window contains two panes: the Watch pane and the Immediate pane. The Watch pane contains the current *watch expressions*—the expressions you want to observe as your application executes. The Immediate pane displays data as a result of your debugging or shows the results of commands you have typed into the pane.

The Title bar shows the present module or form and the associated procedure currently being debugged. You can only work with variables that are in the scope of the Title bar's description. You cannot modify any variables not in the scope of the current procedure, form, or module, except for globals.

The Debug window allows you to examine code and watch expressions. It can be accessed only in break mode.

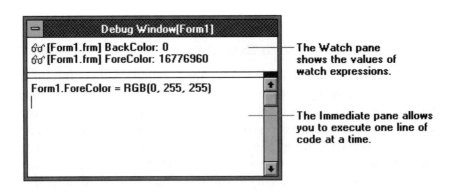

Figure 9.3. Debug window.

9.8.   WATCH EXPRESSIONS

Once again, at times you may find that a bug is not the fault of a single code statement. Thus you may want to monitor only one variable or expression in a procedure. Single stepping through all variables and statements just to monitor one variable could be a tremendous waste of time in such a case. Instead, in break mode you can define the relevant expressions, which are then shown in the Watch pane of the Debug window.

A handy feature of watch expressions is their ability to put the program into break mode automatically when an expression value changes or becomes equal to a specified value. A good example is a loop that executes 2000 times. If you want to check values after, say, 1995 times, you need not single step 1995 times to reach the point desired if you set up a watch expression. Watch expressions will be seen during both design and .EXE versions. If you want design time only testing, consider Immediate pane testing (Section 9.9).

9.8.1.   Adding a Watch

You may add a watch expression in either design or break mode. To add a watch expression:

- From the Debug menu pick Add Watch.
- Enter an expression into the Expression text box.
- Select the appropriate option button in the Context group to set the type of scope.
- Select the appropriate option button in the Watch Type group.
- Click on OK.

9.8.2.   Editing or Deleting a Watch

To edit a watch expression, follow these steps:

- From the Debug menu, pick Edit Watch.
- Click on the expression line you wish to edit.
- Click on the Edit command button.

- Make desired changes to the expression, scope, or type.
- Click on OK.

To delete a watch expression, follow these steps:

- From the Debug menu, pick Edit Watch.
- Click on the expression line you wish to delete.
- Click on the Delete command button.
- Click on OK.

9.8.3.   Instant Watch

During break mode you may find an expression of interest to you that you forgot to put in the Add Watch dialog box. You can use the Instant watch dialog box to check on this expression. Instant watch displays the value of an expression selected from either the Debug window or the Code window. Clicking the Add Watch button in the Instant watch dialog box allows you to continue watching this expression.

To display an Instant watch:

- Pick an expression from the Code window or the Immediate pane of the Debug window.
- Press SHIFT+F9, or select Instant Watch from the Debug menu or the Instant watch button on the Toolbar.
- If you want the expression to be added as a watch expression, click on the Add Watch button.

9.9.   IMMEDIATE PANE TESTING

The Immediate pane (see Figure 9.3.) of the Debug window allows you to test expressions and procedures, and assign new values to variables. The results of expressions are printed in the Immediate pane, which offers certain advantages over using watch expressions. One such advantage is that using the Immediate pane to show immediate results does not interfere with what the future enduser will see during execution. Debug.Print statements (see Section 9.9.1) have *no effect* in the executable (.EXE) version of the application—only during design stage. This option gives you a complete picture of how your application looks and works, but still gives you testing capabilities.

9.9.1.   Immediate Pane Printing Methods

There are two ways to print in the Immediate pane. One is to place print statements in the actual code, and the other is to place print statements directly in the Immediate pane.

To place print statements in actual application code, use the format

```
Debug.Print [items][;]
```

as in the statement:

```
Debug.Print "Name is: "; Emp_Name
```

which will print out an employee's name every time the line is encountered in your code. Note that the name will be printed out only in the Immediate pane.

9.9.2.   Print Statements in the Immediate Pane

While in break mode, click the Debug window to give it the focus or pick Debug from the Window menu. Now you can use the Print statement without using Debug.Print as shown in the preceding section. Entering a code statement or expressions in the Immediate pane and pressing ENTER will cause the expression to evaluate and give the answer on the next line.

> *Note:* A ? character can be used in place of the Print keyword. Thus the statement
>
> ```
> Print XYZ
> ```
>
> can be replaced with the shorthand version
>
> ```
> ? XYZ.
> ```

You can also print property values of objects such as forms and controls that are in scope. For instance, the statement Print

Form1.ForeColor will print the numeric value of the foreground color. One thing to keep in mind is that referencing an unloaded form will load that form, which may not be what you want the system to do at that point.

9.9.3.   Assignments

Not only can you retrieve the values set in objects such as variables and forms, you can also set them. The following code sets a variable and sets the background color to 255 in the Immediate pane.

```
Pi = 3.14158
Form1.BackColor = 255
```

After setting these values, you can continue on with execution to see the results.

9.9.4.   Tips on Using the Immediate Pane

You can reexecute a previously executed statement by giving the focus back (moving the insertion point) to that statement and pressing ENTER. Pressing the PAGE UP or PAGE DOWN key moves the area in the pane up or down by a page. You can thus use either the arrow keys or the mouse to navigate in the Immediate pane. Do not press ENTER unless you are on the line you want executed.

Note that the Print statement can overwrite old statements that you may want to keep displayed in the window pane. This can happen if you have a series of print statements and results in the pane and decide to reexecute a print statement perhaps halfway up the pane. On reexecuting that statement, you will find that a line is deleted right after your result line. You can stop this from happening by adding a semicolon to the end of your print statements. Instead of

```
Print XYZ
```

use

```
Print XYZ;
```

to keep all the information in the pane while still getting your print values.

9.10. TIPS ON AVOIDING BUGS AND DEBUGGING

There are numerous steps you can take to minimize the number of bugs you have to contend with. These include

- During the design phase, when determining what the application will do and how it will act when turned over to the enduser, make diagrams on paper of forms, controls, and procedure functions.
- Use the explicit declaration mode for all variables.
- Use a naming scheme that is consistent for all variables in the application. For instance, decide that all constants must be capitalized.
- Use comments to the point of overkill. What is clear to you now may not be clear in six months. Without clear comments it may be nearly impossible for a new person to understand certain logic areas.

To aid you in debugging, here are some guidelines and helpful tips:

- Single step through the code and use watch expressions to check variables that you assume are acting as wanted, as well as those you suspect are not acting as expected.
- When an application halts without warning, note how far the application ran. Then put watch expressions in various places in the sections preceding the procedures that did not run.
- If a variable does not contain the expected result, define a break expression wherever that variable is used and likely to change in value.
- If you suspect that a variable or expressions used in a Loop structure is wrong, check its value before the loop starts and after the loop is finished.

9.11. REASONS FOR USING ERROR HANDLING

Error handling is the process of trapping problems that could cause your application to stop executing before the expected normal time. The process of trapping errors involves inserting code into your application that makes the application go to special error-handling routines when an error occurs. A very common example of error handling is what happens when the enduser inputs an invalid file or directory name. In another common case, the user is asked to insert or work with an external disk when the application requests it, only to find that the disk cannot be read or written to. You can write error-handling code to handle these situations so that the application can continue despite the error.

9.12. STEPS IN ERROR HANDLING

The general steps needed to code an error-handling routine in a procedure follow. The next section will show an example of such a routine.

1. Enable Visual Basic to start error trapping monitoring by using the statement

    ```
    On Error GoTo Err-routine
    ```

    Err-routine is where the application will jump if an error occurs. For example,

    ```
    Function File-Ok (filename)
    On Error GoTo FixError  'if any error occurs jump to
                            'FixError
      File_Ok = (Dir(Filename) <> "") 'is filename OK?
      .
      .
    FixError:
        'Here is where the code for checking and fixing
        'an error is placed
      If(Err = ERR_DISKNOTREADY) Then
      .
      .
    End Function
    ```

Note: Once you start error trapping in your procedure, it is only turned off when the procedure is finished. If you want to turn error trapping off before that time, there is one statement you can use. That statement is

```
On Error GoTo 0
```

and it can be used anywhere in the procedure or in the error-handling routine itself.

2. Code the Err_routine block. By using If/Then/Else statements check the Err value to determine what happened. Err's value is a number generated by Visual Basic, with each number representing a specific error problem. For instance, if Err is 71, it means the disk drive is not ready for use. This, in turn, could mean that the door to the drive is open or that the requested disk has not been inserted in the drive. By writing the routine to address all the errors you can imagine could possibly happen, you can decrease the chances of application failure. Each error you think of should have code that fixes the problem or uses a legal default, then retries the statement that caused the error or bypasses the offending statement and continues on in the procedure.

9.13. ERROR HANDLING EXAMPLE

This example handles disk problems that may result when an invalid drive is specified or a disk drive door is open.

```
Function Check_File (filename)
Dim Msg As String
''''''''''''''''''''''''''
On Error GoTo WhichError        'on any error go to
WhichError
''''''''''''''''''''''''
    '
    Check_File = (Dir(filename) <> "")
    Exit Function               'all Ok, exit the function
    '
    '
''''''''''''''''''''''''''''''''''''''''''''''''''''
WhichError:                     'start error routines '
''''''''''''''''''''''''''''''''''''''''''''''''''''''
```

```
'
'    Give names to Visual Basic generated error numbers
     Const ERR_DISKNOTREADY = 71
     Const ERR_DEVICEUNAVAILABLE = 68
'
'    Make constants for Message box types
     Const MB_EXCLAIM   = 48
     Const MB_STOP      = 16
     Const MB_OK_CANCEL = 1
     Const BUTTON_OK    = 1
'
'
  If (Err = ERR_DISKNOTREADY) Then
    Msg = "Insert a disk in drive and close door."
    '
    'show a Message box with OK and Cancel buttons and
    'an exclamation mark
    '
    If MsgBox(Msg, MB_EXCLAIM+MB_OK_CANCEL) = BUTTON_OK Then
      Resume (0)  're-try statement that caused error
    Else
      Resume Next 'execute the statement that is one line
                  'AFTER the line that caused the error
    End If
    '
  ElseIf Err = ERR_DEVICEUNAVAILABLE Then
    Msg = "Drive or path does not exist."
    MsgBox Msg, MB_EXCLAIM
    Resume Next
    '
  Else
    Msg = "Unexpected error #" & Str(Err) & ": " & Error
    'show a Message box with OK button and Stop sign
    MsgBox Msg, MB_STOP
    Stop                    'halt program execution
    '
  End If
  Resume (0)
End Function
```

Table 9.2. Exit error handling.

Statement	Function
Resume (0)	Resumes program execution with the statement that caused the error, or the most recently executed call out of the procedure containing the error-handling routine.
Resume Next	Resumes program execution at the code statement immediately following the one that caused the error; must be in the same procedure as the error handler.
Resume line	Resumes program execution at the label specified by *line*. *Line* must be a nonzero line number or line label.
Error Err	Forces a runtime error. When executed within the error-handler routine, the application looks among the calls list for another error-handling routine. The calls list is the list of procedures called as of the time of the error. If an error-handling routine is found going back to other procedures, it is used. You probably will not have to use this very often, as the other three options are adequate for most application exit methods.

In the preceding function, the Err function returns the error number and a string message. As can be seen error handling can either ask the user to change a condition or it can change the condition itself.

9.14. WAYS TO EXIT ERROR-HANDLING CODE

To exit the Err-routine code block, the example in Section 9.13 used the Resume (0) and Resume Next statements. Other statements that can be used to exit the Err-routine block are listed in Table 9.2.

There is more to learning about error handling, but this gives you a good background in its basics and enough information to allow you to place some key error-handling routines into your own applications.

10

Basics of
Communicating with
Other Applications

10.1. INTRODUCTION

This and the remaining chapters of this book discuss subjects that beginners may not wish to use in applications until they have achieved a fair level of proficiency and confidence. These chapters are thus intended only as primers, to give you a basic understanding of their topics and to make you think of how a certain topic may be of value in your future or present applications. The purpose of this book is to get you up and programming—and understanding essential programming concepts—fast. That cannot be done if you read *everything* in the reference books but understand nearly *nothing* due to the resulting technical overload.

This chapter looks at how Visual Basic can communicate with other applications and their data, objects, and libraries. Three areas are covered in this chapter: DDE (Dynamic Data Exchange), OLE (Object Linking and Embedding), and DLL (Dynamic-Link Libraries).

10.2. DDE

Visual Basic allows you to exchange data and information manually between applications by copying and pasting using its DDE (Dynamic Data Exchange) facility. Using DDE, you can automate this process through code statements in your application. DDE is a method supported by MS Windows that enables two programs to communicate with each other. You can use DDE to import or export data from another application, do data updates, and send commands to control other programs.

One important point about DDE in visual Basic needs to be discussed before going on. Unfortunately, this involves one area where beginners may have trouble. The basics of using and understanding DDE in the Visual Basic environment is not one of the easiest areas for beginners to grasp. If you find yourself confused at certain points, go back to the beginning of the DDE section and make sure you understand the terminology. Confusing the terms *source* and *destination* may be another problem area. Reread each section as you progress and if you still find this topic confusing, at least learn the basic concepts of DDE and what it can do for applications. Do not be discouraged if everything covered is not immediately clear. Take away from the sections what you can and invest more time in the DDE process when and if you need it.

If you have Visual Basic, you can run the sample DDE example, DDE Experimenter, by running its make file, DDE.MAK, in the \vb\samples\dde subdirectory. The opening screen is shown in Figure 10.1 with the Application choice of ProgMan, the Windows Program Manager.

DDE Experimenter allows you to exchange text or graphics in another application. Figure 10.2 shows all the various applications that can be chosen to use the data contained in the Destination Data box (in this case, text characters in Text1).

Note as you read through this section that many of the DDE terms discussed, such as application, topic, and so on, are on the sample application form. You will understand the terms betters if you periodically look at Figures 10.1 and 10.2 as you read the subjects discussed. If you have Visual Basic, run the sample program using the application ProgMan after reading about DDE to get a better understanding of how DDEs work.

10.2.1. Source and Destination

When two applications exchange information using DDE, this process is called a *conversation*. The program that initiated the conversation is called the *destination*, and the program that re-

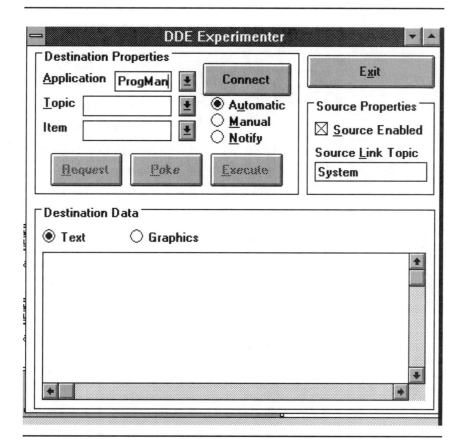

Figure 10.1. DDE Experimenter application.

sponds to the destination is called the *source*. A program (application) can be used in multiple conversations, acting as a source for some and a destination for others. In the Visual Basic language any label, text box, or picture box can be the destination, while any form can be the source.

Another way to think about a conversation is that the destination calls the source, and the source responds to the destination's call.

10.2.2. Application, Topic, and Item

Two things must be specified when a destination begins a DDE conversation. One is the name of the *source application* (pro-

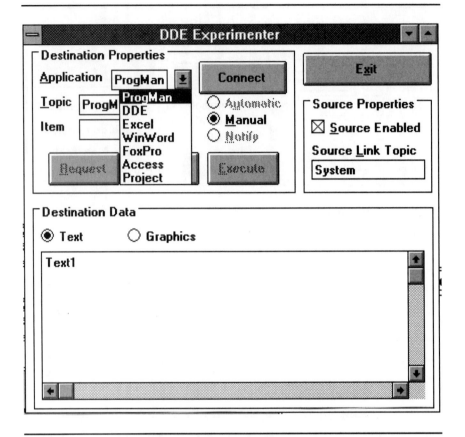

Figure 10.2. Application property list.

gram) that the destination wants a conversation with. The second is the subject of the conversation, the *topic*.

Once a conversation is started, the topic and application cannot be changed. The combination of the application and topic creates a unique identifier for that conversation, which remains until the conversation is done.

While in a conversation, destination and source can exchange data with what are called items. *Items* are references to information (data) that have meaning to both applications. For example, files with the extensions .txt would be understandable to both applications if both applications allowed text data files as input and/or output. Items can be changed by either the source or destination without disturbing a conversation. The application, topic, and item uniquely identify the information being passed between the applications involved.

10.2.2.1. Application. Any application that is a DDE source has an *application name*. It is usually an executable file with no extension. The Applications in the DDE Experimenter are shown in the drop down list in Figure 10.2. The DDE application name and its associated, regular name appear in Table 10.1.

When a form is the source, the application is the name you picked for the executable. If running within Visual Basic, the application is the name of the project.

10.2.2.2. Topic. A *topic* defines the subject of a conversation. Many applications can use a document name as a topic. For example, Word for Windows can be used with only the document name, as long as the extension—and any needed path—is .DOC or .DOT. When a form is the source in a conversation, you may specify the topic by setting the LinkTopic property for that form.

A topic supported by many applications is called *System*. Use this topic to get information about an application, such as what data formats the application supports. You can provide a system topic in your own application by including a form with the

Table 10.1. DDE application name and actual application name.

DDE Application Name	*Application Name*
ProgMan	MS Windows Program Manager
Excel	MS Excel
WinWord	MS Word For Windows
Project	MS Project
MSAccess	MS Access
FoxPro	MS FoxPro for Windows

LinkTopic property set to System, and controls with names that correspond to different supported system items.

10.2.2.3. Item.   The data actually passed during a conversation is called the *item*. Item examples are a certain row and column reference (R1C1), or a file extension such as .DOC for Word for Windows.

10.2.3. Links

A conversation is also called a *link* because the two applications are linked together by the data being exchanged. The three types of links differ in how the source updates the destination when data in the source changes. They are:

- Automatic link: Source supplies information to destination every time data changes
- Manual link: Source supplies information only when destination requests it
- Notify link: Source notifies destination when data changes but supplies the data only on request

> ***Important:*** Please reread the last preceding sentences. In this most common way a link is used, the destination application requests information from the source and the source gives this information to the destination in, for example, a text box. This procedure is called using a *destination link*. If you want *your* application to send information *to* another application a *source link* must be established. More on that later, but understanding who calls what to receive and send data is critical.

10.2.4. Design Time and Links

During design time, the data links you can create are saved as values in the different Link properties of the forms and controls in your program. These are automatically set up when the application is run again. This approach can be very time-saving, since it requires no programming code. Its drawback is that you cannot control the order of the links nor do any error checking. The basics of using code statements for links and DDE will be covered in Section 10.2.5 but for now we will cover only design time data linkage.

10.2.4.1. Retrieving data by links.   Having your Visual Basic application use data supplied by other applications requires you to make a destination link wherein your application (destination) requests data or other information from the source application. As an example your application may need a data field value from a spreadsheet. Your application needs to request the spreadsheet to send the required cell reference value back to your Visual Basic application so that you can use that value. Creating a link at design time will make it a permanent part of your application. However, for this approach to work you must have your application open in the Visual Basic environment, and the other application—in this case the spreadsheet—must also be running.

To create this link between your application and another:

- Select the data item you want in the other application (e.g.: click on the desired spreadsheet cell).
- From the Edit menu in that application, pick Copy.
- In *your* application, select the control (e.g.: text box) that you want to receive the data item.
- From Visual Basic's Edit Menu pick 'Paste Link.'

If all has been done correctly, the value in the control (the text box) will display the information that the other application contains (e.g.: the spreadsheet cell value). This process is termed an *automatic link*, since any time the other application changes this value (e.g.: the cell value) the Visual Basic application control (e.g.: the text box) also changes immediately.

The preceding link is permanent. Every time your application is opened in either design or runtime, the link will try to reestablish itself to exchange data.

10.2.4.2. Sending data by links.   A *source link* allows your Visual Basic application to send information to another applica-

tion. A source link is where the other (destination) application requests data from your (source) application. Like the destination links described in the preceding section, source links can be made a permanent part of your application.

Detailed coverage of this approach is not provided here, as it was not in the preceding section because it is best to use code statements in your application to set up source links. The reason for this is that source links you make at design time may not work at runtime. When you are designing an application, why bother setting up source links that may not work during runtime? Coding the link into your application so that you know it will execute as desired is a better choice. No problems have been mentioned in this area when using destination links; problems occur only when using source links.

10.2.5. Methods and DDE Operation

Functions and methods (code routines) exist that make coding DDE actions easier to understand and apply in your Visual Basic application code. You can use DDE to manipulate other applications in a remote control fashion. With an established destination link, you can send and request commands and data. In this section we discuss the functions and methods used in DDE: Shell function, LinkPoke method, LinkRequest method, LinkSend method, and LinkExecute method.

10.2.5.1. Starting applications. If you attempt a link with an application that is not running, you will get an error message (error #282). The following code shows how to check for this error, activate the StartIt routine if an error occurs, and prevent your application from crashing.

```
Sub BeginApp (Link As Control, AppName As String, Topic As
String)
    Dim a
    Const App_Not_Running = 282
    On Error GoTo StartIt
    Link.LinkMode = NONE
```

```
   Link.LinkTopic = AppName & "|" & Topic
   Link.LinkMode = MANUAL
   Exit Sub              'if ok exit Sub
StartIt:
   If Err = App_Not_Running Then
     a = Shell(AppName) 'if needed start the application
     Resume               'retry the link
   Else
     MsgBox "Undetermined Error Occurred."
     Stop
   End If
End Sub
```

10.2.5.2. *Poking data.*   As mentioned before, the usual flow of data is from the source to the destination. Poking can reverse this so that the destination can send data to the source by using the method LinkPoke. LinkPoke sends the value of the control to the source, updating the data referenced in the LinkItem property. The following example code changes a cell (R1C1, row 1:column 1) in an Excel spreadsheet to the value newVal.

```
Sub ChangeCell (Link As TextBox, filename As String,
               newVal As String)
 '
 Const NONE = 0, MANUAL = 2
 Link.LinkMode = NONE
 Link.LinkTopic = "Excel|" & filename
 Link.LinkItem = "R1C1"
 Link.LinkMode = MANUAL
 Link.Text = newVal       'new value for R1C1
 Link.LinkPoke
 Link.LinkMode = NONE
 '
End Sub
```

10.2.5.3. *Sending commands.*   You can send commands to an application that supports DDE. When a destination link is established you can use the LinkExecute method on the control that is

maintaining the link. As an example, you can send macro commands to Excel, as shown in the following sample code statement, which uses the LinkExecute method on a control named Link to tell Excel to close the currently active spreadsheet:

```
Link.LinkExecute "[File.Close()]"
```

The following example establishes a DDE link with Microsoft Excel, places some values into cells in the first row of a new worksheet, and charts the values. LinkExecute sends Microsoft Excel the command to activate a worksheet, select some values, and chart them. To try this example, Microsoft Excel must be installed and in your path. Now press F5 and click the form, called Form—created from TOOLS | FORM on the Menu Bar.

```
Sub Form_Click ()
  Const NONE = 0, LINK_MANUAL = 2  'Declare constants.
  Dim Cmd, I, Q, Row, Z  'Declare variables.
  Q = Chr(34)  'Define quote marks.

  'Create a string containing Excel macro commands
  Cmd = [ACTIVATE(" & Q &"SHEET1" & Q & ")]"
  Cmd = Cmd & "[SELECT(" & Q & "R1C1:R5C2" & Q & ")]"
  Cmd = Cmd & "[NEW(2,1)][ARRANGE.ALL()]"

  If Text1.LinkMode = NONE Then
    Z = Shell("Excel", 4) 'Start Excel.
    Text1.LinkTopic = "Excel|Sheet1"  'Set link topic.
    Text1.LinkItem = "R1C1"  'Set link item.
    Text1.LinkMode = LINK_MANUAL  'Set link mode.
  End If

For I = 1 To 5
  Row = I  'Define row number.
  Text1.LinkItem = "R" & Row & "C1"  'Set link item.
  Text1.Text = Chr(64 + I) 'Put value in Text.
  Text1.LinkPoke  'Poke value to cell.
  Text1.LinkItem = "R" & Row & "C2"  'Set link item.
```

```
    Text1.Text = Row 'Put value in Text.
    Text1.LinkPoke  'Poke value to cell.
  Next I

    Text1.LinkExecute Cmd  'Execute Excel commands.
  End Sub
```

10.2.5.4. Error handling. Two kinds of errors can occur when using DDE. The first is the normal type that can occur in any executing code. These errors can be handled with the usual error-handling routines discussed in Chapter 9. The second kind of error occurs when no code is being executed. It may seem strange that an error can occur when nothing is being executed. But due to the way Windows operates, such errors can occur. When using automatic links, for example, errors can occur if the file is so large memory runs out, or if data has the wrong format. Link errors such as these and others generate a LinkError event. You can write procedures to handle this type of error using DDE error numbers, which are different from runtime error numbers. Checking for these numbers in the procedure is done in the same way as with any other error-handling procedure. All the link error numbers and their meanings are listed in the Visual Basic *Reference Manuals*. You may also access Help in the Visual Basic menu and look under DoEvents. The main point here is that you must find and use the LinkError event numbers in procedures to check for errors when using DDE links.

DDE and system sharing: Visual Basic allows other applications to run when a DDE operation occurs. Remember, Windows can have more than one application running at a time, causing system resource sharing. This sharing may cause some DDE links not to complete their part of a conversation, causing a system timeout error. To avert this, you can use the DoEvents statement. DoEvent causes Visual Basic to yield, for a short time, enabling other applications to execute and finish their work without interfering with your application.

For example, the following code segment uses the variable retryCount to keep track of how many times the application will yield briefly to let another application finish. The variable may need to be increased above the shown value of 10 if other applications are system-intensive.

```
Dim i, retryCount
Const ERR_TIMEOUT = 286   'fixed system # (not user chosen)
'
On Error GoTo ErrHandler
  'ExecuteStrings() is an array representing different
  'areas to execute
  For i = 0 To UBound(ExecuteStrings)
     Link.LinkExecute ExecuteStrings(i)
  Next i
Exit Sub
'
ErrHandler:
  If Err = ERR_TIMEOUT And RetryCount < 10 Then
    DoEvents             'try to finish other apps
    retryCount = retryCount + 1   'track how many DoEvents
    Resume               'try again the failed execute
  Else
    Error Err
  End If
```

10.2.6. Sending Keystrokes to Applications

Not all applications support DDE, but since they all run under the same environment (Windows 3.x or 4.x), basic communication is always possible. For those applications that do not support DDE, the easiest way to interact is by sending keystrokes to them. The only limitation to this approach is that you cannot send keystrokes to MS-DOS applications running in Windows.

Sending keystrokes to another application simulates typing the keystrokes directly into the other application. Thus any operation that the other application can accept directly can be simulated using keystrokes. For example,

```
SendKeys "XYZ", True
```

immediately sends XYZ to the active application. If this is not the application wanted, you must make the desired application active (see Section 10.2.7.)

10.2.7. Activating Applications

Even though an application may be running, it may not be the *active* application—the one that has the focus. To send keystrokes to the desired application, it must be running and activated. You can use the Shell function to run an application and the AppActivate statement to activate it as in:

```
x = Shell("Terminal")
AppActivate "Terminal"
```

The Shell function is not needed if the terminal program is already running.

10.3. DLL

DLLs (Dynamic Link Libraries) are libraries of procedures that programs can link with and use at runtime, *not* at compile time. Since a DLL is a separate file, if your program calls a DLL, it must be included when you give your executable application file to anyone else. If you do not include the DLL, your program will request a certain procedure in a DLL file and will fail since it will not be able to access the DLL file.

DLLs can contain many different procedures. However, you need not access all the routines in a DLL, just the ones you wish to use. Adding to or changing the procedures in a DLL is a different matter. Many programmers are used to going into the source code of their application, finding the particular routine that needs changing, changing and testing it, and finally recompiling their application. Programmers who want to change a procedure called from a DLL must go into the DLL to change it, but test it from the application that calls the procedure.

DLLs save space, since the code required to execute a procedure is not embedded in your application, but rather in the DLL file, and is used only when called. Also, many applications can use a procedure in a DLL, but only your application can use the procedures contained in your executable application file.

10.3.1. Overview of Using DLLs

Since a DLL is a collection of routines, you must have some way to tell the DLL which routine your application wants to use. The Declare statement accomplishes this. After you have declared which routine you want to use from the DLL, that routine can be used as any other built-in function, routine, or procedure that Visual Basic has to offer. You declare the routine once in your application, but once declared, it can be called and used any number of times from then on.

Some of the code examples in the following sections are taken from CALLDLLS.MAK, located in directory \vb\samples\calldlls. The example in Figure 10.3 uses DLLs to call procedures after one of the three pictures is chosen. Figure 10.3 shows the introductory Calling DLL Procedures screen.

Figure 10.4 shows the information received on a system after the middle picture was called and Windows was clicked on from the given menu list.

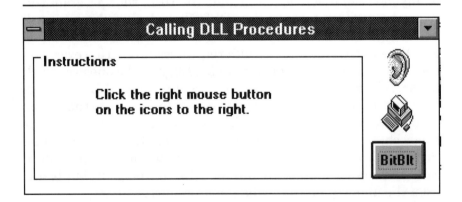

Figure 10.3.   DLL procedure example.

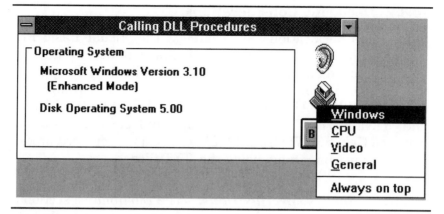

Figure 10.4.   Computer Windows result.

10.3.2. Declaring

Place the Declare statement for a DLL in the Declaration section of your form or procedure. If it is put in a form, it is private to that form. If it is put in a code module, it is public and can be called anywhere from your application.

If the routine does not return a value, declare it as a Sub:

```
Declare Sub CalcN Lib "Math" (N As Double)
```

If the routine does return a value, declare it as a Function:

```
Declare Function CalcY Lib "Math" (N As Double) As Double
```

10.3.3. Calling

When a DLL procedure has been declared, you can call it as if it were part of the Visual Basic system.

```
Sub Do_N (N As Double)
'
   CalcN (N) 'was declared above
'
End Sub
```

10.3.4. Declaring Considerations

Since some declarations are complex, the Visual Basic Professional Toolkit has files to make it easier to declare and call DLL procedures in the Windows API (Application Programming Interface). You can find these files in the \winapi subdirectory: WIN30API.TXT, WIN31API.HLP, WIN31EXT.TXT, and WINMMSYS.TXT. You can copy and paste declarations from the Help file WIN31API.HLP, or use a text or word processor to do the same thing, using the .TXT files.

10.3.4.1. Library specifications. The Lib *libname* section of the Declare statement tells your application where to find the DLL file. Some of the operating environment DLLs are "User", "Kernel", and "GDI". Other system DLLs include files such as "MMSystem."

DLLs from other sources, such as third-party vendors, may include the name and path as in:

```
Declare Sub Xyz Lib "d:\math\xyz\math.dll" (N As Integer)
```

10.3.5. Passing Arguments

When passing arguments in Visual Basic, the default is by reference, which supplies a 32-bit far address. Some DLLs need the arguments to be passed by value. To pass an argument by value, put the keyword ByVal in front of the argument declaration of the Declare statement. For example, the following statement passes the first argument by value and the second by reference:

```
Declare Sub Abc Lib "Math.dll" (ByVal N%, M As Double)
```

> ***Reminder:*** A % placed at the end of a variable is a shortcut for declaring it as type Integer.

> ***Note:*** Using DLL procedure instructions requires the C language syntax. Remember that C passes all arguments by value except for arrays.

10.3.6. Flexible Types

To work around the fact that some arguments in a DLL can accept more than one type of data, the 'As Any' phrase is used in Visual Basic code. If you declare a procedure as:

```
'

Declare Function SendMessage Lib "User" (ByVal hWnd%,
          ByVal msg%, ByVal wp%, lp As Any) As Long
'
```

the function can be called with the last argument (lp As Any) being any Type from a string to a structure, as long as that type is supported by the procedure.

When you remove Type restrictions as was done above with lp, the argument is assumed to be passed by reference. Use the 'By Val' phrase in actual calls to the procedure to pass the argument by value or when passing strings.

10.3.6.1. Alias.   The keyword Alias is used in a number of cases, for example: when a DLL has an illegal character such as a hyphen; an identifier that starts with an underscore; or a Visual Basic reserved word. To work around these problems use the keyword Alias before the illegal word, as in Alias "_Math".

Using a DLL's procedure name is not the only way to identify it. It can be referenced by what is called an ordinal number, which indicates the position of a procedure in a DLL. Some DLLs only use the ordinal number to reference procedures in the DLL file.

To declare a procedure by ordinal number, the Alias clause is used with a string containing the # character and the desired ordinal number. For example the number 132 is the ordinal number for the function GetWinFlags in the Windows kernel DLL file. To declare it in Visual Basic, use:

```
Declare Function GetWinFlags Lib "kernel" Alias "#132" ()
                                                    As Long
```

10.3.7. String Data Types

Visual Basic has a wide variety of data types, but not all can be used in DLLs. Currency is a case in point. You must be aware of what is compatible or your application will not work. The first Visual Basic type we will consider is Strings.

All DLL procedures in Windows API, and in most other DLLs, want strings to be terminated with a NULL (in Visual Basic, ByVal 0&), also referred to in the C language as an ANSI zero. If this is the case with a DLL you are working with, use ByVal to pass the argument as a null-terminated string. For example, the following statement converts a variable length string (lpsound) to the required, null-terminated string.

```
Declare Function sndPlaySound Lib "MMSystem" (ByVal
        lpsound As String, ByVal flag%) As Integer
```

Now you can use statements such as those below to use regular Visual Basic strings to call the procedure to play sound in proper syntax.

```
Dim MusicFile As String, a As Integer
MusicFile = "c:\music\Bach.wav"      'set music file string
a = sndPlaySound(MusicFile, 1)       'play Bach music
```

It is important to note that unless the DLL was specifically written for Visual Basic, DLL procedures cannot return Strings. As you can see from all of the preceding Declare statements, none has Functions that return a String. You can write your own DLLs for Visual Basic so that they can return a String data type variable. The procedure for doing so is explained in Visual Basic's documentation.

10.3.8. Arrays

You may pass individual elements of an array just as you would any other variable. The following code uses the sound example code you just looked at to play multiple sounds.

```
Dim i As Integer, x As Integer
   For i = 0 to UBound(MusicFiles) 'play 0 to top index
      x = sndPlaySound(MusicFiles(i), 1) 'play the i one
   Next i                               'get another
```

You cannot pass an entire array unless the DLL was made for Visual Basic. You can, however, pass an entire array if it is a numeric array.

One restriction on passing an array is that passing cannot handle a Huge array (greater than 64K). If you attempt to do so, only the first 64K of data can be accessed.

10.3.9. User-Defined Types

Some DLLs may use user-defined types, otherwise known as Structs, structures, or records in other languages. As in the sound array example, you may pass individual arguments that are user-defined. You can pass the entire user-defined type if it is passed by reference.

Most DLLs that accept user-defined types do not expect string data. You can pass a user-defined type that includes string elements only if the string elements are fixed-length strings. Unless written specifically for Visual Basic, a DLL cannot accept user-defined types with variable-length strings.

10.3.10. Null Pointers

At times a DLL procedure requires a NULL pointer as an argument. If this is the case, use an 'As Any' clause when you declare the procedure, and use ByVal 0& when passing arguments. You cannot send the DLL a "" (zero-length string) because that would send a pointer to a null string—not a null pointer. For example, the procedure FindWindow accepts two strings as arguments. The correct way to declare this and call it as the following code, which passes a Null pointer as an argument:

```
Declare Function FindWindow Lib "User" (Class As Any) As
                                                    Integer

hWndExcel = FindWindow(ByVal 0&, ByVal As "MS Excel")
```

10.3.11. Handles

The DLLs in the operating system (Windows 3.x, 4.x), use handles such as hWnd a great deal. Handles are unique numbers defined by the operating system to refer to objects such as controls and forms. Always declare an argument that requires a handle as a ByVal Integer.

Handles are ID numbers, not numeric values or pointers. Do not perform math operations on them. As with any other property, when passing handles to DLL procedures you can only pass them by value.

10.3.12. Properties and Objects

Properties are passed by value, and if the corresponding argument uses ByVal, you can pass the property directly. For example, the following code determines the size of the screen in pixels:

```
Declare Function GetDeviceCaps% Lib "GDI" (ByVal hDC%,
                                           ByVal nIndex%)
```

Passing a string property by reference requires a temporary, intermediate value, so you can assign the property to a string intermediate and then pass that variable to the procedure.

Object variables are complex data structures and cannot use forms or controls passed to them. Unless the DLL has been written specially for Visual Basic, you cannot pass form or control variables. The same restriction applies to special objects such as Clipboard, Printer, and so forth.

10.3.13. Converting Declarations

The C language is the usual standard for the syntax in DLL declarations. To use such declarations in Visual Basic you need to know the conversion equivalents. Table 10.2 summarizes the C language declaration argument types, Visual Basic's equivalent declaration, and how to call the declaration in Visual Basic. This will help you when you wish to use a DLL routine that only talks in terms of C syntax.

Table 10.2. Declaration equivalents in C and Visual Basic.

C Declaration	Declare in Visual Basic	Call With
Pointer to String (LPSTR)	ByVal S As String	A String/Variant variable
Pointer to Integer (LPINT)	I As Integer	An Integer/Variant variable
Pointer to long Integer (LPDWORD)	L As Long	A Long/Variant variable
Pointer to a Struct (Ex. LPRECT)	S As Rect	A variable of that user-defined type
Integer (INT, UINT, WORD, BOOL)	ByVal I As Integer	An Integer/Variant variable
Handle (hWnd, hDC, hMenu, etc.)	ByVal h As Integer	An Integer/Variant variable
Long (DWORD, LONG)	ByVal L As Long	A Long/Variant variable
Pointer to an array of integers	I As Integer	The first element of an array, Array(0)
Pointer to a void (void *)	As Any	A Variable using ByVal
Void (function return value)	Sub procedure	n/a
NULL	As Any	ByVal 0&

10.4. OLE

OLE 2.0 (Object Linking and Embedding) is a way to operate between Window applications that allows you, from your Visual Basic application, to display data from other applications. OLE Automation also allows you to program other applications.

Object linking and embedding (OLE) is a technology that allows a programmer of Windows-based applications to create an application that can display data from many different applications, and allows the user to edit that data from within the application in which it was created. In some cases, the user can even edit the data from within the Visual Basic application. The Visual Basic OLE control provides an interface to this technology.

You use the OLE control to display an OLE object on a form. You create the object either at design time using standard OLE dialogs (Insert Object, Paste Special) or at runtime by setting the appropriate properties.

10.4.1. Using the OLE Control's Pop-up Menus

Each time you draw an OLE control on a form, the Insert Object dialog box is displayed. You use this dialog box to create a linked or embedded object. If you choose Cancel, no object is created. At design time, you click the OLE control with the right mouse button to display a pop-up menu. The commands displayed on this pop-up menu depend on the state of the OLE control as displayed in the following list:

Command	Enabled in pop-up when
Insert Object	This command is always enabled.
Paste Special	The Clipboard has a valid OLE object.
Delete Embedded Object	OLE control has an embedded object.
Delete Linked Object	OLE control contains a linked object.
Create Link	SourceDoc property is set.
Create Embedded Object	Class or SourceDoc property is set.

10.4.2. OLE Automation

Some applications provide objects that support OLE Automation. You can use Visual Basic to manipulate the data in these objects programmatically. Some objects that support OLE Automation also support linking and embedding. If an object in the OLE control supports OLE Automation, you can access its data using the Object property. You can create an OLE Automation object without the OLE control by using the CreateObject function.

10.4.3. Class

An object's class determines the application that provides the object's data and the type of data the object contains. The class names of some commonly used Microsoft applications include MSGraph, MSDraw, WordDocument, and ExcelWorksheet. You can get a list of the class names available to your application by selecting the Class property in the Properties window and clicking on the three dots in the Settings box.

10.4.4. Container Application

An application that receives and displays an object's data is a *container application*. For example, a Visual Basic application that uses an OLE control to embed or link data from another application is a container application. In Visual Basic 2.0, applications that provide access to objects were called server or source applications. Applications used to contain objects were referred to as client or destination applications.

10.4.5. Linked and Embedded Objects

You use an OLE control to incorporate data into a Visual Basic application by linking or embedding data from another application. Data associated with a linked object is stored by the application that supplied the object; the OLE control stores only link references that enable the display of snapshots of the source data. Data associated with an embedded object is contained in an OLE control and can be saved by your Visual Basic application.

When an object is linked,the object's data can be accessed from any application containing a link to that data and can be changed from within any of them. For example, if a text file is linked to a Visual Basic application, it can be modified by any other application linked to that application. The modified version of the file will appear in all the documents linked to this text file.

When you use an OLE control to create an embedded object, all the data associated with that object is contained in the OLE control. For example, if a spreadsheet were an embedded object, all the data associated with the cells would be contained in the OLE control, including any necessary formulas. The name of the application that created the object is saved along with the data. If the user selects the embedded object while working with the Visual Basic application, the spreadsheet application can be started automatically for editing of the object's cells. When an object is embedded into an application, no other application has access to the data in the embedded object. Embedding is useful when you want only your application to maintain data that is produced and edited in another application.

10.4.6. Objects and OLE

An OLE object refers to a discrete unit of data supplied by an OLE application. An application can expose many types of objects. For example, a spreadsheet application can expose a worksheet, macro sheet, chart, cell, or range of cells all as different types of objects. You use the OLE control to create linked and embedded objects. When a linked or embedded object is created, it contains the name of the application that supplied the object, its data (or, in the case of a linked object, a reference to the data), and an image of the data. An OLE control can contain only one object at a time. There are several ways to create a linked or embedded object:

- Use the Insert Object or Paste Special dialogs (runtime and design time).
- Set the Class property in the Properties window, then click the OLE control with the right mouse button and select the appropriate command (design time only).
- Set the Action property of the OLE control (runtime only).

The new data type is called "object." You establish a connection with an OLE 2.0 defined object, and then control it with a variable of type Object. You can establish this connection to an OLE 2.0 defined object by what is called OLE Automation, and assign it to an Object variable in one of two ways:

- Create an OLE 2.0 control and set the appropriate properties.
- Call object creation functions such as CreateObject in code statements.

Once the object is made, you can set properties and call methods on the OLE 2.0 object with regular object type syntax. OLE 2.0 objects support various properties that can be assigned, and methods that usually return values.

10.4.7. OLE Automation by a Control

The custom control file that must be in your project is called MSOLE2.VBX. When this file is added, it produces the following icon in the Toolkit:

The most important features that are now available in OLE 2.0 but were not in OLE 1.0 allow you to clip, autosize, stretch, and select the desired OLE object from a standard dialog.

When you click on the OLE 2.0 icon in the Toolbox and place an area for it on a form, you will see an Insert Object window similar to the example shown in Figure 10.5.

When the OLE control has an OLE 2.0 object assigned to it, that object is then easily manipulated, as shown in the following code, which sets a spreadsheet cell to a value, then makes the cell boldface. XyOLEControl is the name of the OLE container control.

```
XyOLEControl.Object.Cell(1,1) = 50   'set cells value to 50
XyOLEControl.Object.Cell(1,1).FormatBold()   'set to Bold
```

10.4.8. OLE Automation by Object Functions

Another way to make a connection with an OLE 2.0 object is to declare a variable as type Object. Then you can set the Object

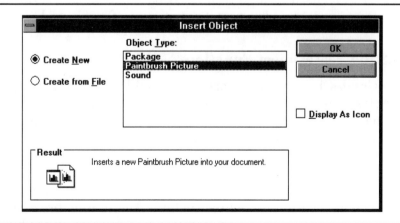

Figure 10.5. OLE Insert Object window.

with one of the two object creation functions, CreateObject or GetObject, as shown here.

```
Dim My_obj as Object
Set My_obj = CreateObject("Excel.Worksheet")
```

or

```
Set My_obj = GetObject("c:\mydoc.doc", "Word.Document")
```

When the variable My_obj is set, you control the OLE 2.0 object in the same way as with the OLE Container control.

```
My_obj.Cell(1,1) = "Text For The Cell" 'put text in cell
My_obj.forecolor = 15   'set foreground color
```

10.4.9. OLE Objects As Controls

An OLE 2.0 object is basically a control if it supports in-place editing and OLE Automation. Thus OLE 2.0 can become an open extension mechanism for developers.

Custom-solution developers can use any OLE 2.0 enabled applications as first-class components in their application, because now developers can use OLE Automation to control these applications as *objects*. For example, an OLE 2.0 enabled word processor object can be used as a powerful text box control, or an OLE 2.0 enabled spreadsheet object can become a very flexible grid control.

10.3.10. CreateObject Function

The CreateObject function creates an OLE Automation object. The class argument used to accomplish this is a string indicating the name of the application used to create the object and the object's type. To specify an object's class, use the syntax:

```
appname.objecttype.
```

Each application that supports OLE Automation provides at least one type of object. For example, a word-processing application may provide an application object, a document object, and a toolbar object. To get a list of OLE Automation objects an application supports, consult the application's documentation.

Use the CreateObject function to create an OLE Automation object and assign the object to an object variable. To do this, first dimension a variable of type object. Then use the Set statement to assign the object returned by CreateObject to that object variable. For example:

```
Dim MyObject As Object
Set MyObject = CreateObject("WordProc.Document")
```

When this code is executed, the application creating the object (WordProc.Exe in this example) is started if it is not already running, and an object of the specified type is created. In this case, unlike the case of a linked or embedded object created by using the OLE control, the object's image is not displayed anywhere in Visual Basic, nor is the object's data maintained by Visual Basic.

Once an object is created, you can reference it in Visual Basic code, using the object variable you defined. For instance, you access properties and methods of the new object in the preceding example using the object variable, MyObject, as shown here:

```
MyObject.Bold
MyObject.Insert "Hello, world."
MyObject.Print
MyObject.SaveAs "C:\WORDPROC\DOCS\TEST.DOC"
```

10.4.11. GetObject Function

GetObject retrieves an OLE Automation object from a file. Use the GetObject function to access an OLE Automation object from a file and assign the object to an object variable. To do this, first dimension a variable of type object. Then use the Set statement to assign the object returned by GetObject to the object variable. For example:

```
Dim MyObject As Object
Set MyObject = GetObject("C:\WORDPROC\DOCS\OLETEST.DOC")
```

When this code is executed, the application associated with the specified file name (WORDPROC.EXE in this example) is started, and the object in the specified file is activated. If the filename argument is set to an empty string (""), this function returns the currently active object of the specified type. If no object of that type is active, an error occurs.

The preceding example shows how to activate an entire file. However, some applications allow you to activate part of a file. To do this, add an exclamation point to the end of the file name, followed by a string that identifies the part of the file you want to activate. For information on how to create this string, see the documentation for the application that created the object. For example, in many spreadsheet applications, you specify the rows and columns of a range of cells using an R1C1 syntax. You could use the following code to activate a range of cells within a spreadsheet called REVENUE.SPD:

```
Set Sheet =
GetObject("C:\ACCOUNTS\REVENUE.SPD!R1C1:R10C20")
```

If you do not specify the object's class, the OLE 2.0 DLLs determine the application to invoke and the object to activate based on the file name you provide. Some files, however, may support more than one class of object. For example, a spreadsheet may support three different types of objects: an application object, a worksheet object, and a toolbar object, all of which are part of the same file. To specify which object in a file you want to activate, use the optional class argument. For example:

```
Set Sheet = GetObject("C:\ACCOUNTS\REVENUE.SPD",
"SPDSHEET.WORKSHEET")
```

In this example, SPDSHEET is the name of a spreadsheet application, and WORKSHEET is one of the object types it supports. Once an object is activated, you can reference it in Visual Basic code using the object variable you defined. In the preceding example you access properties and methods of the new object using the object variable, MyObject. For example:

```
Sheet.Row = 4
Sheet.Column = 2
```

```
Sheet.Insert = "Hello, world."
Sheet.SaveAs "C:\WORDPROC\DOCS\TEST.DOC"
Sheet.Print
```

10.4.12. Files

OLE object data is not permanent. When the form with a control closes, the data associated with that control is gone. To save the information from the object to a file, use the Action property. Note that you only can use the binary file type for this purpose. When the object has been saved in a file, you can then open and restore the file's object information.

10.4.12.1. Save.   To save the information from an OLE object:

- Open a file in binary mode.
- Set the FileNumber property to the same file number used above.
- Set the Action property to OLE_SAVE_TO_FILE(11).

The following code is an example of these steps.

```
Sub Save_My_Object()
   FileNum = FreeFile  'find a free file # and assign it
   Open "CONTROL.OLE" For Binary As #FileNum 'open a file
   OleClient1.FileNumber = FileNum 'set file to same file
   OleClient1.Action = OLE_SAVE_TO_FILE 'save the file
   Close #FileNum 'close the file
End Sub
```

10.4.12.2. Read.   The following code reads back the object saved in Section 10.4.12.1.

```
Sub Read_My_Object()
   FileNum = FreeFile  'find a free file # and assign it
   Open "CONTROL.OLE" For Binary As #FileNum ' open a file
   OleClient1.FileNumber = FileNum 'set file to same file
   OleClient1.Action = OLE_READ_FROM_FILE 'read the file
   Close #FileNum 'close the file
End Sub
```

11

ODBC

11.1. INTRODUCING ODBC

ODBC (Open DataBase Connectivity) is a component of WOSA (Microsoft Windows Open Services Architecture). ODBC allows you to interface with DBMS (DataBase Management Systems). The ability to use SQL (Structured Query Language) is also provided.

A single application can access data in different DBMSs through one interface. Your application can be independent of the DBMS through the use of drivers. *Drivers* are modules that link the application to the chosen DBMS.

ODBC is a more specialized form of data handling. For many of your general applications, the data handling discussed in Chapter 5 will be adequate. File handling involving aspects such as SQL and networking will require ODBC for effective processing. However, with Visual Basic 3.0, the data-aware controls (see Sections 8.7 and 8.8) may provide the same functionality and at the same time be much easier to set up and use.

This chapter discusses ODBC in a way that gives you an understanding of the terms and concepts of ODBC and how it is used.

11.2. COMPONENTS OF ODBC

The five components of the ODBC architecture are:

- *Your Visual Basic application:* By OBDC object properties and methods, performs data definitions and data manipulations.
- *Visual Basic internals:* Send requests from an ODBC object in your application to the Driver manager for executing.
- *Driver manager;* Gets and sends an ODBC object request submitted from Visual Basic internals to the correct driver.
- *Driver:* Executes ODBC functions, sends out SQL requests to data, and returns the results.
- *Data source:* The data the application wants to use, the operating system, the DBMS, and if needed, the network platform.

11.3. APPLICATIONS

Your Visual Basic application can use ODBC statements, objects, functions, and methods to manage data and various database structures.

You can use objects to send SQL requests, terminate connection to the data, and execute rollback and/or commit operations for transaction control.

You can use dynasets (see Section 11.11) to report results back to the user, and define storage areas and data formats for the results of SQL requests.

Visual Basic internals (the programming system) serve as an interface to data sources, drivers, and Driver managers. It sends requests from an object to the Driver manager for execution.

11.4. DRIVER MANAGER

The *Driver manager* is a DLL whose purpose is to load drivers. It also provides entry points to ODBC functions for each driver, maps a data source name to a specific driver, initializes ODBC calls, and validates the parameters and sequence of ODBC calls.

11.4.1. Drivers

A *driver* is a DLL that executes ODBC function calls along with their appropriate data sets. When the code statement function OpenDataBase is called, the Driver manager calls the driver DLL.

A driver establishes and sends a request to the data, changes data formats if this is requested, returns results, formats errors into standard error codes, and allows for explicit transaction initiation.

11.5. DATA SOURCE

A *data source* is a unique combination of a DBMS with any remote operating system and network needed to access it. In this chapter, a DBMS refers to any SQL database management system.

11.6. DRIVER CONFIGURATIONS

There are two types of ODBC drivers: one for single-tier and the other for multiple-tier configurations. In a single-tier configuration, the database file is processed directly by the driver. In multiple-tier configurations, the driver sends SQL requests to a server that executes SQL requests. Most of the time, though not always, in multiple-tier configurations the installation is divided into multiple platforms. The application, driver, and Drive manager are on a system called the *client*, while the database and software access are on another system called the *server*.

11.7. REFERENCE OVERVIEW

The following sections give you an overview of ODBC and how ODBC elements work together. If you have Visual Basic, run the VISDATA.MAK application. As shown in Figure 11.1, this is a very good example of some of the features you can use in your application with ODBC.

Figure 11.2 shows the File options available for the Visual Data example application. If you plan to run this program, it can be found in the subdirectory \sample\visdata.

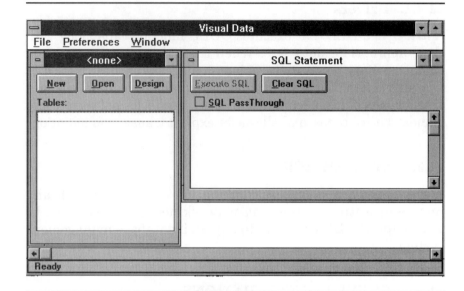

Figure 11.1. Visual Data ODBC example.

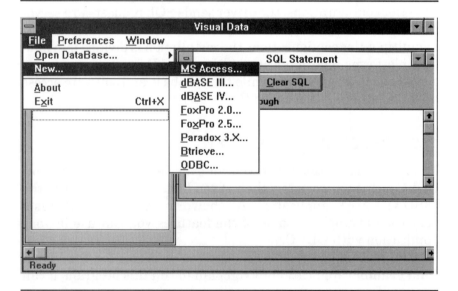

Figure 11.2. Visual Data and files.

11.8. DATABASE STRUCTURE

An *ODBC database* is a collection of tables. A table has fields and their indexes. The database can have multiple tables, each described in a TableDef statement, and each representing an object. The set of *all* TableDef objects is called the *TableDefs collection*.

A TableDef object includes one or more fields called *Field objects*. *Index objects* describe the organization of the table. All the fields in a table are called a *Field collection*, and all the indexes are called the *Index collection*.

11.9. OBJECTS

The *Database object* contains information about which database is open, how it can be accessed, and how it is structured. It also has information on the methods that you can use to manipulate and close a database. Information about the tables in a database is in the TableDef collection.

The *TableDef object* defines a table. It defines it by name, the collection of fields, and the indexes collection.

Field objects have a name, data type, and size. Field objects in TableDef objects do not contain data values. Instead, they describe structures into which values are put. How to use these so-called structures will be seen in Section 11.13.2.

Index objects define a key or keys which maintain and access the actual data within a table. They will be discussed in Section 11.13.3.

11.10. COLLECTIONS

A *collection* is a list of related objects. The following example will give you a better understanding of collections, an essential concept for using ODBC objects and their methods.

Assume that there are 30 data processing employees in a company called ABC. Data about these employees is kept in a listed in numbered order. Because this list involves a collection of dp employees, it will be called DPemp. The employees in the DPemp collection are objects that have properties. That is, each dp employee object has the properties name, department, salary, title, and so on. The collection also has *methods*, or actions, such as programming, debugging, managing, and so forth.

Now some code examples will show how to refer to some of the dp employees to retrieve information about them. The following code gets the salary of the third dp employee in the collection list, using an index value.

```
thisdpemp = DPemp(2).salary
```

Knowing the person's name, you could use the following *method* to set the person's task to programming.

```
DPemp("Thomas Torgerson").program
```

If each dp employee has a phone extension, the collection could use the Count property to print the names of all the dp employees and their phone numbers.

```
For i = 0 to DPemp.Count - 1
   Printer.Print DPemp(i).employeename
   Printer.Print DPemp(i).phone_ext
Next i
```

The DPemp collection can be related to the TableDefs in a database. TableDefs is a collection of objects, each of which describes a table. The TableDefs.Count gives the number of objects in the collection, just as DPemp.Count gave the number of dp employees in company ABC. There, to refer to a particular employee, the index or name was used. This is basically the same way you access data with a TableDef collection.

11.10.1. Create or Delete ODBC Objects

The structure of your database is contained by the database's TableDefs collection. The tables are defined by the contents of their Fields and Indexes collections. Adding or deleting objects from collections changes the structure of the database. You can create a new TableDef Object, add the Field and Index objects to it, then append it to the TableDefs collection. Deleting a TableDef from the TableDefs collection removes the table and all associated table data.

11.11. DYNASETS

You can access data only by creating a temporary, new object called a dynaset. A *dynaset* is one or more tables in which the number of fields depends on how the dynaset was created.

The set of fields in a dynaset is also called a *Field collection*. These field objects differ from a TableDef object in that dynaset objects have a value property whereby you can access and work with real database values. As an example, Table 11.1 is an employee table with three fields and three records. The Sales_Commission represents the percentage bonus that each employee receives.

One way a dynaset can be created is by using a SQL SELECT statement that performs as a filter of sorts, determining which records to put into the dynaset, and which to reject from tables. In this case, the dynaset will contain two of the three records in Table 11.1 because of the restriction that only employees with a sales commission greater than 5% can be included. Table 11.2 shows the results of this sample code.

```
Dim selectStr As String
'
selectStr = "SELECT Name, Id, Sales_Commission FROM
          Employee WHERE Sales_Commission > 5"
'
MyDS = db.CreateDynaset(selectStr)
```

Table 11.1.   Employee table.

	Field-1 Name	*Field-2 Id*	*Field-3 Sales_Commission*
Row 1 —	Johnson	231	10
Row 2 —	Frabens	685	3
Row 3 —	Lorens	378	11

Table 11.2. Samples created dynaset.

	Field-1 Name	Field-2 Id	Field-3 Sales_Commission
Row 1 —	Johnson	231	10
Row 3 —	Lorens	378	11

11.12. INTRODUCTION TO DATA MANIPULATION

To make data manipulation easier, Visual Basic has *object variables* that represent databases and dynasets. Using the methods of these object variables you can open, close, and get information on a database, extract subsets of data, and add, delete, and edit data fields and records.

For the remainder of this chapter a hypothetical database called CUSTDB_A will be referenced. It will contain four fields: First_Name, Last_Name, Customer_ID, and Phone.

11.12.1. Opening and Closing a Database

A Database object is needed to use the functions associated with a database. Declare a Database object as you would any other object variable, and then use the Set statement to assign it to the return value of the OpenDatabase function. The following code shows how to accomplish this.

```
Dim db As Database    'db is now a Database object
Dim DBName As String
Dim DBConnect As String
'
DBName = "\\SALES\PUBLIC\NEW\CUSTDB_A"
DBConnect = "UID-TOM;PWD=TT"
Set db = OpenDatabase(DBName, False, False, DBConnect)
```

The database CUSTDB_A is found on the server \\sales\public in the \new directory. It will be opened in read-write mode with the user Id TOM and the password TT.

When you are done with a database, close it with the statement

```
db.Close
```

11.13. INFORMATION ABOUT A DATABASE

A database is referenced by the number and structure of its member tables. Tables are described by the fields and indexes they contain. ODBC can provide information about the structure of a referenced database. This data is put into the Database object when the OpenDatabase code statement is used. The TableDef object provides some of this information about a database table, including the name of the table (stored in the Name property), a collection of Field objects, and a collection of Index objects.

> *Note:* Please remember that the Field objects referred to here do *not* have value properties and therefore do not hold database values. Dynasets are the objects that hold such values and allow you to access data.

11.13.1. TableDefs Collection

The TableDefs property collection contains one TableDef object for each table in the database. A TableDef object can be used to learn about the field structure of a table, index information, and so on.

The following example code finds all the table names in a database and puts them in a list box.

```
Dim db As Database    'db is now a Database object
Dim DBName As String
Dim DBConnect As String
Dim i As Integer
'
DBName = "\\SALES\PUBLIC\NEW\CUSTDB_A"
DBConnect = "UID=TOM;PWD=TT"
'
Set db = OpenDatabase(DBName, False, False, DBConnect)
'
'
'''''''Put all database table Names in the listbox''''''
For i = 0 to db.TableDefs.Count - 1
   TableList.AddItem = db.TableDefs(i).Name
Next i
''''''''''''''''''''''''''''''''''''''''''''''''''''''''
```

11.13.2. Information about a Field

To obtain information about a field, retrieve the field's Name, Type, and Size properties. The following code declares a TableDef object (tDef), sets it to the first table, and retrieves the names of all the fields in this first table.

```
Dim db As Database    'db is now a Database object
Dim DBName As String
Dim DBConnect As String
Dim i As Integer
Dim tDef As TableDef
'
DBName = "\\SALES\PUBLIC\NEW\CUSTDB_A"
DBConnect = "UID=TOM;PWD=TT"
'
Set db = OpenDatabase(DBName, False, False, DBConnect)
'
Set tDef = db.TableDefs(0)  'go to the first Table
tDef.Fields.Refresh         'update the field list
'
''''''''Put all database Field Names in the listbox''''''
For i = 0 to tDef.Fields.Count -1
   FieldList.AddItem = tDef.Fields(i).Name
Next i
''''''''''''''''''''''''''''''''''''''''''''''''''''''''
'
db.Close
'close the database and any associated db files
```

The Type and Size of the fields can also be accessed by:

```
type_of_field = tdef.Fields(i).Type
size_of_field = tdef.Fields(i).Size
```

11.13.3. Information about Indexes

An index has three properties: the name (usually the table name), a list of one or more key fields separated by semicolons, and a True or False value for a property called Unique.

The following code shows the first index name, the key field, and the Unique value for the table Customer, the only table in the CUSTDB_A database.

```
Dim tDef As TableDef
Dim IndexName As String
Dim IndexFields As String
Dim IndexUnique As String
'
Set tDef = db.TableDefs("Customer")
tDef.Indexes.Refresh
''''''''''''''''''''''''''''''''''''''''''''''''''''''''
'
' If there is a index, assign the first name and field
' to two variables
'
If tDef.Indexes.Count > 0 Then
  IndexName = tDef.Indexes(0).Name
  IndexFields = tDef.Indexes(0).Fields
''''''''''''''''''''''''''''''''''''''''''''''''''''''''
'
'Now check Unique property
 If tDef.Indexes(0).Unique = False Then
  IndexUnique = "FALSE"
 Else
  IndexUnique = "TRUE"
'
 End If
End If
```

11.14. CHANGING THE DATABASE STRUCTURE

You can add new fields, delete or add tables and indexes, and so on using ODBC methods. If you wanted to add a "customer phone calls" table to the database CUSTDB_A, you would create a temporary TableDef object. Next add new Field and Size objects for each new item in the table, in this case Call_Number and Call_Date. Finally, Append will add the new table, CustCalls, to the database's TableDefs collection.

```
Dim tempDef as New TableDef    'temporary TableDef object
Dim tempIndex as New Index     'temporary Index object
Dim f1, f2                     'temporary FIELD objects
'
tempDef.Name = "CustCalls"     'new table name
'
f1.Name = "Call_Number"        'New field name assignment
f1.Type = DB_SINGLENUMBER      'Constant, equals 6
f1.Size = DB_SINGLENUMBERSIZE  'Constant, equals 4 bytes
tempDef.Fields.Append f1       'add to the collection
'
f2.Name = "Call_Date"
f2.Type = DB_DATE
f2.Size = DB_DATESIZE
tempDef.Fields.Append f2       'add to the collection
'
'Create an index on the call number field
'
tempIndex.Name = "Call_Number_Index"
tempIndex.Fields = "Call_number"
tempIndex.Unique = True
tempDef.Indexes.Append tempIndex 'add index to collection
'
'''''''''Below appends the new table definition'''''''
'       to the TableDefs collection - and a new
'       table CUSTCALLS is created, with 2 fields
'       and one index.
'..................................................
db.TableDefs.Append tempDef
```

11.14.1. Adding a Field

The last section showed how to create new fields by creating a new table. You can also add a new field to an existing table. The following code adds the field Operator_Code to the Customers table.

```
Dim f as New Field
'
f.Name = "Operator_Code"
```

```
f.Type = DB_TEXT
f.Size = 8
'

'''''''''''''Append the new field to the TableDef''''''
db.TableDefs("Customers").Fields.Append f
```

11.14.2. Adding an Index

Tables can have multiple indexes. The following code adds another index (Operator_Index) to the Customers table.

```
Dim tempIndex as New Index
'

tempIndex.Name = "Operator_Index"
tempIndex.Fields = "Operator_Code"
tempIndex.Unique = False
'

'''''''Append the new index to the TableDef'''''''''
db.TableDefs("Customers").Indexes.Append tempIndex
```

11.14.3. Deleting a Table or Index

If you delete a table, all of its fields and indexes are also deleted. The following line of code deletes the Customers table.

```
db.TableDefs.Delete "Customers"
```

The next example removes the index created in Section 11.14.2.

```
db.TableDefs("Customers").Indexes.Delete "Operator_Index"
```

11.15. DYNASET OBJECTS

As previously mentioned, you can only access values in the database by creating Dynaset objects. The dynaset can be created from any table, subset of a table, or combination of tables.

A dynaset can contain all the records and fields of the original table along with the field values if set up as shown in the following code, which declares MyDS as a dynaset and then creates it.

```
Dim MyDS As Dynaset
Set MyDS = db.CreateDynaset("Customers")
```

A dynaset may also contain only some records and some fields if you use the SQL SELECT statement. This was shown in Section 11.11, where only a portion of the records were put into a dynaset but all of their fields were included.

11.16. GETTING AROUND IN A DYNASET

Getting around in a dynaset refers to the ways of moving among its records. When the dynaset is first created, the first record becomes the current, or active, record. The content of that first record is automatically set and available for viewing. The next few sections refer to ways to get other wanted records from a dynaset.

11.16.1. Go to First Record

Many times it is necessary to go to the first record in a dynaset. This can be accomplished easily by closing and then recreating the dynaset, as shown below. This approach moves you to the first record.

```
MyDS.Close
Set MyDS = db.CreateDynaset("Customers")
```

11.16.2. Go to Next Record

The MoveNext method causes the next record in the table to become the current record. Be careful not to use this method if you are at EOF (End Of File) because doing so will cause an error. The following code uses a grid control to place data in column and row format and lists the first and last names of all customers.

```
Dim MyDS As Dynaset
Dim gridrow As Integer
gridRow = 1
```

```
'
Set MyDS = db.CreateDynaset("Customers")
'
Do While MyDS.EOF = False           'do a loop until EOF
  browseGrid.Rows = gridRow + 1     'add new row
  browseGrid.Row = gridRow          'move to it
  browseGrid.Col = 0                'column for last name
  browseGrid.Text = MyDS("Last_Name")
  browseGrid.Col = 1                'column for first name
  browseGrid.Text = MyDS("First_Name")
  MyDS.MoveNext                     'move to next record
  gridRow = gridRow + 1            'next row
Loop
```

11.16.3. Go to Desired Record

When you want to go to a particular record and you know the
record number, you can use a For loop to make it current. If you
wanted record number three, use the following code structure:

```
Nmoves = 2  'three minus one is needed for the loop
MyDS.Close
Set MyDS = db.CreateDynaset"(Customers") 'record now at #1
'
For j = 1 to Nmoves
  MyDS.MoveNext                            'next record
Next j
```

If you wanted record number 1265, then Nmoves would be 1264.
    If the record number is unknown then all the records in the
dynaset may be checked for a specified value in one of the
records' fields as follows:

```
Do While MyDS.EOF = False
  If Last_Name = "Torgerson" Then GoTo Found_Wanted_Record
    .            '
    .
Loop
```

11.16.4. Closing a Dynaset

To close a dynaset, use statements such as

```
MyDS.Close
```

as shown in the preceding examples. If you do not close all the dynasets but simply stop the application, dynaset memory space will not return to the system as it should.

11.17. MANIPULATING RECORDS

A number of methods exist for adding, editing, and deleting records in dynasets. However, you can use these methods only if the Updatable property of the dynaset is set to True. If this property is set to False, data values are then read-only for the dynaset.

Other rules that must be observed if you intend to update a dynaset are:

1. The dynaset cannot be created from the SQL SELECT statement; it must instead be made directly from a table.
2. The table used to create the dynaset must have an index with a unique key field.
3. Both the database and the dynaset must open with the read-only flags assigned to False.

11.17.1. Add a Record

To add a new record, append that record's information to the end of the dynaset. To accomplish this, first use the AddNew method to create a blank record, assign values to this record, and save the record to the dynaset with the Update method. The following example code adds a new customer to the end of the dynaset.

```
Set MyDS = db.CreateDynaset("Customers")
'
MyDS("First_Name") = "Tom"
MyDS("Last_Name")  = "Torgerson"
MyDS("Customer_ID")= "1234"
```

```
MyDS("Phone")       = "(612) 521-3109"
MyDS.Update           'append this new record to Customers
                      'table
```

11.17.2. Edit Current Record

To edit the current record in a dynaset, first set up the record for editing by using the Edit method. Next, assign the new values you want to the appropriate fields, and then use the Update method described in Section 11.17.2. This examples changes the ID assigned in the original code from 1234 to 4321 *only if* the record's position has been changed to that of first record in the table.

```
Set MyDS = db.CreateDynaset("Customers") '1st record set
'
MyDS.Edit             'set up for editing
MyDS("Customer_ID") = 4321      'change Id number
MyDS.Update                     'make permanent
```

Grid controls that display the order of your data will be incorrect after this edit update and need to be rebuilt to show the data correctly.

11.17.3. Delete a Record

To delete a dynaset record, you need only find the record you want deleted and use the Delete method, as shown below.

```
Set MyDS = db.CreateDynaset("Customers") '1st record
MyDS.MoveNext    'get the second record
MyDS.Delete      'delete the second record
```

11.17.4. Transaction States

Changes in data are reflected immediately in the records of the dynaset. However these changes may or may not be reflected in the "actual" database table immediately. Whether or not the database table changes immediately depends on a property called the *transaction state*. If the transaction state is auto-commit—the default—then the changes are made immediately and are permanent. If there is what is called a *transaction* open, the changes are not made immediately. They can be batched into a group, so that later all the changes are made—or possibly, undone.

11.17.5. Data Locking

Data locking takes the worry out of wondering if other users are making conflicting changes to data. It allows you to have the only updatable copy of data, while others have only "read" access to the data. This feature is available only at the dynaset level and is set by making the second parameter of the CreateDynaset statement True.

```
Set MyDS = db.CreateDynaset("Customers", True)
```

11.17.6. SQL Commands

You can pass SQL commands directly to the underlying database, without the dynaset commands. This is accomplished by using the ExecuteSQL method of a Database object as shown.

```
db.ExecuteSQL "DELETE" * FROM Customers WHERE First_Name
                                LIKE 'T*';"
```

This will delete any record that has a first name starting with T.

11.18. LARGE DATA FIELDS

Sometimes Memo fields can exceed the 64K size limitations of string variables. Three methods for dealing with Memo fields are: FieldSize, GetChunk, and AppendChunk.

The FieldSize method returns the size of a Memo field. If it is greater than 64K, the GetChunk method is used to access the memo field a portion at a time.

The AppendChunk method adds a string to the end of an existing Memo field. This allows you to add your own comments, or a user's comments, to a preexisting Memo field.

11.19. TRANSACTIONS

A *transaction* is a recoverable series of database activities. Transactions can be useful in situations where the default setting of changing the underlying database and the dynaset immediately is undesirable. A case in point may be a banking application in which the operator enters dozens of new credit applications. By exercising the option not to commit all these applications to immediate database changes, the bank has a chance to review the applications for errors before making the transactions permanent.

The three commands to support transaction processing are: BeginTrans, CommitTrans, and RollBack. You need to make sure that the database will support transactions, and that the Transaction property of the database is set to True.

11.19.1. BeginTrans

BeginTrans takes the database out of the default auto-commit and starts the beginning of a transaction. When you use BeginTrans you must at some point thereafter use CommitTrans or RollBack before you close the database or an error occurs. To begin an example transaction code, use:

```
BeginTrans
```

11.19.2. CommitTrans

CommitTrans saves to the underlying table the dynaset changes made since the transaction began with BeginTrans. The following line of code saves all table actions:

```
CommitTrans
```

11.19.3. Rollback

Rollback undoes, or takes back, all data changes in the current transaction. If you found major mistakes while working with your dynasets, this statement could be a major timesaver. Call the command as:

```
Rollback
```

11.20. CONNECT FAILURE AREAS

Four possible problem areas can contribute to a failure to connect to a database server when using ODBC and Visual Basic. Check to be sure that you:

1. Have correct .INI file settings
2. Have the correct DLLs in the right place
3. Have the server information needed to connect to a server correctly
4. Meet the needs of Microsoft and Sybase SQL Servers

11.20.1. INI Settings

Two .INI files, ODBCINST.INI and ODBC.INI, must reside in the Windows directory and contain correct information about the installed ODBC drivers and servers.

ODBCINST.INI contains the ODBC driver information needed to register new servers using the RegisterDataBase() statement in Visual Basic. Here is an example .INI file for the SQL Server driver that ships with Visual Basic:

```
[ODBC Drivers]
SQL Server=Installed

[SQL Server]
Driver=D:\WINDOWS\SYSTEM\sqlsrvr.dll
Setup=D:\WINDOWS\SYSTEM\sqlsetup.dll
```

The [ODBC Drivers] section tells the driver manager the names of the installed drivers. The [SQL Server] section tells the ODBC driver manager the names of the dynamic link libraries (DLLs) to use to access data from a server set up as a SQL Server. The order of the two sections and their entries is arbitrary.

ODBC.INI contains the data for each installed driver. The

driver manager uses this information to determine which DLL to use to access data from a particular database backend. Here is an example of a file containing three data sources, all using the SQL Server driver:

```
[ODBC Data Sources]
MySQL=SQL Server
CorpSQL=SQL Server

[MySQL]
Driver=D:\WINDOWS\SYSTEM\sqlsrvr.dll
Description=SQL Server on server MySQL
OemToAnsi=No
Network=dbnmp3
Address=\\mysql\pipe\sql\query
[CorpSQL]
Driver=D:\WINDOWS\SYSTEM\sqlsrvr.dll
Description=SQL Server on server CorpSQL
OemToAnsi=No
Network=dbnmp3
Address=\\corpsql\pipe\sql\query
```

The first section tells the driver manager which sections appearing below it define the data source. As you can see, each entry has a value (in this case, SQL Server) that matches a value from the ODBCINST.INI file.

If the information on a data source is incorrect or missing, you may get the following error:

```
ODBC - SQLConnect failure 'IM002[Microsoft][ODBC DLL] Data
source not found and no default driver specified'.
```

If the DLL listed on the Driver=... line cannot be found or is corrupt, the following error may occur:

```
ODBC - SQLConnect failure 'IM003[Microsoft][ODBC DLL]
Driver specified by data source could not be loaded'.
```

11.20.2.   ODBC and Driver DLLs

The following DLLs must be on the path or in the Windows system directory in order for ODBC to be accessible from Visual Basic:

ODBC.DLL   —   Driver manager
ODBCINST.DLL   —   Driver setup manager
VBDB300.DLL   —   Visual Basic programming layer

If VBDB300.DLL is missing or corrupt, you see the following error in Visual Basic when you try to run the application:

```
ODBC Objects require VBDB300.DLL.
```

If either the ODBC.DLL or ODBCINST.DLL file is missing or corrupt, you see the following error in Visual Basic when you try to run the application:

```
Cannot Find ODBC.DLL, File not Found.
```

The SQL Server driver requires the following files:

SQLSRVR.DLL   —   Actual driver
SQLSETUP.DLL   —   Driver setup routines
DBNMP3.DLL   —   Named pipe routines needed by SQL
                    server

If the SQLSRVR.DLL is missing or corrupt, you see the following error when calling the OpenDataBase() function with a SQL Server data source:

```
ODBC - SQLConnect failure 'IM003[Microsoft][ODBC DLL]
Driver specified by data source could not be loaded'.
```

If the SQLSETUP.DLL is missing or corrupt, you see the following error when calling the RegisterDataBase statement with SQL Server as the driver name:

```
The configuration DLL (C:\WINDOWS\SYSTEM\SQLSETUP.DLL) for
the ODBC SQL server driver could not be loaded.
```

11.20.3. Server Information Needed

Certain information is needed to connect to a data source using the OpenDataBase() function. This information is obtainable from the server administrator in the case of SQL Server. The following is an example of a call to the OpenDataBase() function to connect to a SQL Server called CorpSQL as a user named Guest with password set to mypw:

```
Dim db As DataBase
Set db = OpenDataBase( "corpsql", False, False,
        "UID=guest;PWD=mypw")
```

If any of this information is missing, an ODBC dialog box appears to give the user a chance to supply the needed data. If the information is incorrect, the following error occurs:

```
ODBC - SQLConnect failure '28000[Microsoft][ODBC SQL Server
Driver] [SQL Server] Login failed'.
```

11.20.4. Microsoft and Sybase SQL Servers

For Microsoft and Sybase SQL Servers, you must add stored procedures to the server itself by running a batch file of SQL statements to make a Microsoft or Sybase SQL Server ODBC-aware. In other words, before you can run a Visual Basic ODBC application using the SQL Server driver, you must first update the ODBC catalog of stored procedures. These procedures are provided in the INSTCAT.SQL file. The system administrator for the SQL Server should install the procedures by using the SQL Server Interactive SQL (ISQL) utility.

If the INSTCAT.SQL file is not processed on the server, the following error occurs:

```
'ODBC - SQL Connect Failure'.
"08001" [Microsoft ODBC SQL Server Driver]
'unable to connect to data source'number: 606'
```

To install the catalog of stored procedures by using the INSTCAT.SQL file, run INSTCAT.SQL from the command line using ISQL. Do not use the SAF utility provided with the SQL Server. Microsoft SAF for MS-DOS and OS/2 is limited to 511 lines of code in a SQL script, and INSTCAT.SQL contains more than 511 lines of code.

Run ISQL from the OS/2 command line using the following syntax, entered in a single line, and do not include the angle braces, <>. Your command will scroll into 2 lines but the command will execute it as one line.

```
ISQL /U <sa login name > /n /P <password> /S <SQL server
name> /i <drive: \path\INSTCAT.SQL > /o <drive:\path\output
file name>
```

In this statement, the switches have the following values:

/U	The login name for the system administrator.
/n	Eliminates line numbering and prompting for user input.
/P	Password used for the system administrator. This switch is case-sensitive.
/S	The name of the server to set up.
/i	Provides the drive and fully qualified path for the location of INSTCAT.SQL
/o	Provides ISQL with an output file destination for results, including error listings.

Here is an example of that syntax:

```
ISQL /U sa /n /P squeeze /S BLUEDWARF /i C: \SQL\INSTCAT.SQL
/o C: \SQL OUTPUT.TXT
```

12

Limitations in Visual Basic Systems

12.1. APPLICATION LIMITATIONS

This chapter covers the various limitations of which you should be aware while constructing your applications. Many of the maximums cited here are not only subject to the stated number, but also to your own system resources. A system with two megabytes of RAM usually will not be able to reach some of the maximum limitation numbers stated for tables, especially in large applications.

The next few sections state the limitations of objects, forms, and procedures that apply to applications.

12.1.1. Objects

Your application cannot have more than 256 objects. Objects include forms, global objects, and controls (but not multiple instances of controls on your forms).

12.1.2. Forms

The limit of forms per project is approximately 230. Up to 80 forms can be loaded at once.

12.1.3. Procedures

The sum of all modules, procedures, forms, and DLL declarations must be 5200 or less.

12.2. FORM LIMITATIONS

Each form in Visual Basic has control, open forms, and property limits given in the next three sections.

12.2.1. Control Numbers

The limit on the number of controls on a single form is 470 or less, depending on the type of control, and the limit on control names is 254. A control array counts as only one name because the array elements share a single, common control name.

Since each nongraphical control (except shape, image, line, and label) uses a window, a limit also exists on the number of windows there can be in a single form. Windows 3.1 limits windows to 600, while Windows 3.0 has a limit of 475. All windows in existence count toward this limit, including forms and windows executing in other applications.

12.2.2. Open Forms

In all open forms the maximum number of controls allowed is about 600, but this figure does not include graphic labels and controls.

12.2.3. Properties

One data segment (64K) is used for all the data in form properties plus the properties for all controls. Excluded from this figure are the List property of combo box and list box controls and the Text property of multiline text box controls.

12.3. CONTROL LIMITATIONS

The next few sections describe limits on Visual Basic controls.

12.3.1. List

The List property of a list box or combo box is 64K. The maximum number of items in a list is 5440. Each of these items is limited to 1K; anything over this limit is cut off, or truncated.

12.3.2. Text

Each text box has a limit of 32K. Set the MultiLine property to True so that each multiline text box is stored in its own data segment. If you do not, the 64K (one data segment) total will soon be exceeded when all the other controls are summed up within the one data segment.

12.3.3. Caption

The Caption property of command buttons, check boxes, option buttons, and frames is limited to 255 characters. The Caption of a label is limited to 1K.

12.3.4. Tag

The Tag property has a limit of 32K; anything over will cause an Out of Memory error.

12.4. CODE LIMITATIONS

There can be up to 64K of p-code (a shorthand representation of your code inside the machine) for a procedure. Module Declaration sections for forms and code modules also have this 64K limit. If you exceed this level an Out of Memory error appears. This can be fixed by breaking up your module into smaller modules or procedures. You can get a rough estimate of the size of a procedure or module by looking at its size in ASCII form. For instance, use the DOS dir (directory) command on the file, which will give you its size, as in

```
dir myfile.bas
```

or use the File Manager.

12.5. SYMBOL TABLES

Symbol tables are used to store the names of identifiers, such as variables, in your code. Each such table also has a 64K limit.

12.5.1. Module

The module symbol table contains the names of Sub and Function procedures, module and local level variable names, module level DLL declarations, and line numbers and labels.

12.5.2. Global

Your whole application uses one symbol table that contains all global names. These include all global names and variables, user-defined type definitions, module names, and global DLL declarations.

12.6. DATA LIMITATIONS

The following sections describe limits for Visual Basic variables.

12.6.1. Global

An application uses up to one data segment (64K) for each global constant and variable.

12.6.2. Form and Code

Every form and module has its own data segment (64K). The data segment contains: module-level fixed-length string variables and constants, static local variables, module-level variables other than arrays and variable-length strings, and tracking data for controls and nonstatic local variables.

12.6.3. Size of Variables

There are seven standard variable types. The following list shows the names and size limits of each.

Type	Size
Integer	2 bytes
Long	4 bytes
Single	4 bytes
Double	8 bytes
Currency	8 bytes
String	4 bytes, plus 0–64K bytes (1 byte/character)
Variant	16 bytes, plus 1 byte/character if a string

12.7. STRING DATA

A string has a maximum size of 64K. This limit applies to a regular string variable, an element in an array, or an element in a user-defined type. By following certain criteria, the sum of the lengths of the groups of strings that follow can be larger than 64K.

- The total of all global variable-length string variables
- The total of all module-level variable-length strings
- The total of all local variable-length strings
- The total of all variable-length string elements in user-defined types

The groups of strings that follow cannot exceed 64K:

- The total of all global, module-level, or local fixed-length strings
- The total of all elements of each variable-length string array in a user-defined type.

If you initially assign a small number of characters to a string, then assign a large number to the string later on, you could get an Out of string space error because of the manner in which memory is allocated in the system. To overcome this problem, assign a larger string of characters initially.

12.8. ARRAYS

The index to any array can be from –32,768 to 32,767. For huge arrays (greater than 64K) the maximum size is 64MB for Windows Enhanced mode and 1 MB for Windows Standard mode.

12.9. USER-DEFINED TYPES

No user-defined type variable can exceed 64K, though the sum of variable-length strings in a user-defined type *can* exceed the 64K limit. User-defined types defined in terms of other user-defined types are also limited to 64K.

12.10. STACK SPACE

Each application has a 20K stack space. No options exist to change this value. If your application uses recursion a great deal, you may get an Out of stack space error. Arguments and local variables take up stack space at runtime. Static, global, and module variables do not use stack space because they are located in the data segments for modules and forms.

Visual Basic itself also uses a portion of the stack for tasks such as storing intermediate values. This space is used more while you are in the development environment than when the compiled .EXE file is being run. This means that if you do not run out of stack space while developing an application, you need not worry about a stack error during .EXE runtime.

12.11. WINDOWS LIMITATIONS

Microsoft Windows 3.x/4.x itself creates some limits on applications, and they vary with the particular version of Windows in use.

12.11.1. Resources

Windows resources come into play every time a window opens and uses some system resources (data areas set aside for Microsoft Windows). If you use up all the system resources you receive an

Out of memory error. The percentage of resources still available can be found by choosing About from the Help menu in the Program Manager. You can reclaim some system resources by making sure you close unused open windows.

12.11.2. Run and Shell Settings

You can automatically start your applications using the SHELL= in the SYSTEM.INI file, or RUN= in the WIN.INI file statements. SHELL= is supported in Windows 3.1 or greater, and RUN= is supported in Windows 3.0 and above.

12.11.3. MDI Applications

When the MDIChild property in a form is set to True, the CommandBox, BorderStyle, MinButton, and MaxButton are fully supported only in Windows 3.1 and above. These features work differently in Windows 3.0. See your MDI reference material for details if you are using Windows 3.0.

13

Advanced Area Introductions

13.1. GRAPHICS

Graphics can give an application that added dimension that says "This is a professional program." Visual Basic offers you many ways to create graphics in your applications. This section looks at some of them. Figure 13.1 shows an example called BLANKER.MAK that you can run if you have Visual Basic. This file is in the directory \vb\samples\graphics and shows various graphic examples.

13.1.1. Fundamentals

The two basic ways to create graphics in your application are: graphical controls or graphical methods. Though the ways in which they create graphics differ, they basically still accomplish the same task—using or creating graphics in your application. The next few sections discuss areas that are common to both styles.

13.1.1.1. Twips. All graphical drawing statements, sizing, and movement by default use a unit called a *twip*. A twip is 1/20 of a printer's point. One inch equals 1440 twips. The size of a twip

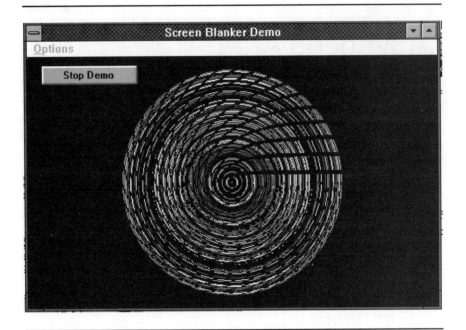

Figure 13.1.   Graphics Screen Blanker Demo.

on a monitor screen varies, depending on the size of the screen. If you wish, you can change to a unit of measure other than twips.

13.1.1.2. Coordinate system.   All graphical operations use the coordinate system of the drawing area or container. The coordinate system is a two-dimensional grid that defines locations on a form, screen, or other container such as a Printer object. The syntax used is x,y where x is the location of the point along the *x*-axis, with a default location of 0 at the extreme left, and y is the location of the point along the *y*-axis, with the default location of 0 at the extreme top.

13.1.1.3. Color.   There are four ways to assign a color value at runtime:

- RGB function
- QBColor function

- Use a previously defined constant from CONSTANTS.TXT
- Insert a color value (long integer) directly.

Only the first two ways will be discussed here, since they are powerful and easy to use and remember, especially if you have used other Basic dialects such as QuickBasic.

RGB. The RGB function can be used to create any color. To use this function, first give each of the three primary colors (red, green, and blue) a number indicating intensity from the lowest, 0, to the highest, 255. Next, assign these three numbers to the function, in the order red, green, then blue. Finally, assign the result to the color property or color argument wanted as follows:

```
Form1.BackColor = RGB (255,255,0)   'background now yellow
Form2.BackColor = RGB (0,128,0)     'background is green
PSet(100,100), RGB (0,0,64)         'set point - dark blue
```

QBColor. If you have used QuickBasic, you can use its color values by calling the QBColor function. This function uses a single number between 0 and 15, returning a long integer that can be used in any color argument or color property setting. For example:

```
Form1.BackColor = QBColor(4)
```

13.1.2. Graphical Controls

Three controls you can use to create graphics for your application are:

1. The image control

2. The line control

3. The shape control

13.1.2.1. Advantages. Graphical controls are very useful during design time. Two advantages are that controls require fewer system resources and less code to implement in your program.

13.1.2.2. Limitations. The limitations of using graphical controls are that they cannot receive focus at run time, appear on top of other controls, serve as containers for other controls, or have an hWnd property.

13.1.2.3. Image control. The *image control* is a rectangular area where you can load picture files, similar to a picture box. Note, however, that with an image control you can stretch pictures to fit the control's size—something you cannot do with a picture box.

Picture files use any of the three standard formats: bitmap, icon, or metafile.

13.1.2.4. Line control. The *line control* is a straight line drawn at design time. The position, length, style, and color can be set to desired parameters. One common use for the line control is to separate screen items or common group items.

13.1.2.5. Shape control. The shape control can be one of several shapes: a rectangle (square or rounded corners), oval, square (square or rounded corners), or a circle. You can determine the shapes' size, color, transparency, and fill and outline colors.

13.1.2.6. Placing pictures in forms. You can display a picture in three places in your application: a picture box, a form, or an image control. The pictures can originate from clip-art libraries, PC Paintbrush, or other graphic programs. Visual Basic itself includes many icons in a separate directory that you can use as ready-made graphics.

You can add a graphic at design time in two ways: load a picture from a picture file, or use the Paste method.

You can add a graphic at runtime with the LoadPicture function, copying a picture from one object to another or from the Clipboard.

13.1.2.7. Animation. Simple animations can be done by changing pictures at runtime. Toggling between two images is the easiest way. An example is a hand waving, created by using one image of a hand facing up and another image of a hand facing down.

When you toggle back and forth, the hands look as if they are waving. You can also use a series of pictures to create animation, and if you move the picture dynamically, more sophisticated effects can be achieved.

13.1.3. Graphical Methods

Other than the graphical controls available to you, other methods you can use to create graphics are:

Control	Effect
Cls	Clears all graphics and any Print output
PSet	Sets the color of a pixel
Point	Returns color value of a specific point
Line	Draws an ellipse, circle, or arc

13.1.3.1. Advantages.   There are times when using a control for a graphic would entail too much work as compared to using a method. Graph gridlines are an example. Using controls would require using a large number of line controls. Conversely, only a few codelines are required using the Line method.

Methods have additional features not available in controls. Among these are the ability to create arcs or to paint individual pixels.

13.1.3.2. Limitations.   Since graphic methods reside in your code, you must run the application to see the results of your work. Using graphical controls, you can see the result of your work from the control on the form at design time rather than run the application as you must with methods.

13.2. MDI

Multiple-Document Interface (MDI) allows you to have multiple forms within a single container, or "main," form. Excel, MS Word for Windows, and many other applications use the concept of MDI.

An MDI program allows you to show multiple documents at the same time, with each document in its own window. Document windows are contained in a *parent window*. As the "main" form, the parent window provides a place to work in and is the largest physically to accommodate the document windows that it will display.

An example of a MDI application, MDINOTE.MAK, is included in your Visual Basic system in the \vb\samples\mdi directory. Figure 13.2 shows a document window called "Untitled" from this application.

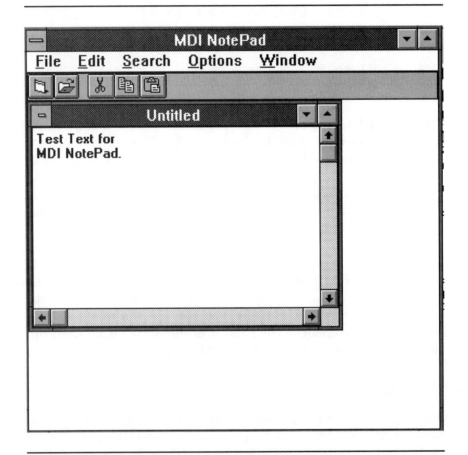

Figure 13.2. MDI NotePad example.

13.2.1. MDI in Visual Basic

An application can have only one MDI form, the *main form*, which contains all other *child forms*. A child form is a regular form with its MDIChild property set to True. Multiple child forms can be associated with the main form. At runtime, the child forms are shown within the MDI form, the area inside its borders and below the caption and menu bars.

13.2.2. Creating MDI Forms

To create a MDI form choose New MDI Form from the File menu. Then create child forms inside the MDI Form by creating new forms and setting their MDIChild property to True.

13.2.3. Design-Time Child Forms

At design time you can find out if a form is a child form by looking at its MDIChild property or at the Project window. Visual Basic displays special icons in the Project window for the MDI Form and child windows.

13.2.4. Runtime Child Forms

Child forms have special characteristics at runtime, among them:

- You can move and size child forms like any other forms: you are restricted only by screen area of the main MDI Form.
- When a child form is maximized, its caption is combined with the MDI Form caption name and shown on the MDI Form's menu bar.
- When a child form is minimized, an icon appears within the MDI Form—not in your desktop area.
- You cannot hide a child form.

13.2.5. Windows Compatibility

The look of your MDI applications depends on which version of MS Windows you are using. Windows 3.1 supports all functions as stated in reference manuals, whereas Windows 3.0 users may find that some areas not supported.

13.2.6. Document-Centered Applications

MDI, as the name infers, was designed especially for document-centered applications. These applications, such as MS Excel, allow the user to open many similar documents at the same time.

Creating such applications requires a MDI Form and a child form. During design, you create the MDI Form, which contains the application, and a child form to serve as a template for your application's documents. At runtime, the user can request a new document, usually with the File|New menu options, which creates a new instance of the child form, as is the case in the example mentioned previously, MDINOTE.MAK.

13.3. OBJECTS

When working in Visual Basic you work with objects. You make form objects and use control objects for those form objects. You can extend the power of these objects by declaring and using variables that represent those objects. Called object variables, these allow you to manipulate forms and controls as easily as if they were an Integer or Double type of variable. With object variables you can create multiple instances (copies of an object), modify a form or control, and make data structures from them.

13.3.1. Introduction to Objects

Object variables give you added capabilities such as creating additional instances of forms in your application. An *instance* is a copy that has its own existence, as if you had made it from the design section.

For an example showing the utility of object variables, create a command button as shown in Figure 13.3. Then add the following code:

```
Sub Command1_Click()
Dim Nf As New Form1    'Nf is declared a new form object
                       'variable - an instance from Form1.
    Nf.Show            'show a new instance on screen
    Nf.Move Left + (Width\10), Top + (Height\10) 'move it
```

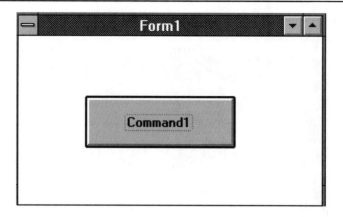

Figure 13.3. Command1 button.

```
    Nf.BackColor = RGB(Rnd*256, Rnd*256, Rnd*256) 'color it
End Sub
```

This code shows a new instance of the form and displays it when the command button is clicked. It also moves and colors the new instance form so that you can see it in respect to the old form. If this were not the case, the new form would completely cover up the old form. Figure 13.4 shows what can happen if the command button is clicked a few times to create new instances of Form1.

Figure 13.5 shows another sample application that creates new instances whenever the New Instance command button is clicked.

13.3.2. Declaring an Object

You declare an object in the same way as any other variable, using Dim, Static, ReDim, or Global. The difference is that you can use the optional New keyword. The syntax is:

```
{Dim|Static|ReDim|Global} variablename As [New] objecttype
```

Here are some example declarations:

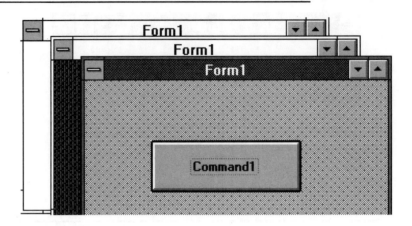

Figure 13.4. Multiple form instances.

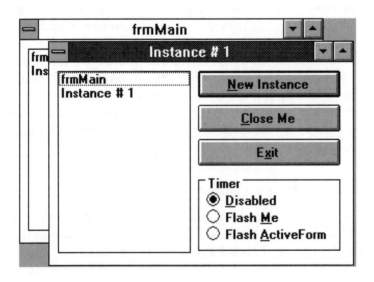

Figure 13.5. New instances creation.

1. Declares an object variable referring to a form called myMain:

   ```
   Dim FormVar As New myMain
   ```

2. Declares an object variable that can refer to any form:

   ```
   Dim anyForm As Form
   ```

3. Declares an object variable that can refer to any text box:

   ```
   Dim anyText As TextBox
   ```

4. Declares an object variable that can refer to any control:

   ```
   Dim anyControl As Control.
   ```

You cannot refer in your declaration to a particular control, but only to a particular *type* of control such as a Text box or other control. This approach does not apply to forms, nor can you include objects in user-defined types.

13.3.3. Object Types

Object variables have an object type, but can also have a *specific* or *generic* type. A specific object variable must refer only to one specific type of object, but a generic object variable can refer to one of many specific types of objects such as any form or any control on any form.

13.3.4. Arrays

You may declare arrays on objects just as you do on any other data type. The arrays can be fixed-length or variable. The only restriction is that you cannot use huge arrays.

13.3.5. Using Objects

Once your objects are declared, they can be used as any other variables. You can also do other operations with objects, such as making object variables refer to other objects, passing objects to procedures, comparing two objects, and testing the type of object variables.

13.3.6. System Objects

Five special system objects let you manipulate and get information about the environment in which your application is running. These system objects are:

1. App: Gives specific information about the program
2. Clipboard: Gives access to the Clipboard
3. Debug: Enables printing to the Debug window
4. Printer: Enables printing text and graphics to printer
5. Screen: Gives form, control, and other screen-related data

13.4.   PRINTING AND DISPLAYING

As you develop your applications there will be times when you want the enduser to be able to print out information, such as the example in Figure 13.6 which shows the Print Card command button. Printing includes printing to the screen as well as to the printer. This section deals more with an introduction to using the printer to output desired information instead of the screen. However, as you will see, both devices have common traits to deal with, such as type sizes and fonts.

13.4.1. Fonts

Text is still the most common way to relay information to a user. There is more to using text than simply putting out or receiving strings of characters. Deciding what font to use, and in what size, is also important in making a useful, attractive application.

13.4.1.1. Printer and screen fonts.   Fonts are especially important to you if you decide to use the WYSIWYG (what you see is what you get) process. Bear in mind that there are screen fonts and printer fonts. How close the screen output is to the printed output will depend on how closely the screen fonts match the printer fonts. For instance, if you have a font on the screen such as Bold Roman, but the user's printer does not have that font, the printer's output will not match what the user sees on the screen.

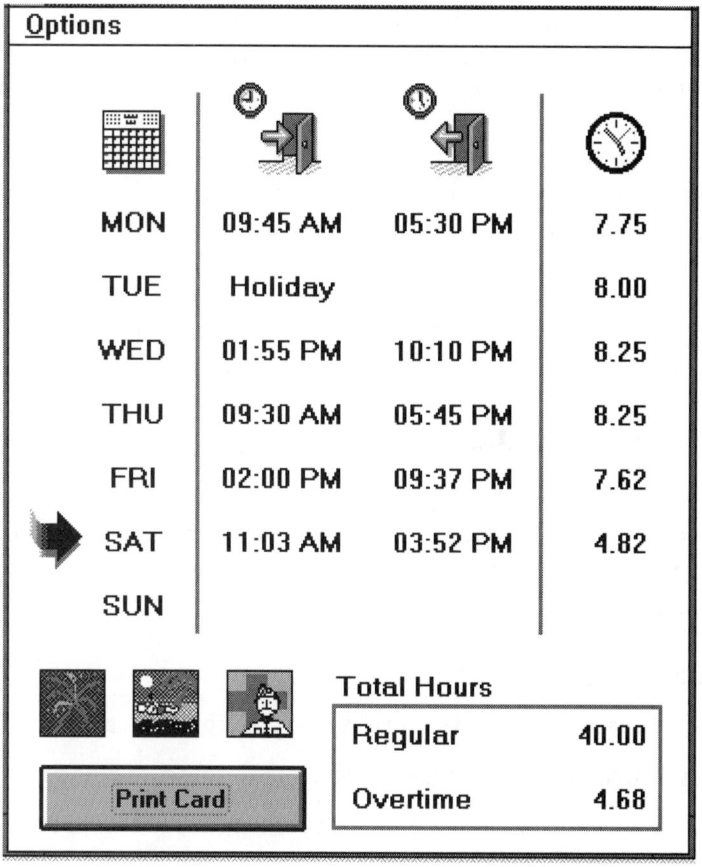

Figure 13.6. Print a timecard example.

The system will decide what available printer typeface comes closest to Bold Roman and use that font for the user's printer. Thus true WYSIWYG is not guaranteed, but instead depends on hardware constraints.

13.4.1.2. Font characteristics. Forms and most controls display text. Caption or Text properties are used to set fonts for controls. Forms, controls that show text, and the Printer object (described in Section 13.4.5.1) support font properties. The visual look of your application and its output is determined by fonts and their properties. These properties include the font it-self (which typeface), the font size, and any special setups such as bold, italic, or underlines.

13.4.1.3. Setting fonts. You can set the fonts either by setting properties in a form or control at design time, or at runtime by using code statements as shown below.

```
Total_Count.FontName = "Modern"  'set font to modern
Total_Count.FontBold = True      'set bold on
Total_Count.FontItalic = True    'set italics on
```

13.4.2. Print Method

To print on a form, picture box, or the Printer object (your printer, for instance, LPT1), you can use the print method, usually pre-ceded by the object's name. Here are some examples. To print messages to:

- A form named CalcForm:

  ```
  CalcForm.Print "This prints on the form CalcForm."
  ```

- A picture box named picMypic:

  ```
  picMypic.Print "This is a picture box called picMypic"
  ```

- The current form:

  ```
  Print "Hello, this is the current form."
  ```

- The Printer object:

  ```
  Printer.Print "Send this line to my Epson printer."
  ```

13.4.3. Tabs

The built-in print zones of Visual Basic make it easy to print tables. A print zone is 14 columns wide. When you use a comma between print items in your print commands, the next item prints at the beginning of the next print zone. In the following statement are three items, each item printing 14 characters, for a total of 52 columns. Since all these items are less than 14 characters long, they are printed left-justified with blanks to their right to fill in the needed 14 characters of their respective print zone.

```
Form1.Print "First", "Second", "Third item."
```

13.4.4. Format Number, Time, Date

You have many options for formatting data. The Format$ and Format function allow nearly any type of formatting you may wish to do. Format$ gives you control over the appearance of data, while Format converts a numeric value into a Variant data type. The following examples show some of the ways in which you can use Format$.

```
Format$(768.0,"000.00") -> 768.00

Format$(768.0,"$#0.00")   $768.00

Format$(Now,"m/d/yy")      1994

Format$(Now,"hh:mm AM/PM") 09:10 AM

Format$(Now,"ddddd ttttt") 12/29/94 9:10:34 AM
```

13.4.5. Introduction to Printing

Printing (e.g.: to LPT1) involves three areas: the start of the printing process initiated in code statements, the Windows 3.x/4.x printer drivers that are installed in both your system and the enduser's, and the ability of a printer to use Windows print features and drivers.

13.4.5.1. Printer object.   There are two ways to send information to your printer: the Printer object and PrintForm.

The Printer object can send both text and graphics to the printer (e.g.: Printer.Print "This text line will be printed") and provides the best print quality due to its device independent drawing space. The Printer object is translated to best match the resolution and abilities of the printer online.

13.4.5.2. PrintForm. You can put the results of your application on a form and then print that form using the PrintForm method. This is the easiest way to send data to your printer; it merely prints out the form without having you set up any parameters.

13.4.5.3. Printing a printer object. When you have placed your text and/or graphics on the Printer object, the EndDoc method will advance the page and send all ready output to the print spooler.

```
Printer.Print "First line to be printed as a set."
Printer.Print "Second and final line of the set."
Printer.EndDoc    'advance page and send above to spooler
```

13.4.5.4. Multipage documents. When a new page is needed, either for long documents or as part of your formatting scheme for reports, the NewPage method is used.

```
Printer.Print "This will be page 1, containing one line."
Printer.NewPage
Printer.Print "This is the second page, also one line."
Printer.EndDoc
```

13.4.5.5. PrintForm method. Printing the entire form is made possible by using the PrintForm method. The entire form is printed, even if parts are not visible. However, if graphics are present they will only be printed if the AutoRedraw property is set to True.

```
Print "Some text on a form."
PrintForm
```

If your printer has better resolution than your screen, the clarity achieved in your document may suffer when using PrintForm.

13.5. HELP COMPILER

You can make your applications easier to use by adding a Help system. The procedure for doing so is available only in the Professional Versions of Visual Basic. A Help system answers common user questions, gives definitions, and assists on matters of correct usage of areas in an application. The more complicated the application, the more a Help system is needed. Figure 13.7. shows an application where the user can get assistance by clicking on Help.

Figure 13.8 shows a typical Help screen explaining how to use Help in an application. The actual help items related to the application are accessed by selecting another option from the main Help menu items.

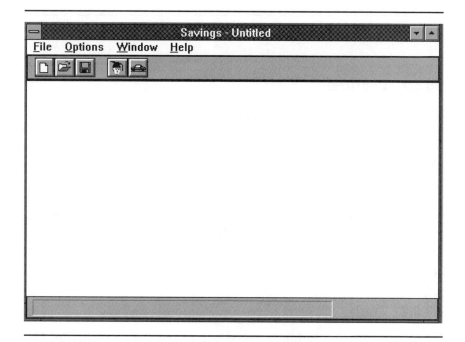

Figure 13.7. Savings application with Help ability.

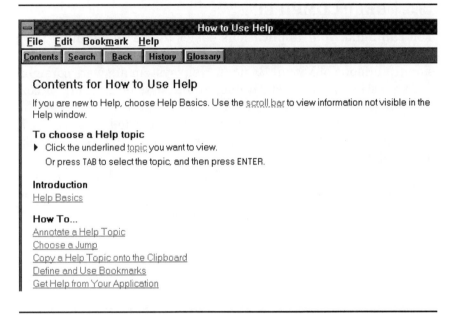

Figure 13.8.   Getting help on using Help.

13.5.1. Features

The Windows Help compiler (HC31.EXE) is included in Visual Basic Professional. With it, you can make a system of online Help for your endusers. Windows Help version 3.1, or WinHelp (WINHELP.EXE), shows and displays the compiled Help system made by HC31.EXE.

WinHelp provides graphics, text with font properties, macros to automate portions of the Help system, hot-spots (such as hypertext areas), secondary windows, and keyword search ability all designed to enable the enduser to find specific information quickly.

13.5.2. Tools

Three tools are available to assist you in creating a Help file. The Help compiler (HC31.EXE) compiles all the topic and graphic files that are in the project file into a Help file that can be used in your WinHelp application. The aim is to create a .HLP file so WinHelp can use it in your application. If no bugs are found in the finished .HLP file, your job is done and you have a useful Help file.

The Hotspot Editor (SHED.EXE) links graphics to topics in the Help file.

The Multiple resolution bitmap compiler (MRBC.EXE) compiles bitmap graphics of different screen resolutions and makes them common and useable to the user's screen resolution.

13.5.3. Creating the Help System

Making a help file entails many tasks. The following list describes these tasks in general terms.

1. Plan the information needed for the help topics.
2. Plan the structure of the help system.
3. Set up your application so that it can access the help system.
4. Type the text files needed for the topics.
5. Enter needed control codes into your text files.
6. If needed, create your graphics.
7. Create or use any wanted macros to aid your help system.
8. Build and compile the help source files.
9. Test and debug the compiled help files you have created.

13.5.4. Topics

A *topic* is the main unit of information in a help file, a self-contained area of text and graphics much like a page in a book. A topic can contain as much information as needed. Scroll bars are used if the information exceeds a full screen of information.

Topics can contain *hot spots* that if clicked, will give information about the hot spot. You can tell a hot spot by its broken underlining and brief title—usually just one or two words. When a hot spot is selected, a pop-up window or overlapping window appears explaining the meaning, or giving further information, about that hot spot.

You can also create *jumps*, or cross-references, to related topics. To activate these topics, simply click on them, just as on hot spots.

13.5.5. Planning the Help System

There is no one way to plan the content of a help system. For instance, your application may be intended for experienced, intermediate, or novice level users. Each of these groups requires a different amount of information and topics to give adequate help to the intended user audience.

If your application is intended for users at all levels, it may be wise to put more topics in the help system than you think necessary, since for some users there is no such things as too much help. Types of information should include documentation topics on terms, menus, features, and the steps required to use the various routines your application offers.

13.5.6. Creating Topic Files

Your text files must be created only with certain text editors or word processors, because these files must be saved in Rich Text Format (RTF). With RTF you can insert the necessary coded text for help terms, pop-up definitions, keywords, and jumps. Some of your RTF choices are:

- MS Word MS-DOS, version 5.0+
- MS Word for Windows, version 1.0+
- MS Word Macintosh series, version 3.0+
- Any other word processor that supports RTF.

13.5.7. Hypergraphics

A hypergraphic is a graphic with embedded hot spots that users can click on to:

- Display a pop-up window
- Jump to another help topic

- Activate DLL routines
- Execute a help macro

You create a hypergraphic with the Hotspot editor. The graphics must be made before you start using the editor. When the graphic is saved as a hypergraphic, using the Hotspot editor, it can no longer be read by any regular MS drawing or painting program.

13.5.8. WinHelp Macros

WinHelp macros give you the ability to add or remove custom buttons and menus, change the function of buttons and menus, execute applications from within Help, and so forth. One example is the Back macro. It displays the previous topic in the back list. The back list includes the last 40 topics that the enduser has displayed while in Help.

13.6.   Grid

There are times when you need to present your information in column and row formats. The grid control allows an easy way to accomplish this. Figure 13.9 shows an example using a grid to make the output easier to read. If you have Visual Basic, the name of this example program is LOAN.MAK, located in \vb\samples\grid.

13.6.1. Grid Control

The grid control lets you display information in row and column format. Special rows and columns can also display headings. You program the application to change the grid's values using properties and methods. If you plan to distribute your application, do not forget to include the file GRID.VBX in the users' copies.

13.6.2. Sizing

Two types of column and row sizing options are available. The more common is *nonfixed*, meaning that a row or column scrolls if

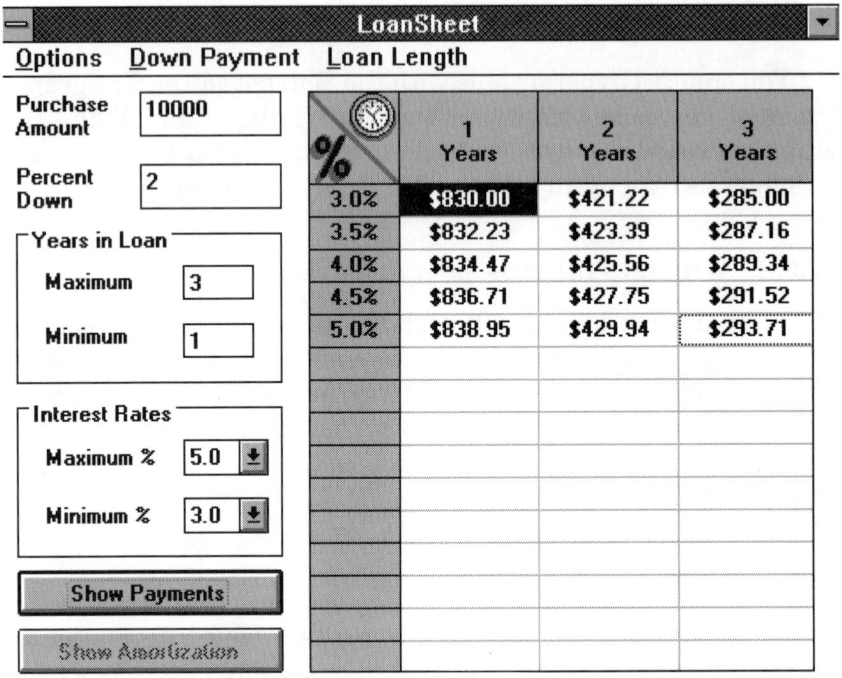

Figure 13.9. Grid loan sheet example.

the scroll bars are active in the control. The fixed column or row type does not allow scrolling at any time. Look at Figure 13.9, where the nonfixed rows and columns are in the default color, white, while the fixed columns and rows are in gray.

13.6.3. Changing the Grid Size

With the grid control the height of a row is set by the RowHeight statement, and the width of a column by ColWidth. These values can only be set at runtime. In the example application in Figure 13.9, before the program displays the monthly loan payments, it resizes the width of columns with code statements.

13.6.4. Text in Grid Cells

The easiest way to add text to a cell is to set the grid control Text property to the text string desired using a code statement. You cannot add text to a grid control at design time; that is why a code statement is needed.

13.6.5. Alignment

Two properties control the alignment of text in the columns of a grid control. These properties are ColAlignment (for nonfixed columns) and FixedAlignment (for fixed columns). With these properties you can align flush left, flush right, or centered in the cells of the selected column.

13.6.6. Adding Graphics

Using the Picture property, you can add a graphic to a cell. The following code puts a graphic in the Loan program in cell 0,0.

```
grdPayments.Rows = 0
grdPayments.Cols = 0
grdPayments.ColWidth(0) = imgGraphic.Width
grdPayments.RowHeight(0) = imgGraphic.Height
grdPayments.Picture      = imgGraphic.Picture
```

13.6.7. Adding and Removing Rows

You can add new rows and their values at runtime using the AddItem method. Removing rows is done with the RemoveItem method. As an example, the following code removes the fourth (starting from 0) row every time the Command1 button is clicked.

```
Sub Command1_Click()
   Grid1.RemoveItem 3
End Sub
```

13.7. CONTROL DEVELOPMENT KIT

The Control Development Kit (CDK) allows you to write custom controls. Using the CDK requires some background in the Applications Programming Interface (API), as well as a solid background in Visual Basic.

13.7.1. Custom Control Defined

A custom control adds another tool, and its icon, to the Toolbox. Such controls operate in the same way as the other standard controls, but can add a completely new function to the Toolbox
    As programmer of a new custom control you have control over:

* How the control will be displayed in the Toolbox
* The control's events and properties
* The behavior of the small set of regular Visual Basic methods these controls support

    Once written, a custom control has its own control file with a .VBX file extension, which must be added to your project if your new control is to function. In fact, a custom control file is actually a DLL made specifically to interact with Visual Basic.

13.7.2. Needed Software Background

To create your own custom controls, you need a background in particular software areas, namely:

* MS Windows Software Development Kit (SDK)
* A programming language such as C or C++
* Visual Basic

13.7.3. Software System Requirements

To develop a custom control, you need the following software on your system:

- MS Windows Software Development Kit (SDK)
- A programming language such as C that will create DLLs
- Visual Basic Professional Version

13.7.4. Installing CDK

CDK files (found in directory \cdk) mostly provide you with examples and documentation. A couple of the files that must be on your hard disk to create a control are:

- VBAPI.LIB: A library of intermediate function calls that link into the host development environment
- VBAPI.H: A header file containing all the prototypes to functions in VBAPI.LIB, plus the constants and structures of needed definitions

13.7.5. Fundamentals

Programming a custom control is like writing a standard Windows application. Both react to messages and use API call functions.

The differences are that a custom control is a DLL and is specific to Visual Basic.

13.7.6. Control Class

Writing a custom control is actually equivalent to writing a *control class*. When a control class is loaded into a project, multiple instances of that class can be created. Just as you can create many Text box controls on your form, they are all still only instances of the Text box class. The same is true with custom controls, since they too are control classes.

13.8.   DATA MANAGER

The Visual Basic Data Manager helps Visual Basic users to create new databases (.MDB format) and examine or map the structure of existing external databases in a variety of formats. The formats that you can either create or modify with the Data Manager are:

294 VISUAL BASIC PROFESSIONAL 3.0

Database Format	Create	Modify
Microsoft Access V1.0	Yes	Yes
Microsoft Access V1.1	Yes	Yes
Paradox 3.0 and 3.5	No	Yes
dBASE III and IV	No	Yes
FoxPro 2.0 and 2.5	No	Yes
Btrieve	No	Yes

Visual Basic shares its database engine with Microsoft Access, so databases created with Visual Basic or the Data Manager can be manipulated using Microsoft Access. In addition, databases created with Microsoft Access can be manipulated using Visual Basic and the Data Manager.

Many external databases exist as directories on your disk. To create databases in these formats, use the File Manager to create a directory (this directory becomes the database). Once the database directory is created, you use the Data Manager to add tables and indexes, which become files in this directory.

13.8.1. Creating a Database

To create a database using Visual Basic:

1. Choose the Data Manager option under the Window menu. From the submenu, select the type of database you want to create (Microsoft Access version 1.0, or Microsoft Access version 1.1). (See Figure 13.10.)
2. Enter the name of the database you want to create in the displayed dialog. The file extension must be .MDB. Do not enter or choose the name of an existing .MDB file.
3. Press OK to accept the new database name, or press Network (if available) to connect to a network drive.

Once the database file has been created, use the Data Manager to add new tables and indexes to contain the data to be stored.

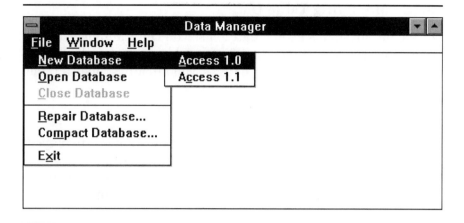

Figure 13.10. Data Manager.

To create an external database (dBASE III/IV, FoxPro, or Paradox), note that many external databases are simply disk directories. To create these types of databases, use the File Manager to create a directory. Once the database directory is created, you can use Data Manager to add tables and indexes, which then become files in this directory.

13.8.2. Opening a Database

To open an existing database:

1. Choose the Data Manager+Open Database command from the Windows menu. From the submenu, select the type of database you want to open.
2. Enter the name of the database you want to open in the displayed dialog. If you are opening an external database (dBASE III/IV, FoxPro, Paradox), use the dialog to select the database directory. To open a BTRIEVE database, use the dialog to select the desired .DDF file.
3. Press OK to open the database, or press Network (if available) to connect to a network drive. Once the database file has been opened, use the Data Manager to add new tables and indexes or to modify the existing tables or data.

13.8.3. Modifying Table Data

Once a database has been created, use the Data Manager to add records to a table, delete records from a table, or modify the data in a table. To perform any of these tasks, you must first open a table.

13.8.3.1. Opening a table.   To open a table:

1. Open an existing database. The Tables window is displayed.
2. Select the table you want to modify and click the Open button. The Table Access Window is displayed. This window displays each of the table's fields and any data it contains.

13.8.3.2. Adding a record to a table.   To add a record to a table:

1. Click the Add button.
2. Enter data as desired in each field.
3. To save the new record, click the Update button or move to another record. To return the table to its previous state, without saving your changes, click the Refresh button.

13.8.3.3. Deleting a record from a table.   To delete a record from a table:

1. Select the record you want to delete. There are two ways to locate a record in the Table Access window. Use the data control at the bottom of the Table Access window to view the first, previous, next, or last record in the table. Use the Find button to locate a record in a large database. The syntax for the search expression is identical to the Find method described in Visual Basic help. Generally, these statements follow the syntax for Structured Query Language (SQL) WHERE clauses. For example, in the Authors table in BIBLIO.MDB, you can locate the tenth record by entering "AU_ID > 9" as the search expression.
2. Click the Delete button and respond to the prompt. If you answer 'Yes,' the record is immediately deleted and cannot be recovered.

13.8.3.4. *Modifying the data in a record.*   To modify a record:

1. Select the record you want to modify (see step 1 in Section 13.8.3.3).
2. Enter data as desired.
3. To save the new record, click the Update button or move to another record. To return the table to its previous state, without saving your changes, click the Refresh button.

13.8.3.5. *Viewing the current records in the table.*   Click the Refresh button. Use the Refresh button to retrieve the current records from the table. If the database is being used by more than one person, use the Refresh button to ensure that you are working on the most recent data.

If you add or change a record and the values in the record's fields do not meet the requirements set by the data type or violate a restriction established by the index, an error occurs. The maximum length for a record is 2000 characters.

Appendix

A.1. INSTALLING VISUAL BASIC

The Visual Basic manual addresses the installation process, but certain aspects of installing are not mentioned. Thus this section deals with the regular install process and aspects of it not mentioned in the manual. Hardware and software requirements for installing Visual Basic are:

- An IBM-compatible machine with 80286 or higher processor
- Hard disk drive
- A 3 1/2" or 5 1/4" floppy drive
- EGA (or better) monitor
- One megabyte of memory (preferably, 4 MB RAM)
- Mouse
- MS-DOS 3.1 or later
- Windows 3.0 or higher running in standard or enhanced mode

A.1.1. Backup Disks and Miscellaneous Issues

Before running setup or installing Visual Basic, make backup copies of the master disks that came with your Visual Basic package.

Use the DISKCOPY command to copy all files to your backup set. Use the backup set for the setup process.

Insert the first disk, turn on your printer, and enter the command TYPE README.TXT>PRN. This will give you a hard copy of the latest information concerning the Visual Basic package for ease of reading and later future reference.

A.1.2.   Running Setup

SETUP.EXE is a Windows program that must be run from Windows, not from the DOS command line. It must also be run with Windows in either Standard or Enhanced mode. You can tell which form you are in by choosing 'About' from the 'Help' menu in the Program Manager.

> *Warning:* Do not write-protect the disks you use for installing. If you do, Visual Basic cannot be installed successfully.

Insert disk one in drive A. From the File menu of the Program Manager or File Manager, choose Run. Type A:SETUP, press the ENTER key, and follow instructions. You will be told when all areas are installed in your system and you can then consider Visual Basic Professional 3.0 ready to use.

A.1.3.   Other Text Files

I have already mentioned that you should print out the READ ME.TXT file, but there are other text files worth mentioning here that you should also print out. The PACKING.LST file lists all the files on the system and is useful when you want to reinstall only one or two files but do not know where they are. This list is also helpful in showing you all the general sample program names on the system you can run for learning purposes. The file SAMPLES.TXT in the Professional Version tells you about eight, more complex sample applications, ranging from graphics to a database using the ODBC object layer. Other files you may want to print out include WIN30EXT.TXT, WIN31EXT.TXT, CONSTANT.TXT, and CDK(Control Development Kit).TXT.

The files on your distribution and backup disks are compressed, so you cannot merely copy a file from one of these disks to your hard drive. If you need to reinstall a file, you can do so by running SETUP from the File Manager or Program Manager and following these steps:

1. Pick the Run item from the File menu.
2. Type SETUP.EXE /Z [source file] [destination file]. The extension /Z activates the decompression process. SETUP.EXE must be run from Windows, not DOS.

A.1.4.   Checking Setup

To make sure all items have been installed, go to Windows Program Manager and look for a new icon. Double-click on the Visual Basic 3.0 icon and verify that all accessories are installed as shown in Figure A.1.

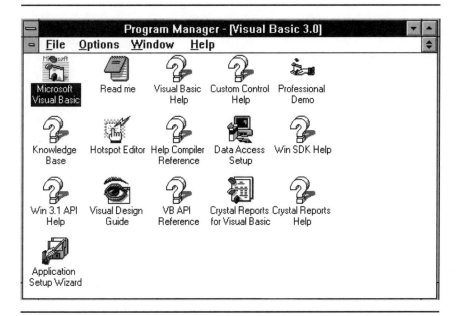

Figure A.1.   Visual Basic Professional 3.0 group items.

Index

Access keys, 80
Alias, 223
An executable, 93
Array, 144

BASIC, xxiii
BASICA, xxiii
Binary access, 153
Bound custom control, 34
Break mode, 189
Breakpoint, 193
Buffer, 160

CDK, 34
Check boxes, 48
Class, 228
Collection, 241
Combo boxes, 53
Command line, 12
Comment symbol, 116
Constants, 150
Container application, 229
Context-sensitive, 10
Control arrays, 64
Control structures, 121
Controls, 33
Conversation, 208
Coordinate system, 270
Crystal Reports, 5, 183
Custom control, 33

Data control, 173
Data Manager, 293
Data types, 131
Data-aware controls, 5, 173
DDE, 207
Debug window, 196
Debugging, 187
Declaring a variable, 132
Design time, 189
Destination, 208
Dialog boxes, 82
DLL, 6, 34
Driver manager, 238
Drivers, 237
Dynamic arrays, 146
Dynaset, 243
Dynaset object, 172

Environment, 102
EOF, 160
Error handling, 187
Event-driven programming, 108
Extension, 11

Field object, 173
File allocation table, 169
File, 11
Focus, 27, 63
Forms, 14
Functional procedures, 113
Fundamental data types, 140

General procedure, 112
Grid, 289
GUI, xxiii

Handles, 226
Help menu, 9
Hot spots, 287
Hypergraphic, 288

Icon, 2
If/Then block, 122
Image control, 42
Immediate pane, 196
Index object, 173
Installing, 299

Label, 44
Lifetime, 133
Link, 212
List property, 57
LOF, 161
Loop structures, 124

MAPI, 4
Menu, 69
Menu Bar, 13
Menu separators, 80
Microsoft Access 1.1 Engine, 5, 170
Modal, 82
Modeless, 82
Modules, 94
Multidimensional arrays, 145
Multiple-column list boxes, 58
Multiple-Document Interface (MDI),
    273

Nested structures, 127
NULL pointer, 225

Object box, 25
Object layer, 171
Object variables, 244
Objects, 147
ODBC (Open DataBase Connectivity),
    4, 237
ODBC database, 241
OLE, 1
OLE 2.0 (Object Linking and
    Embedding), 227
OLE 2.0 Automation, 6
Online documentation, 8
Online tutorials, 10
Option buttons, 50

Passed by value, 144
Poking, 215
Print method, 282
Private procedures, 116
Procedures, 29
Programmatic, 171
Programmatic layer, 5
Project, 11, 21
Project window, 14
Properties, 25
Properties window, 14
Public procedures, 116

Random access file, 151
Rollback, 255
Runtime mode, 189

Scope, 133
Select Case, 123
Sequential access files, 153
Settings box, 26
SETUP.EXE, 300
SetupWizard, 104
Shortcut keys, 81
Sizing handles, 23
SQL (Structured Query Language), 237
Startup form, 110
Submenu, 79
Subroutine procedures, 113

Tab order, 63
Template, 29
Text boxes, 46
Text property, 57
Toolbar, 13
Toolbox, 14
Topic, 287
Transaction, 171
Twips, 269

User-defined data types, 148

Validation, 180
Variables, 131
Variant, 120
Visual Basic Professional 3.0, 1
Visual layer, 5
Visual programming, 4

Watch pane, 196
Windows API, 222
Windows Help compiler, 286
WOSA (Microsoft Windows Open
    Services Architecture), 237